PRINTING NUEVA YORK

AMERICA AND THE LONG 19TH CENTURY

General Editors: David Kazanjian, Elizabeth McHenry, and Priscilla Wald

Referenced Sites of Nineteenth-Century Nueva York in Manhattan

Ambas Américas - 58 and 60 Fulton St.

La América - 756 Broadway

La América Ilustrada - 41 Park Row

Cacara Jícara - 81 New St.; 115 and 117 Park Row

El Educador Popular - 40 and 42 Broadway

Doctrina de Martí - 122 W. 33rd St.

El Mundo Nuevo - 537 Pearl St.

Patria - 214 Pearl St.; 120 and 122 Front St.

Revista Ilustrada de Nueva York - 116 Reade St.; 124 Chambers St.

La Revolución - 40 and 42 Broadway

Néstor Ponce de León's Print Shop and Spanish-Language Bookstore - 17 E. 16th St.; 23 Union Square; 40 and 42 Broadway

Imprenta América Print Shop - 285 and 286 Pearl St.

Map of key sites of New York City's nineteenth-century Spanish-language press. Courtesy of the author. From The Ground Beneath Our Feet (GBOF.pace.edu), Pace University, created with Performant Software Solutions. Base map, Egbert L. Viele, "Sanitary & Topographical Map of the City and Island of New York," courtesy of David Rumsey Map Collection, David Rumsey Map Center, Stanford Libraries.

Printing Nueva York

Spanish-Language Print Culture,
Media Change, and Democracy
in the Late Nineteenth Century

Kelley Kreitz

New York University Press

New York

NEW YORK UNIVERSITY PRESS
New York
www.nyupress.org

Please contact the Library of Congress for Cataloging-in-Publication data.

ISBN: 9781479830466 (hardback)
ISBN: 9781479830527 (paperback)
ISBN: 9781479830541 (library ebook)
ISBN: 9781479830534 (consumer ebook)

This book is printed on acid-free paper, and its binding materials are chosen for strength and durability. We strive to use environmentally responsible suppliers and materials to the greatest extent possible in publishing our books.

The manufacturer's authorized representative in the EU for product safety is Mare Nostrum Group B.V., Mauritskade 21D, 1091 GC Amsterdam, The Netherlands. Email: gpsr@mare-nostrum.co.uk.

Manufactured in the United States of America

10 9 8 7 6 5 4 3 2 1

Also available as an ebook

For Weston, Theo, and Felix

CONTENTS

A NOTE ON TRANSLATION

The translations from Spanish in this book are mine unless otherwise noted. In my translations from Spanish-language archival texts throughout this book, I have not modernized the spelling. In addition, I have found that the goal of translation is a bit different in the context of close readings of archival sources. At times, I found making the translation sound as fluid as possible in English, as is more typical, at odds with highlighting word choices, rhythm, and sentence structure considered in my analysis. As a result, if a hint of the Spanish lingers in the English translations I have offered here, so much the better.

Introduction

> Paradoxically, it was not through the book but through the
> development of the mass press, particularly the telegraph
> press, that poets found artistic keys to the world of simulta-
> neity, or of modern myth.
> —Marshall McLuhan, *The Gutenberg Galaxy*

When the *Paris Herald* launched in 1887, Venezuelan writer and editor Nicanor Bolet Peraza, contributing as a New York correspondent to
the Havana-based Cuban literary weekly *La Habana Elegante* (Elegant
Havana), waxed rhapsodic about the *New York Herald*'s use of the new
transatlantic telegraph cable to deliver news from New York City to
Paris: "Esa hoja puede atravesar en segundos el Atlántico, volar de un
hemisferio á otro hemisferio . . . y unir á dos mundos en el pensamiento."
(This sheet can cross the Atlantic in seconds, fly from one hemisphere to
another . . . and join two worlds in thought.)[1] Propelled by what McLuhan called the "telegraph press," news from the Western Hemisphere
could land in Europe a few hours later, putting the burgeoning world
powers of the West on a level playing field: "El producto de los cerebros
se difunde como atmósfera por todas las latitudes, no existiendo ya el
pasado, siendo todo presente, viviendo toda la creación en un solo día."
(Mental production spreads like an atmosphere across all latitudes, with
the past no longer existing, everything being the present, all creation
living in a single day.)[2]

This new world of simultaneous experience enables the exchange of
ideas in all directions, and Bolet Peraza notes that this ability does not
belong to the *Herald* alone: "Parecería de magia si no estuviésemos fa-
miliarizados con los fenómenos de la electricidad, si no perteneciéra-

mos como pertenecemos á esta centuria de titanes que han subido á los cielos." (It would appear to be magic if we were not familiar with the phenomenon of electricity, if we did not belong as we do belong to this century of Titans who have risen to the heavens.)[3] The *Paris Herald* is less magical feat than provocation to explore the possibilities afforded by the new world of print in the age of electricity. Bolet Peraza, writing for a Cuban publication that maintained close connections to New York's Spanish-language publishing community and that circulated throughout the hemisphere, invites his readers to join in imagining those possibilities. In turn, as readers looking back on Bolet Peraza's musings from the perspective of the twenty-first century, we are led to imagine the feelings of possibility—and even hope—that may have been provoked in a readership that traversed the national, regional, and linguistic boundaries that have shaped the study of literary and media history in the United States and Latin America.

Printing Nueva York brings together Spanish- and English-language periodicals published in—or in conversation with—New York City print culture to restore their lost connections to the period of media transition in which Bolet Peraza participated. During the final decades of the nineteenth century, visions of the changing world of print, and of what it might be harnessed to achieve, abounded across local, national, and transnational circuits. The electric telegraph, first demonstrated in the United States by Samuel Morse in 1837, was half a century old when Bolet Peraza penned his letter from New York about the *Paris Herald* for *La Habana Elegante*. Yet the installation of reliable undersea telegraph cables starting in 1866, followed by the invention of the telephone in 1876, expanded further the possibilities of simultaneous experience; the telegraph thus continued to inspire a sense of novelty and possibility.[4] Those new technologies, along with a range of innovations introduced into the printing process throughout the nineteenth century—including cheaper paper, steam- and hand-powered cylinder presses, rotary presses, and a variety of innovations that facilitated the reproduction of images— brought major changes to printing practices.

What exactly these changes would mean for the cultural producers who were already invested in the world of print, and for new participants who saw opportunities in the period's new media, remained to be seen. As Lisa Gitelman has observed, the last decades of the nineteenth

century were characterized by "an unfixity of print perhaps unprecedented since the seventeenth century."[5] Even as print still dominated the
period's media system, its earlier forms and conventions became unstable.[6] On this uneven footing, writers and editors representing a wide
range of ambitions and interests contributed to developing the forms
of what would become twentieth-century mass media. They also produced a trove of once promising and since forgotten ideas about identity,
community, publics, forms of expression, and means of enacting social
and political change that might have transformed modern media, and
indeed the modern world.

One constellation of such alternatives radiated from New York
City's thriving community of Spanish-language periodicals, which
first appeared in the early nineteenth century and grew in size and
influence in the context of late nineteenth-century media change. This
book seeks to reignite the ideas and dreams of that community. I hope
it will also lead to more research on the patterns and possibilities generated in additional nodes in the hemispheric network of periodicals in
which New York's Hispanophone publishing community participated,
such as Havana, Mexico City, Caracas, and Buenos Aires—and also
on communities of print that published in languages other than Spanish and English within the multilingual print culture of nineteenth-
century New York City.[7]

Printing Nueva York uncovers the leading role played by US-based
writers and editors of Latin American descent in the media innovation
of the late nineteenth century. Visionary writers and editors, including
Bolet Peraza, Teófilo Domínguez, Sotero Figueroa, José Martí, Néstor
Ponce de León, Amalia Puga de Losada, Rafael Serra, and María de la
Torriente, saw the changing world of print as a means of achieving independence from Spain for Cuba and Puerto Rico, while empowering the
hemispheric community that Martí named "nuestra América" to participate in the spread of Latin American ideas and culture throughout the
hemisphere and beyond. At the very moment when Anglophone daily
newspapers like the *Herald* drew a stark line between producers and consumers in the forms of mass entertainment they developed, the network
of Hispanophone writers and editors in what I am calling nineteenth-
century Nueva York emphasized quality over quantity, collective mobilization over private edification or mass entertainment, and most

importantly and experimentally for the time, reader participation over passive consumption. Their ideas help to situate nineteenth-century US-based Spanish-language publishing in relation to the emergence of mass media. In that context, they contribute to recent interest in nineteenth-century Latinx writing by locating US-based Spanish-language publishing within a story that has long been dominated by English-language newspapers and magazines including the *Herald*, the *New York Sun*, the *New York World*, the *New York Journal, Frank Leslie's Illustrated Newspaper*, and *Harper's Weekly*.

Reanimating the period's US-based Spanish-language innovations in late nineteenth-century print culture also introduces fresh perspectives on contemporaneous Anglophone journalistic and literary communities of print. As we will see, forward-thinking writers and editors including Joseph Pulitzer, William Randolph Hearst, Nellie Bly, William Dean Howells, and Henry James explored the possibilities of a print culture that had not yet drawn the lines that would later solidify between writer and reader, producer and consumer, mass and high culture. In addition, the ideas about the future of news and literature that I recover here reveal the limits of print, especially for those whose stories the widest-circulating Anglophone publications—and many Hispanophone publications as well—refused to tell. To circulate their stories, Black, Indigenous, and people of color (BIPOC), women, and anarchist writers and editors also created their own publications. These included *Minerva*, a Havana-based magazine by and for Afro-Cuban women that circulated in Cuba and among Afro-Cuban and African American women in Tampa, Key West, and New York City; Teófilo Domínguez's collection of biographical essays, *Figuras y figuritas: Ensayos biográficos* (Big and small figures: Biographical essays), which documented the contributions of Afro-Cuban leaders of the Cuban separatist movement; and newspapers of the radical labor press, like the New York-based *El Despertar* (The Awakening).[8] These texts that are rarely considered in a literary context are the fragments that enable scholars today to piece together another story of the transformation of print culture in the age of electricity—one that locates ideas in motion rather than the end points reached by the most successful of the period's ideas, experiments, and literary forms.

Many of the ideas and ambitions that *Printing Nueva York* will uncover may be unfamiliar or seem inchoate or unintentional compared to those that achieved long-lasting success, which have the teleological advantage of looking as if they had been better planned. The emergent, imperfectly realized visions and forms of writing that are the primary object of study in this book require attentive looking. Once seen for what they are, they provide new vistas on late nineteenth-century print culture. Hispanophone print culture, focused through the lens of Nueva York, reveals more collaborative and collectivist models of print and media change at the end of the nineteenth century; they are unbounded by and often run counter to those of the progressive, capitalist emerging mass media of the period—even as both models claimed to be fulfilling a democratic vision.[9] Such models also demonstrate that, although local and national contexts shape technological infrastructure and media institutions, the work of cultural producers in imagining new uses for media technologies—or of mediating change—operates within larger, transnational spheres of circulation and exchange of ideas.

Hemispheric Latinidad and Nineteenth-Century Nueva York

In the late nineteenth century, US-based writers of Latin American descent envisioned new formations of media and community. Those formations included new audiences, which John Alba Cutler has described as "Latino/a reading publics [that] were constituted at the crossroads of U.S. and hemispheric American literary history."[10] This book works at that crossroads, at times showing how Hispanophone and Anglophone texts from the period inform each other. Throughout its chapters, *Printing Nueva York* demonstrates the centrality and enduring presence of Latinx writing in a US-based print culture characterized by routes of circulation and exchange that traversed national boundaries and connected Spanish-speaking communities throughout the hemisphere and beyond. In this way, the book's analysis also contributes to what Carmen Lamas describes as "recuperating and reclaiming the complex and intertwining histories of the Americas and of Latina/os in that history specifically" to pursue understanding of the "deep and constitutive imprint that the Latinx experience, their lives and works, had and continue to have across the Americas and the world."[11]

A recognition that there is not just one monolithic print culture, but many print cultures, undergirds this work of recovering what Anna

Brickhouse has called a "forgotten Spanish-language print culture throughout the United States" and a "lost Latino public sphere."[12] Carl F. Kaestle and Janice A. Radway have argued that "after 1880, what emerged in addition to the mass-market newspapers, magazines, and books . . . was a variety of *specialized* networks for printing, publishing and circulating material that often were quite focused and had more narrow audiences."[13] As one such network, the Spanish-language publications that radiated from New York City at the end of the nineteenth century reveal that late nineteenth-century print culture was far less stable and much more diverse than often presumed. Moreover, they indicate that the publics shaped by these specialized networks sometimes reached farther geographically than their mass-market counterparts, even as the former typically reached much smaller circulation numbers.

In Latinx studies, the hemisphere provides an important conceptual framework for exploring this diversity and instability of nineteenth-century print culture. Claire Fox has argued that the term *hemispheric* is more useful as a designation of "a field for locating particular trajectories rather than an object of analysis itself."[14] While Fox's assessment describes an earlier formulation of hemispheric American studies in the US literary field, her notion that the hemisphere can be a lens through which to identify new patterns of "transit, commerce, and dynamism" has continued to hold true as scholars in Latinx studies have turned their attention toward nineteenth-century and earlier print cultural history.[15] According to Rodrigo Lazo, the archive of what he calls "the Latino nineteenth century" demands "engagement with hemispheric geographies, a variety of textual production, and multiple archival sites."[16] From such a hemispheric vantage point, it becomes possible to locate previously overlooked local, regional, and transnational—especially transamerican—publications, careers, routes, and spheres of influence relevant to Latinx history.[17]

The terms *Latinx*, *American*, and *Latin American*, as I employ them throughout this book, refer to categories of community and identity that were emerging, unstable, relational, and contested in the nineteenth century. Scholars of nineteenth-century US-based Spanish-language print culture have engaged in a rich discussion about the application of the terms *Latina/o*, *Latinx*—or most recently, *Latine*—to this time period. As Raúl Coronado has noted, "'Latino,' in this sense, refers less to a subject-position than it does to a literary and intellectual culture that emerges in the interstices between the United States and Spanish America."[18] Following this line of thought, I employ the term *Latinx* to recognize its increasing (and widely debated) use in Latinx studies in the years since Coronado made his observations in his 2013 book—while acknowledging that the writers and editors considered herein would not have recognized the sense of a unique US-based subject position for individuals of Latin American descent, or the gender neutrality conveyed by the term.[19] The search for a common sense of purpose, community, and identity among people of Latin American descent precedes, but also informs, more recent terms and debates about their use. Engaging with scholars who have worked, as Kirsten Silva Gruesz has explained, to "test out the possibility of a meaningful commonality of the idea of Latino expression, even before the term was invented," my purpose is to situate nineteenth-century Hispanophone publications within a longer trajectory of the development of notions of *latinidad*.[20] In particular, I am interested in ideas of *latinidad* that emerged as direct responses to the possibilities envisioned by Hispanophone writers in the United States and by their interlocutors throughout the hemisphere as a result of their changing world of print.

As they explored the convergence of electric and mechanical innovations that were transforming nineteenth-century print culture, Hispanophone writers and editors of the period constructed notions of *latinidad* that demonstrate Robert McKee Irwin's insight that "in the context of both the nineteenth century and the present . . . Latinidad is perhaps most productively addressed not only as a fixed ethnic identity but also as an unstable, sometimes volatile, and often incomplete transnational process."[21] Scholars have located some of the earliest notions of a shared identity among the nations that experienced Spanish colonialism in the independence movements of the early nineteenth century.[22] Although those foundations clearly influenced late nineteenth-century writers as they made their own attempts to create what Gerard Aching has called "a Spanish American cultural space," neither the terminology for describing the region and its people nor the sense of common experience that such terminology was meant to evoke had found solid ground by the end of the nineteenth century.[23] In *La Habana Elegante* and in the periodicals that served as its interlocutors, the language showed the variability of a still inchoate idea. At times, writers employed phrases such as "nuestra raza, la noble raza hispano-americana" (our people, the noble Hispano-American people).[24] Writers also employed the adjective *hispano-americano/a* (sometimes spelled without the hyphen), and the adjective *latino/a* appeared somewhat less often. *Latinidad*, in this context, constitutes a possibility that was still unfolding—one inseparable from attempts by publications like *La Habana Elegante* and *La Revista Ilustrada de Nueva York* to establish a more interactive media system throughout the hemisphere. As an editorial note published in *La Revista Ilustrada de Nueva York* makes explicit, the point was to find new ways to unite and empower "los pueblos de nuestra raza en este hemisferio" (the people of our race in this hemisphere).[25]

A similar instability and sense of possibility characterizes the meaning of *americano/American* and *América/America* in many of the texts considered throughout this book. In the Spanish-language press, *América* or *americano* references the United States at times, while more typically applying to the entire hemisphere with an emphasis on the Hispanophone part of it. The latter meaning, for example, appears in the title of the New York-based illustrated magazine *La América Ilustrada* (Illustrated America), discussed in chapter 1. That publication's idea of hemispheric *latinidad* accompanies its articulation of Hispanophone América—in contrast to a US Anglo America that had already clearly demonstrated its imperial designs on Latin America. The term *Latin America* also dates back to this period, when it emerged alongside—and in tension with—shifting notions of América/America.[26] While some historians prefer to employ the term *Spanish American* in a nineteenth-century context, I have chosen to use *Latin America* as another emerging category of identity from the period, which participates in the longer history of community and identity formation.

The challenges confronted in this book in choosing words to describe the region and its people provide a reminder that the period's geospatial struggles are inseparable from the possibilities and potential dangers that the editors and writers of Nueva York saw in their changing world of print. In the mid-nineteenth century, the United States acquired nearly half of Mexico's territory through the 1848 Treaty of Guadalupe Hidalgo, which ended the Mexican-American War. By the final decades of the century, the former Mexican citizens of what became US territory were experiencing widespread, violent oppression and refusal by the US government to recognize Mexican land ownership, as the treaty had promised.[27] These realities formed the backdrop against which the period's Spanish- and English-language press debated the potential role of the United States in Cubans' and Puerto Ricans' fight for independence from Spain. Writers and editors within and outside this movement, including those from Venezuela, Nicaragua, and other parts of Latin America, developed new ideas about how modern media might aid in this effort. Some saw opportunities to mobilize new audiences—or to expand the ranks of those who participated in the production of print—in pursuit of goals that transcended (or were not exclusively focused on) increasing circulation and advertising rates. In some cases, they also rethought authorship as a collaborative or collective endeavor, in contrast to contemporaneous efforts to elevate the author or artist in a separate sphere. Those alternate visions of what print could achieve aligned with communitarian ideas of democracy and contrasted with individualist-capitalist narratives associated with Anglophone emerging mass media.[28]

An important site of the formation of these alternate visions of culture and community was New York City, which by the 1870s had long served as a hub of media innovation for writers, editors, and printers of newspapers and magazines in English and Spanish. In Lower Manhattan, where Newspaper Row became the bustling center of the English-language emerging mass press, an active Spanish-language press thrived in the same area—in a few cases, in the same buildings. That community of print included writers from Cuba and Puerto Rico who sought greater freedom in their publishing activities than they could find under Spanish colonial rule.[29] The most famous contributor to New York City's Spanish-language press in the late nineteenth century, Cuban writer and revolutionary José Martí, chose New York as a base starting in 1880 largely because of the well-established Spanish-language publishing community—led, in part, by Cuban exiles like himself—that welcomed him there. Yet the community that surrounded Martí has long been understudied, and its participants pursued their own ideas of how to harness the potential of an expanding and increasingly interconnected world of print.[30] Alongside the emerging mass-circulation English-language press in New York City, the writers and editors of the

Spanish-language press designed and pursued their own vision of the future direction of modern media that would reach beyond the United States, especially to Latin America. At this key historical moment of possibility fueled largely by anticolonial struggle against Spain, that community of print helped to shape and produce influential images of what Esther Allen has described as a "Nueva York [that] is consubstantial with New York: it walks down the same streets, endures the same blizzards, hunches over tables in the same libraries, stares out of windows at the same rivers, is blinded by the same hard, glittering light."[31] As an alternative to the Anglophone New York, Nueva York is a place, as well as an idea of a more communitarian, inclusive print culture whose visions of democracy—and of future independent Cuban and Puerto Rican democratic republics—had some overlaps into anarchism.[32]

Nueva York, as an idea of a more inclusive print culture, reached far beyond the geographical borders of New York City—into a hemispheric community of writers and editors for whom pursuing the possibilities of print and exploring new formulations of community and identity intertwined. As one reviewer put it in praising the New York-based illustrated magazine *La América Ilustrada*, such a publication that "se publica en Nueva York, sin pertenecer a ningun pueblo de los de la América latina, pertenece no obstante, a todos" (is published in New York, without belonging to any Latin American nation, belongs nevertheless to all).[33] As a city whose connections were not limited to any one Latin American nation, Nueva York thus belonged to writers and readers throughout the hemisphere, including those in Havana, Cuba, which boasted one of the largest populations and print cultures in Latin America at the time. Even as Spanish colonial censorship heightened in the context of Cuba's war with Spain that began in 1895, Havana served as an important node in the hemispheric Spanish-language print culture of the period. Other nodes in Nueva York's network included Tampa and Key West, Florida, which were important sites of organizing for Cuban independence, and Buenos Aires, Argentina, where *La Nación* (The Nation) became one of the most prominent Latin American newspapers of the era—in addition to Caracas, Lima, Mexico City, Philadelphia, San Francisco, and Santiago de Chile, among others. Within that wide-ranging network of Nueva York, writers and editors considered the possibilities of their changing world of print in the context of Cuba's and Puerto Rico's anticolonial struggle, as well as the shift toward authoritarianism within some of the Latin American nations that had achieved their independence from Spain earlier in the century. They also grappled with the United States as a representation of democracy, finding hope in US democratic institutions centered on education and press freedom while also critical of the nation's imperialistic endeavors in and beyond the hemisphere and of violent racial discrimination within its own borders.

The word *democracy* appears in late nineteenth-century Nueva York's publications that participated in such experimentation as another shifting and slippery term. It is important to recognize, as an August 1896 article in *Doctrina de Martí* explains, that among Cubans who supported independence from Spain at that stage in the island's decades-long struggle, "no todos esos mismos cubanos, convenimos por igual, en el breve establecimiento en Cuba, de una República absolutamente democrática" (not all of those same Cubans agree equally in the brief establishment in Cuba, of an absolutely democratic Republic).[34] Also worth noting is that the form of government pursued by the Cuban and Puerto Rican movement as Cuba embarked on its third independence war with Spain was a democratic republic, while democracy also served as a more abstract concept linked to ideas of liberty and equality. Among those who held up democracy as an ideal, some employed the term to signal the need for the Cuban and Puerto Rican independence movement to focus on equality and justice, as was the case in *Doctrina de Martí*. Anarchist papers like *El Despertar* critiqued US democracy as corrupted beyond repair and envisioned a world organized solely through community collaboration and exchange; yet they also recognized some democratic institutions in the United States as "todo cuanto de bueno existe en el país: bibliotecas, museos, universidades, instituciones filantrópicas" (all the good that exists in the country: libraries, museums, universities, philanthropic institutions).[35] In their pursuit of an egalitarian future for their overlapping communities, these and other publications evoked what Donald Pease has described in the context of Martí's writing as "an American democracy that has yet to come."[36] That ideal of democracy remains unrealized, in part, because of US influence following the 1898 intervention in Cuba's war with Spain. It was also stalled because of racism among Cuban leaders of the new nation, which compromised the egalitarian vison for the future of Cuba, Puerto

Rico, and Latin America more broadly that Nueva York's publications circulated. As Vanessa Valdés has explained, "Postindependence Cuba had failed to achieve José Martí's dream of a united nation; in the years following the establishment of the Cuban republic in 1902, the Cuban government had actively encouraged Spanish immigration in efforts to whiten the country, passing over those men who had fought in the Ten Years War of 1868–1878, the Little War of 1879–1880, and what has come to be known as the Spanish-American War of 1898."[37]

Before that political turning point, an article reprinted in *Doctrina de Martí* from a US Anglophone publication dedicated to the period's single tax movement, captures something of the potentiality of the ideas about participation and democracy that thrived in Nueva York: "Probable es que los cubanos tengan una envidiable oportunidad de aprovecharse de nuestros errores, y á no ser que su anhelo de Libertad sea meramente librarse de una forma de tiranía para abrazar otra, establecerán la igualdad de derechos al uso de la tierra." (It is likely that Cubans have an enviable opportunity to learn from our mistakes, and unless their desire for freedom is merely to get rid of one form of tyranny to embrace another, they will establish equal rights to land use.)[38] It is not difficult to see why *Doctrina de Martí*'s editor Rafael Serra would have chosen to reprint the article (outside its context of advocacy for a US national single tax based on land value) for its suggestion that Cubans had an opportunity to improve on the shortcomings of the United States and make their own, better form of democracy. Within and outside *Doctrina de Martí*, Serra and his collaborators, who included Figueroa, Juan Bonilla, and Francisco Gonzalo "Pachín" Marín, advocated passionately for what one 1896 editorial note called "la práctica de la verdadera democracia" (the practice of true democracy).[39] This book attends to the ways in which Serra, Figueroa, Martí, and others who participated in Nueva York's publishing community made use of writing and audience building through new publications to pursue their cause—for which "true democracy" provided an intermittent and imperfect shorthand. In that context, the visionary publications of nineteenth-century Nueva York provided powerful resources—both conceptual and material—for making media a tool of democracy.

Nineteenth-Century Media Change and Nueva York's Network

My contention throughout this book is that attention to nineteenth-century media change—brought into focus through the novel ideas that it enabled and inspired in US-based Spanish-language periodicals and their interlocutors—provides a means of recovering the diversity and complexity of the period's print culture and of locating Latinx media innovation within it. The term "media change" draws on the work of scholars who have noted that, while media systems and the social processes to which they contribute are never static, "some moments of change are more revealing than others."[40] As William Uricchio explains, "The history of 'old media' developments, if freed from the teleological determinism which so often accompanies retrospective considerations, can provide a surprisingly diverse range of alternative concepts and consequences," many of which appear in retrospect as "dead ends and spoiled dreams."[41] In Latin American and US film studies, scholars have employed this perspective to consider the early years of cinema, when it was far from a given that film technologies would lead to the kind of theater-based public spectacle that cinema would become in the early twentieth century.[42] Media change also encompasses the "remediation" of older forms of media, as new ones redefine their potential uses.[43] As Richard Menke noted in his study of nineteenth-century British realist novels, "The appearance of newer media helped to alter the meaning of print textuality in the nineteenth-century's media environment."[44] *Printing Nueva York* explores such a transformation of print textuality. It traces the ways in which the telegraph, telephone, wood engraving, cylinder presses, and other electric and mechanical media innovations enabled and inspired wide-ranging and ambitious experimentation and negotiation over new possible uses of the old—and still dominant—medium of print, especially in newspapers and magazines.

Such negotiations and experimentation repeatedly run into questions of power and privilege that also motivate the search for lost voices in Latinx history. As scholars within Latinx studies have enacted "a philosophical move away from the teleological mode of *prediction* into the more complex temporality of *prophecy*," they have also generated discussions of alternative cultural formations.[45] In parallel with the alternative uses of new technologies revealed within media studies, this kind of alternative within Latinx history demonstrates that the notions of community and identity most familiar to us were not preordained. Some of the period's media alternatives, then, converge with the "moments of failure, of dreams that failed to cohere" that Coronado calls upon scholars to pursue in order to investigate "the discursive world of nineteenth-century Latinas/os, a world filled with texts and individuals that held competing, often contradictory, beliefs."[46] Those long-lost dreams demonstrate "culture as struggle and media as means in that struggle—a fabric continually rewoven according to the interests of a given time and place."[47] The late nineteenth-century Spanish- and English-language texts considered here set out to influence whose publications, media practices, ideas, and culture would define hemispheric print culture and played a critical sociopolitical role in the age of electricity.[48]

One source of inspiration for exploring new forms of storytelling was the transformational present. Stephen Kern argues that the present emerged as new imaginative territory starting with the invention of the telegraph in 1836, when it was "the sense of the present [that] was the most distinctively new, . . . expanded spatially to create the vast, shared experience of simultaneity."[49] As undersea telegraph cables expanded the reach of the telegraph and the telephone entered into the media landscape following its invention in 1876, they inspired a new surge of speculation about the present.[50] According to Uricchio, "Although the telegraph before it had transformed Western notions of time and space, the telephone offered something even more radical—the live transmission of voice, the opportunity to direct point-to-point encounters with the simultaneous."[51] This "directable simultaneity" made it possible for anyone who had access to a telephone to do what required vast resources, like those of the most successful daily newspapers around the globe, to accomplish by telegraph. Kern notes, "Telephones break down barriers of distance—horizontally across the face of the land and vertically across social strata."[52]

Even when they did not engage with telegraphs and telephones directly, cultural producers considered them part of the broader media landscape that made their communication possible and inspired them to envision how print could be a vehicle for realizing future dreams. As Janet Murray observes, "Storytellers and theorists build imaginary landscapes of information, writing stories and essays that later become blueprints for actual systems."⁵³ From that perspective, the writers and editors of Nueva York participated in a phenomenon that differs from the formation of national imagined communities that Benedict Anderson attributed to the shared reading experiences of newspapers and novels. In contrast to such communities, which took shape as a by-product of "print-capitalism," late nineteenth-century Latinx editors and writers actively set out to harness the power of print media to mediate new communities, many of which traversed national boundaries by design.⁵⁴ Mediation, in this sense, is not a passive process, but rather a deliberate form of mediating change—through engagement with media to construct an audience, a movement, a community, a nation, a better world.

Gerard Aching has made a similar observation in the context of *modernismo*, the Latin American literary movement that included as participants many of the writers whom I consider here. The images of modern life produced by *modernistas*, he explains, were "not imagined passively, as in Anderson's *Imagined Communities*, but [were] purposefully constructed through a symbolic, utopian discourse."⁵⁵ *Printing Nueva York* extends Aching's recognition of strategic efforts to mediate a new audience into a broader range of nineteenth-century texts—some but not all of which participated in *modernismo*. As they sought to update literary writing, these media innovators also envisioned potential futures of modern media—some designed with hopeful, liberatory intentions—that would never (or have not yet) come to be. Building on Aching's observations, an alternate metaphor to the imagined community that helps to capture the intentionality of Nueva York's writers and editors, as well as the specific period of media change in which they participated, is the network.

Twenty-first-century notions of the *network* and networking date back to the nineteenth century and correspond with the deliberate efforts of Nueva York's editors and writers to connect and empower a community of printers, editors, writers, and readers. As I have noted elsewhere, "First used in the sixteenth century to evoke the interlacing pattern of fabric or netting, by the nineteenth century, network came to mean 'any netlike or complex system or collection of interrelated things, as topographical features, lines of transportation, or telecommunications routes' and also 'an interconnected group of people.'"⁵⁶ John Fagg, Matthew Pethers, and Robin Vandome have argued that "nineteenth-century magazines and newspapers offer . . . a fertile lens through which Americanists can begin to engage with the question of how social connections were forged and furthered in the pre-digital age."[57] Pursuing such a line of inquiry in a US Anglophone context, Stacey Margolis has argued that the period's "emergent social networks foster new forms of political influence and . . . such influence begins to refigure the very idea of participation."[58] Such rethinking of participation and of what kind of collaboration might be possible through print is precisely what happened in the publications of Nueva York starting in the 1870s. As Nueva York's late nineteenth-century publications formed their own social networks, they displayed an interest in privileging creativity and in blurring the line between producer and consumer in ways that early twenty-first-century notions of—and debates about—participatory culture help to elucidate.

The term *participatory culture* emerged near the turn of the twenty-first century initially in relation to fan communities. Henry Jenkins's foundational 1992 study *Textual Poachers: Television Fans and Participatory Culture* defined participatory culture as a process through which "fans cease to be simply an audience for popular texts; instead, they become active participants in the construction and circulation of textual meanings."[59] More recently, in recognizing the characteristics and limitations of participatory culture in a digital context, Jenkins has described participatory culture as "one which embraces the value of diversity and democracy throughout every aspect of our interactions with each other—one which assumes that we are capable of making decisions, collectively and individually, and that we should have the capacity to express ourselves through a broad range of different forms and practices."[60] In describing this phenomenon, Jenkins and others have acknowledged that such practices that promote diversity and democracy are ideals that are rarely fully realized—and that are often in conflict with the individualist, capitalist aims of media companies, including social media platforms. Scholars also recognize that participatory culture existed, albeit far less prevalently, before digital media.[61] In the case of late nineteenth-century Nueva York, its editors' and writers' notions of movement building and enabling collaboration through participation in print might also be said to have delivered more fully than digital fan culture or early social media on the promise Jenkins saw in participation as an alternative to spectatorship or consumption. Nueva York's participants did more than interact with nineteenth-century print culture as what we might call today fans or users. They were innovators who brought together the power of storytelling with new publications that they created and circulated as a means of making the world in which they wanted to live. As they did so, they also extended notions of the public sphere, with its Habermasian associations of open exchange and debate, into participation in the production of those ideas and in the new kinds of publications that circulated them.[62]

These same writers and editors of nineteenth-century Nueva York also raised questions that align with recent critiques of the limits of participation as an ideal. Reflecting on twenty-first-century design processes for civic and other technologies, Sasha Costanza-Chock notes that "many design approaches that are supposedly more inclusive, participatory, and democratic actually serve an extractive function."[63] In a twenty-first-century media system in which many platforms that might be called participatory also profit on data mining and division, even well-intentioned processes of involving community members in generating ideas and reviewing new product designs often create value for the companies leading the work—while failing to produce "community ownership, profit, credit, and visibility" for those who participated.[64] In the very different context of nineteenth-century print culture, similar questions of how to make a publication a site of collaboration and a source of benefit for its community emerge in the most thoughtful publications of Nueva York. At a time when Anglophone mass-circulation publications engaged in their own efforts that might also be considered participatory in their pursuit of mass audiences (through contests and investigative stories aimed at exposing political and business corruption), the idea that a publication might be a means to another kind of end was, itself, revolutionary. It differentiates the publications of Nueva York from the progressive, capitalist model of many of their Anglophone counterparts—and also from similarly motivated notions of participatory culture designed by media companies today.

The unique experiments and questions sparked by electric media by the end of the nineteenth century also help to differentiate earlier formations of US-based Hispanophone print culture from the late nineteenth-century texts considered in this book. In his study of early nineteenth-century Philadelphia, Rodrigo Lazo traces Spanish-language print culture in the northeastern United States to the 1820s, when it emerged at "the intricate intersection of, on the one hand, conditions for a for-profit print culture in Philadelphia, and, on the other hand, the political goals of trans-American intellectuals who . . . moved in tandem with changes in the commerce of Philadelphia printing and political changes brought on by anticolonial battles in Spanish America."[65] This was a market in which communication largely took place through the circulation of personal and published letters at a pace set by ships and horses. Coronado comments on the speed of communications in the early nineteenth century in his consideration of Mexican tejanos in the decades preceding the Mexican-American War, observing that "the temporality of the communication network—the length in time it took for imprints to circulate across the Atlantic—appears to have varied between two to four months."[66] In the print-dominated media system of that time, a sense of belonging to a transnational public sphere did not include the ideas of simultaneity that would emerge later in the century as print entered the age of electricity. By the late nineteenth century, however, media change had transformed the horizon of possibility, as well as the means through which writers and editors might set out to realize new possible worlds.

This is not to say that the late nineteenth century saw a wholesale transformation of the media system. Indeed, late nineteenth-century writers and editors continued to rely on ships and horses—or a walk to the editorial office—to submit their contributions. The figure of the correspondent also loomed large in many of the Spanish-language periodicals analyzed here. The *crónica* (chronicle) genre associated with the literary movement of *modernismo* that emerged from this community generally took the form of letters or regular columns from a foreign correspondent or a local member of the community who reflected on a wide variety of current events, including artistic performances, social gossip, political happenings, and reflections on modern life.[67] These published letters remediated the model of epistolary communication that Lazo locates in the early nineteenth century by redefining the role of such writing in relation to the period's new electric media and the corresponding possibilities that writers articulated in reflections like the one by Bolet Peraza considered at the outset of this introduction.[68] Within the *crónica*—and in a wide range of familiar and unfamiliar publications that circulated in the publications of nineteenth-century Nueva York—writers tapped into hopes and fears that surrounded the tangle of new electric and mechanical media that were transforming their world of print to articulate new ideas of being and belonging, mobilize collectivities to achieve Cuban and Puerto Rican independence, and facilitate the wide-ranging collaboration necessary to make more just democracies throughout the hemisphere. Together, these texts reveal understudied notions of the literary that invite rethinking of the study of nineteenth-century print culture in Nueva York and beyond.

The Democratic Literary Imagination at the Crossroads of Literary and Media Studies

Printing Nueva York shakes up notions of the literary, while also demonstrating the relevance of literary study to understanding the cultural and political dimensions of media change. Literary scholars have demonstrated that "media history and literary history share the same groundwater."[69] Yet within media studies, literature remains marginal to investigations of the media innovations and their cultural implications.[70] If we consider the literary as a category of discourse that is uniquely reflective about its relationship to the broader media system (and therefore constantly shifting in relation to it), writing that engages an imaginative element, regardless of its literary quality or form, provides a vantage point from which to view the complex and diverse processes through which changes in media practices influence notions of identity, community, and the possibility for social and political change. From such a vantage point that connects writing and its forms to historically specific media practices, platforms, and transitions, it also follows that literary innovation is a kind of media innovation. The writers and editors—or more broadly, cultural producers—who engage in such innovation are also media innovators.

To rewire literary and media history in this way requires different starting points and research questions than those that are typical of literary study. For example, an early version of this project examined the commonalities and differences between the concurrent literary movements of Latin American *modernismo* and US realism. As it became clear that the writers and editors associated with these movements approached writing as a means of acting on the possibilities they saw in nineteenth-century media change, however, I began to see Latin American *modernismo* and US realism as two of many possible end points rather than starting points. To avoid privileging these culminating literary configurations in my analysis of the archive, Latin American *modernismo* and US realism are no longer my primary objects of study. In shifting the center of my analysis, I defamiliarize those widely discussed literary formations. They become portals into a world of obsolete ideas about what should become the future of journalism and literature, forgotten notions of identity and community, and lost connections between English- and Spanish-language communities of print centered in the United States, especially in New York City.

A recent archival turn at the intersection of periodical studies, Latinx studies, and US and Latin American literary studies has shown the importance of decentering canonical literary formations. Lazo has argued for the need to consider literature in its broader meaning of "printed matter," emphasizing that "it is important not to relinquish 'literature' to a contemporary historical formulation that emphasizes certain literary genres in the twentieth century."[71] Similarly, Coronado has observed that literary scholars have "fetishized" traditional literary forms such as the novel, poetry, and drama and has called instead for "read[ing] history from the unsure, unfolding perspective of its makers" in order to "discover other worlds, in texts both new and familiar, that can challenge us to see other glistening, brutal, tenuous desires to achieve a sense of immanence."[72] As we will see, late nineteenth-century Nueva York complicates the story of Latin American *modernismo* as a movement focused on achieving literary specialization and distinction.[73] As I have argued elsewhere, "In place of polished literary forms—or even hybrid ones like the literary-journalistic genre of the *crónica*, which scholars have long cited as a defining form of *modernismo*—one finds relics of print culture that might be easy to overlook. They include editorial notes, appeals to readers and sales agents to submit their subscription fees, and hopeful announcements of the possibilities of new media technologies."[74] A wide range of publications of Nueva York, some of which associated themselves with *modernismo* and others that did not, might be considered experiments with the literary in the sense that would have been familiar to writers and editors of late nineteenth-century Nueva York:

as a category of writing that was in flux, shifting along with the new possibilities explored in newspapers and magazines of the period, and that had blurred boundaries with journalistic writing, which was also in transition at the time.

Scholars who have articulated the significance of the *crónica* genre for the Latin American literary field, including Fina García Marruz, Laura Lomas, Julio Ramos, and Susana Rotker, have paved the way for this book's investigation of Nueva York's literary innovations in the context of late nineteenth-century media change.[75] As Lomas has argued in her analysis of what she calls the "Latino modernism" demonstrated by Martí in New York, his writing "moves not only across languages but also across the gap between the existent and the possible to stress the role of the imagination as a force for creative political change."[76] Of course, the role of imagination in the revolutionary work of late nineteenth-century Nueva York—as its leaders raised funds, built coalitions, and planned for Cuban and Puerto Rican independence—reached well beyond the printed page, including speeches, clubs, archiving initiatives, and other organizing activities. Yet a unique kind of imaginative experiment to support these revolutionary efforts took place in the context of late nineteenth-century media change, as some of the most visionary writers and editors of Nueva York set out to write into existence a more equitable world. They pursued an ideal that was democratic—even as the future political formations in Cuba and Puerto Rico for which they advocated were also the subject of much debate—in the sense that they prioritized widespread collaboration and participation in planning an equitable future of Cuba, Puerto Rico, and beyond. Their publications were literary in the sense that they brought together storytelling and strategic engagement within a changing media system to explore the possibilities and limits of newspapers and magazines for creating collaborative processes, and for creating value that was not defined (or at least not only) by a publication's circulation size and profit.

Such literary experimentation took varying forms as the publications of Nueva York shared in what might be called a democratic literary imagination. The writers and editors of these publications made collective and purposeful use of narrative and print media to imagine and promote broad engagement and dialogue in striving for racial, gender, and economic justice in Cuba, Puerto Rico, and beyond. Writing that contributed to this work, even when penned by a single author, did not operate in isolation; it required exchange, revision, circulation, and movement building. It also often involved debate and (not always reconcilable) disagreement. It is important to note that collaboration and collective action do not necessarily mean harmony. Rather, many of Nueva York's publications were dynamic, sometimes cacophonous, platforms for shaping and circulating ideas. Literature in that context is quite the opposite of polished final forms that are the product of an author's solitary genius; literature becomes, instead, multi-authored, unlimited by generic conventions, and always a work in progress.

Magazines and newspapers provided ideal platforms for this kind of experimentation and negotiation guided by the democratic literary imagination of Nueva York. It is worth noting that in Spanish in the late nineteenth century, the words *revista* (magazine) and *periódico* (newspaper) did not signal entirely distinct types of publications—and I have referred to Spanish-language publications as magazines only when they employed the word *revista*. As Carmen Suárez León has explained, "Estos términos aún se empleaban con diversos matices y vacilaciones, y en general, se utilizaba el substantivo *periódico* para nombrar a todo impreso que saliera a la luz cada cierto tiempo." (These terms were still being used with various nuances and hesitations, and in general the noun newspaper was used to name any printed matter published periodically.)[77] The fluidity of these words in Spanish highlights an aspect of magazines and newspapers that was true in Spanish- and English-language publishing communities at the time. These were old forms of print whose roles and conventions were in transition; newspapers and magazines thus provided flexibility for editors, printers, and writers who wanted to explore new possibilities in their changing world of print. As we will see, one idea that took varying forms from the 1870s through the 1890s was that the new publications of Nueva York served as workshops that extended across space and time, providing the opportunity for collaboration on ideas and movement building to take place within their pages.

Because of the prominence of magazines and newspapers as the vehicles of choice for late nineteenth-century writers and editors who tapped into Nueva York's democratic literary imagination, editorial teams and the strategies they articulated play an important role in my analysis. Jim Casey and Sarah Salter have argued that "a better understanding of the archives of editorship can illuminate the role of periodical publishing, and serial media more broadly, in building communities across different nations, languages, and historical periods."[78] In an analysis of the *Colored Citizen*, a Cincinnati-based African American weekly newspaper published in the 1860s, Jewon Woo argues that a focus on "the collective editorship of multiethnic periodicals can reveal how they constantly evolved and revived themselves under communal leadership, responding to the ever changing dynamics of their communities."[79] Such collaboration, negotiation, and transformation, evidenced most clearly in the genre of the editorial note, also characterize the editorial teams of the contemporaneous Spanish-language periodicals of Nueva York. In addition, following Ayendy Bonifacio's observation that advertisements "exist outside complete editorial management in ways that news and editorials do not . . . [and] thus allow us to access a fuller picture of the periodical's social context," I suggest that advertising offers another (often contrasting) angle on editorial strategy in the chapters that follow.[80]

While *Printing Nueva York* largely employs traditional humanities methods of close and contextual reading, I also take inspiration from conversations that position the digital humanities as a field from which scholars might mobilize "new digital worlds."[81] As Roopika Risam has argued, "The opportunity to intervene in the digital cultural record—to tell new stories, shed light on counter-histories, and create spaces for communities to produce and share their own knowledges should they wish—is the great promise of digital humanities."[82] I would add that digital and traditional humanities methods must work in tandem to achieve these ends—particularly through the fields, including Latinx studies, that are built on challenging colonial knowledge structures.

Printing Nueva York thus models what a combined literary and media history looks like when we enter into the archival record to narrate histories of "the multitude, the dispossessed, the subaltern, and the enslaved," which Saidiya Hartman has noted require scholars to "grapple with the power and authority of the archive and the limits it sets on what can be known, whose perspective matters, and who is endowed with the gravity and authority of historical actor."[83] As Thomas Augst has suggested, "Encountered across digital archives, US literature becomes a collection rather than a canon, whose rich materials and extensible organization enable more expansive accounting of formats and contexts of textual circulation."[84] The idea of replacing the canon with a collection—or perhaps many possible collections—captures something of the possibility of our own media moment for research on literary and media history. Within the vast field that literature becomes when we look beyond familiar texts and established notions of literary value, the idea of the collection provides a means of contemplating the multiple pathways and patterns that scholars, their students, and the public might find in exploring that new territory. *Printing Nueva York* represents one of many such possible collections—which draws on texts accessed through a combination of digital archives, microfilm reels, and paper archives located in the United States, Cuba, and Argentina.

To reenter the worlds dreamed up by those texts today is to see what could have been from the perspective of its most hopeful and ambitious moments of emergence. It is also to understand how, as Gitelman suggests, "all new media emerge into and help to reconstruct publics and public life."[85] Our ability to access those worlds—and also the limits we encounter in our attempts to do so—are testaments to Gitelman's observation that new media raise questions of "what (and who) gets preserved—written down, printed up, recorded, filmed, taped, or scanned—and why."[86] Moreover, our current media moment provides new opportunities to employ historical methods that can recover lost and suppressed voices and ideas of the past, especially as digital archives and digital humanities methods expand opportunities to explore the archival record and to contemplate its absences.

Late nineteenth-century Nueva York's innovations provide a reminder that another world is possible. But casting off the structures of oppression that continue to maintain a tight grip on the realm of the possible in our own period of media change, as they did in the past, is not the easy path. In this sense, the story that unfolds in the pages that follow may point to ways to imagine a digital future that pick up where nineteenth-century Nueva York left off. Reconnecting literary and media history, in that light, might also be considered a point of departure for reimagining humanistic inquiry to prioritize engaging researchers, students, and the public in putting the lost voices of our past in conversation with ongoing struggles for social justice in the present. One such collection of voices from the past appears through late nineteenth-century Nueva York's publications that sought to dream up and realize a more just world.

Entering Nineteenth-Century Nueva York

Across this book's five chapters, my analysis reanimates some of Nueva York's most hopeful and ambitious ideas—from early articulations of the magazine as a workshop for enabling collaboration across distances in the 1870s illustrated Spanish-language press, to notions of collaborative rather than individual authorship—or what I am calling the "networked author"—in Spanish- and English-language periodicals and novels of the late 1880s, to emergent notions of a more participatory print culture in literary magazines of that same decade that explored the idea of the magazine as a walking library and as a site of two-way exchange between writer and reader inspired by the telephone. Following those experiments, a more fully realized conception of the magazine as workshop for collaboration and collective action appeared in the Cuban separatist press of the 1890s. Throughout Nueva York during the final decades of the nineteenth century, and in some cases into the early twentieth, ideas of editorship centered on community building and movement making—and of public writing and archival work as important methods of rewriting history and understanding its relationship to the present—supported and extended the work of the democratic literary imagination in the publications of Nueva York.

Chapter 1, "*Taller* Magazines: Networking Nueva York in the 1870s Illustrated Press," considers the 1870s illustrated press, where the idea of a Nueva York with a hemispheric network inspired by the possibilities of electric media began. During this decade, which constituted the heyday of the illustrated press in New York City—in both Spanish- and English-language communities of print—magazines like *El Mundo Nuevo* (*The New World*), which briefly partnered with Frank Leslie's Publishing House, and *La América Ilustrada* (which later merged with *El Mundo Nuevo*) took inspiration from the global connectivity enabled by telegraph cables to create a shared platform for writers, editors, and readers advocating for democracy and Hispanophone culture. The chapter examines three key responses to technological and hemispheric modernity: the rise of the Anglophone mass-circulation press, which featured an individualist-capitalist approach to the future of print and democracy; the Baudelairian observer of modernity, who would later influence Latin American *modernismo*; and the magazine as a *taller*, or workshop, for collective democratic engagement. This latter vision, emerging in *La América Ilustrada* and in the illustrated guidebook *Guía de la ciudad de Nueva York y sus alrededores*, written by Antonio Bachiller y Morales and published by Néstor Ponce de León, laid the groundwork for later publications of Nueva York as they continued the struggle for Cuban and Puerto Rican independence.

Chapter 2, "Heroic Reporters and Networked Authors: Innovations from New Journalism and Its Collaborative Literary Alternatives," turns to the reporter—a much-criticized figure by Spanish-language magazines of the 1880s and 1890s. After Joseph Pulitzer purchased the *New York World* in 1883, that publication, along with its primary competitor, the *New York Sun*, built on the idea of the reporter or special artist from the Anglophone illustrated press and conceptions of romantic individualism in literature to make their reporters stars of news stories that helped to draw a stark line between writers and readers. The chapter contrasts the rise of the reporter in the *New York World* and the *New York Sun* with what I call "networked authors." It analyzes major works that reflect on labor issues of the time, including Henry James's *The Princess Casamassima*, William Dean Howells's *A Hazard of New Fortunes*, and José Martí's *crónicas* "Nueva York bajo la nieve" (New York under snow) and "Un drama terrible" (A terrible drama.) These texts prioritize collaborative or democratic approaches to authorship, challenging the individualistic reporter model. The chapter also introduces the anarchist newspaper *El Despertar*, which critiques the *World* and envisions a more just future for the press.

Chapter 3, "Mobile Libraries and Telephonic Literature: Participatory Futures of Print from *La Habana Elegante* and *La Revista Ilustrada de Nueva York*," compares the participatory futures of print pursued in the 1880s and early 1890s by the New York-based *La Revista Ilustrada de Nueva York* (New York Illustrated Magazine) and the Havana-based *La Habana Elegante* (Elegant Havana), which maintained close connections to the Spanish-language publishing community of Nueva York. *La Revista Ilustrada* promoted democratic participation through collaboration in creating new ideas and democratic models—figured in the magazine by an idea of a walking library. *La Habana Elegante* explored the concept of direct, real-time communication between publications and readers, inspired by the telegraph and telephone and figured by a notion of what I call "telephonic literature." Both periodicals drew from the collaborative foundations of earlier publications like *El Mundo Nuevo* and *La América Ilustrada*, seeking to create a more interactive and democratic relationship between writers and readers. Martí's "Nuestra América," which first appeared in *La Revista Ilustrada* (and soon afterward in Mexico City's *El Partido Liberal*) in 1891, exemplifies this vision. Martí suggests a form of creative production and participation that transcended borders and colonial legacies, for which Figueroa also advocated as a contributing editor of *La Revista Ilustrada*.

The emergent participatory futures of print envisioned in the Spanish-language periodicals of the 1880s and 1890s found further articulation in the newspapers and periodicals that emerged in the buildup to and during Cuba's third independence war with Spain. Chapter 4, "Revolutionary Workshops: The US-Based Cuban Separatist Press in the Age of Yellow Journalism," examines the Cuban separatist press of the late 1890s. This chapter contrasts the scandal-driven, telegraph-based model of yellow journalism, as practiced by the *New York World* and *New York Journal*, with the collaborative, participatory model of the Cuban revolutionary newspapers *Doctrina de Martí* and *La Revista de Cuba Libre*. These Spanish-language publications updated the idea of the newspaper as a *taller*, or workshop, for democratic participation. *La Revista de Cuba Libre*, led by Torriente and her editorial team dominated by women, redefined women's roles in the Cuban independence movement, while *Doctrina de Martí*, founded by Serra and his primary collaborator Figueroa, advocated for labor and racial equality. Both publications embraced anti-imperialist and anti-capitalist ideals, offering a powerful counternarrative to the mass-circulation press and imagining a more just, collective future for Cuba and the Americas. They did so as Cuba's war with Spain became the site in which the yellow press devoted unprecedented resources to developing stories with mass appeal. In that context, Nueva York's publications embraced the newspaper-as-workshop model more fully than their predecessors, making their publications more explicitly anti-capitalist and anti-imperialist.

Although the compromised ending in 1898 of Cuba's final independence war with Spain marked the end of an era of New York-based Spanish-language publishing (in which the shared anticolonial struggle of Cuba and Puerto Rico against Spain had provided a gravitational center), the expressions of the democratic literary imagination within it led to legacies that scholars have not typically recognized as such. Chapter 5, "Work in Progress: Editorship from the Margins of Print and at the Limits of Literature in Nueva York," examines the role of editorship in the publishing community of late nineteenth-century Nueva York. The chapter contextualizes editorship within nineteenth-century Nueva York alongside other forms of activism, including public speaking, protesting, and archiving suppressed histories—and as a vehicle for literary innovation that resisted market-driven literary genres. The chapter explores key examples: *El Despertar*, where editors like Luis Barcia, José Cayetano Campos, and Pedro Esteve bridged print, education, and movement building; and *Minerva*, edited by a team of women, including Etelvina Zayas ("E. T. Elvina") and Úrsula Coimbra de Valverde ("Cecilia"), which advocated for Black women's rights despite systemic barriers to publishing. Finally, it considers how Teófilo Domínguez's *Figuras y figuritas: Ensayos biográficos* (Big and small figures: Biographical essays) and Arturo Schomburg's early twentieth-century essays and letters to the editor of the *New York Times*, along with his curation of African diasporic texts, shifted focus from print media to historical preservation as a means of collective action. An afterword, called "Democracy Now: Twenty-First-Century Legacies of Nineteenth-Century Nueva York," highlights contemporary projects in which storytelling, digital and public humanities, education, and civic engagement intersect to shape democratic futures, arguing that such projects continue the legacy of nineteenth-century Nueva York.

Together, these chapters elucidate the observation made by Marshall McLuhan in the epigraph to this introduction: "Paradoxically, it was not through the book but through the development of the mass press, particularly the telegraph press, that poets found artistic keys to the world of simultaneity, or of modern myth." His words offer a hint of the creative license taken by writers and editors who responded to the many material factors, including new technologies like the telegraph, that contributed to media change in the nineteenth century. In this light, it may not be such a paradox as McLuhan may have thought to see technology and artistic interpretation coming together within the expanding print culture of the late nineteenth century. Their interrelationship offers an illustration of the artistry behind the periods in media history when a major shift in the way people see the world is at hand. In those periods of transition, cultural producers have opportunities to influence the experience of human affairs that can result from media change at its most revolutionary moments. The best of these cultural producers set about doing so with all the intentionality and skill of a mythic bard spinning a tale that captivates, convinces, and inspires as it mediates new possible worlds and accompanying forms of being and belonging.

1

Taller Magazines

NETWORKING NUEVA YORK IN THE 1870S
ILLUSTRATED PRESS

The New York-based illustrated magazine *La América Ilustrada* (Illustrated America) first rolled off its own presses, housed in rented office
space within the New York Times Building at 41 Park Row, in January
1872. During that same month, in the small, bustling plaza across the
street, the city unveiled a statue of Benjamin Franklin, the father of
American printing, whose towering presence heralded the success of
the leading Anglophone daily newspapers nearby, which included the
New York Sun and the *New York Tribune*, in addition to the *Times*.[1] This
was the period when Park Row began to take on a new identity as Newspaper Row, eventually replacing the area's previous moniker, Printing
House Square. *La America Ilustrada*'s editors Juan Ignacio de Armas y
Céspedes and Enrique Piñeyro rooted the identity of their own publication within that same dynamic locale.

The May 15, 1872, issue of *La América Ilustrada* included a two-page
illustration stretching from Brooklyn, across the East River—and including a projection of what the Brooklyn Bridge, whose construction
had begun two years earlier, would look like after its completion—to
its own building in Lower Manhattan. According to the accompanying
note, "El edificio . . . con la bandera americana encima i con la palabra
TIMES en su fachada, es uno de los principales de la ciudad, i en él
estan la redaccion e imprenta de LA AMÉRICA ILUSTRADA." (The
building . . . with the American flag on top and with the word TIMES
on its façade, is one of the main ones in the city, and in it are the news-
room and printing press of LA AMÉRICA ILUSTRADA.)[2] By highlighting *La América Ilustrada*'s site of production within the New York
Times Building, the note brings New York City into focus as a site of the
hemispheric, Spanish-language print culture to which the periodical and

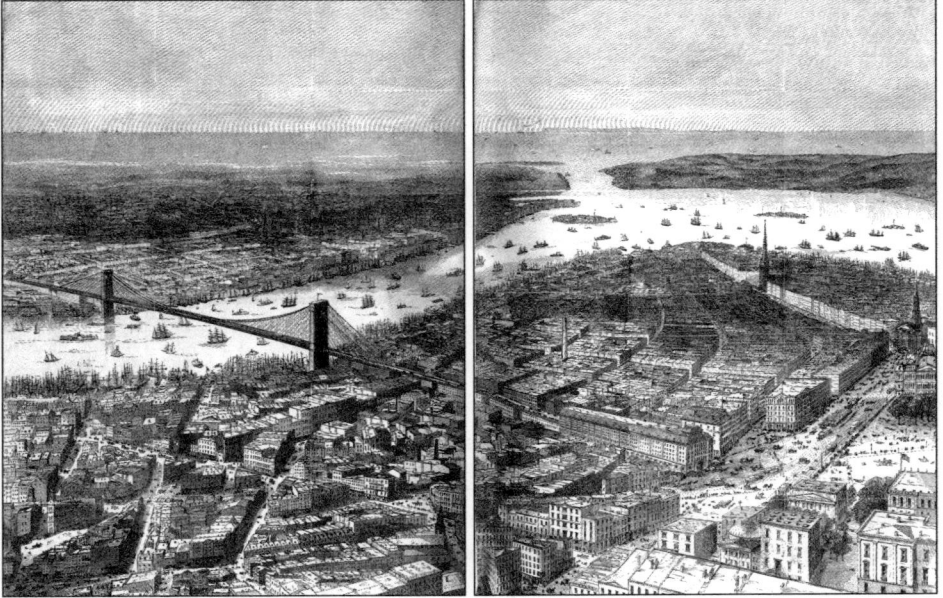

Figure 1.1. Illustration of Lower Manhattan from the Brooklyn Bridge to the New York Times Building. "La metropoli americana," *La América Ilustrada*, May 15, 1872, 136–237.

its readers belonged. The editors position their Nueva York within the boundaries of the hemispheric América that the magazine claims as its territory. From that vantage point they also promoted their own ideas about the purpose of print, which diverged sharply from the emerging Anglophone mass-circulation model celebrated by the statue of Ben Franklin—and, as we will see, from another model with broad reach that privileged individual observers over collaborative teams.

This chapter considers *La América Ilustrada*—along with *El Mundo Nuevo* (The New World), another leading New York-based Hispanophone illustrated magazine of the 1870s edited by Piñeyro, and *Guía de la ciudad de Nueva York y sus alrededores* (Guide to New York City and its surroundings), a guidebook written and published by two major contributors to the city's Spanish-language press, Antonio Bachiller y Morales and Néstor Ponce de León. As the undersea cable projects of the 1870s gave the telegraph global reach, and these and other illustrated magazines tapped into print technologies that made it easier and faster to produce and circulate illustrated magazines, they constructed a Nueva

York that updated earlier notions of hemispheric unity to define active roles for their network of printers, editors, contributors, and readers in shaping the region's future. Despite the limitations of both *El Mundo Nuevo* and *La América Ilustrada*—with their overly hopeful views of technology and their appeal primarily to White, elite readers—in their best moments, they also initiated new thinking about who could participate in print and what those participants might achieve together. One such foundational idea, which appeared in *La América Ilustrada*, was the notion of the illustrated magazine as a *taller*, or workshop, that could facilitate collaboration across Nueva York's América to shape ideas about democracy and hemispheric Hispanophone identity, while preparing those who conducted that work as printers, editors, writers, or readers to participate in the region's current and future democracies. Without yet embracing a multiracial, working-class readership, as later publications of Nueva York would do, the 1870s illustrated magazines provided the foundation for later, more radical efforts to pursue what Vanessa Valdés has described as a rejection of "a highly regimented hierarchy . . . in order to create a region defined by freedom and equality for all."[3]

The chapter's analysis demonstrates how a Spanish-language publishing community in New York City that reached back to the 1820s responded to late nineteenth-century media change to construct a Nueva York whose horizons and affordances expanded along with its architects' changing world of print. It is telling that the use of the word *network* to mean "an interconnected group of people; an organization; spec. a group of people having certain connections . . . which may be exploited to gain preferment, information, etc., esp. for professional advantage" dates back to this period.[4] While the word's denotation of "any netlike or complex system or collection of interrelated things, as topographical features, lines of transportation, or telecommunications routes" emerged in the earlier nineteenth century along with the telegraph, it was in the final decades of the century that editors and writers began to consider the possibilities of the changing world of print for facilitating collaboration for a shared purpose.[5] In the 1870s, writers and editors of New York City's Spanish-language press explored the potentiality of the expanded reach and increased pace of printed publications to support Cuban and Puerto Rican independence from Spain and promote Latin American culture throughout the hemisphere. Building Nueva York as a social network of collaborators from Hispanophone *América* thus also led to new thinking about the magazine as a form.

The illustrated press of Nueva York in the 1870s began to shift the role of the magazine as a kind of receptacle—rooted in sixteenth- and seventeenth-century uses of the word, as "a place where goods are kept in store" and sometimes more specifically "a building, room, or compartment (of a ship, etc.), for the storage of ammunition, or other military provisions"—to that of a virtual space for collaboration where a far-flung network of contributors could work together to forge new ideas.[6] Although the circulation of magazines still took more time than sending telegrams, notions of simultaneous experience inspired new thinking about regular, strategic engagement of a reading public. In that context, the 1870s illustrated press updated earlier efforts to explore the power of print for achieving independence from Spain, such as those that Rodrigo Lazo has linked to the filibustering efforts of the mid-nineteenth century, in which "Cuban *filibusteros* attempted to connect the material of print culture with military organizing and armed combat to gain territorial control. They sent out their articles and poems as weapons in a battle for Cuba."[7] While the idea of newspapers or articles as weapons suggests individualized, if coordinated, interventions, the 1870s illustrated press explored how the magazine might become a site of collective action.

The model of print culture represented by the *taller* magazines of the 1870s Spanish-language illustrated press is best understood in relation to the competing models from which it diverged. One such model forged by *La América Ilustrada*'s Anglophone neighbors in Lower Manhattan, especially the nearby *Frank Leslie's Illustrated Newspaper*, contributed to the rising stardom of the reporter as a figure with exclusive access to the news. Another model, centered in individualized, artistic impressions, reaches back to Charles Baudelaire's 1863 essay "Le Peintre de la vie moderne" (The painter of modern life), which coincidentally took inspiration from the *Illustrated London News*—the newspaper where Henry Carter learned the illustrated news business before he immigrated to New York City and started his own publication under the name of Frank Leslie.[8] "Le Peintre" also served as a more direct source of influence for writers associated with Latin American *modernismo*, including *La Habana Elegante* editor Enrique Hernández Miyares, who promoted their own brand of the privileged observer (at times while also rejecting the brand of reporter that became a feature of New York City's Anglophone press) for the purpose of placing literary writing into its own sphere. In contrast to both the reporter and Baudelairian observer models, which emphasized individual expression, the city's 1870s Spanish-language illustrated press fashioned a divergent course centered on mobilizing collaboration through the magazine. Like *La América Ilustrada*'s physical workshop in 41 Park Row, the metaphorical one provided by the publication itself is a vehicle through which those who participate within it hone their skills to become exemplary participants in democracy. In this way, the 1870s illustrated magazines considered here provide a first stop in this book's exploration of Nueva York's democratic literary imagination, characterized by the collaborative and strategic use of storytelling and print media to envision and advocate for a more equitable future that included widespread participation and negotiation in the pursuit of racial, gender, and economic equality for Cuba, Puerto Rico, and beyond.

In addition, this chapter's wide-ranging itinerary demonstrates how slippery emergent concepts—especially those that competed only fleetingly, and ultimately unsuccessfully—can be as objects of study. One challenge is that obsolete ideas have a way of slipping into new packaging, if not disappearing altogether. In the case of *La América Ilustrada* and its interlocutors, the increasing separation of literary and journalistic discourse by the 1880s and 1890s—which *cronistas* like Hernández Miyares and Manuel Gutiérrez Nájera encouraged as they promoted the literary value of their articles and publications—makes it a bit mindbending from today's perspective to envision a world where *La América Ilustrada*'s editorial team and its network might have shared discursive common ground with writers and editors whose locations and reputations are as widely dispersed as Charles Baudelaire and Frank Leslie. When periods of rapid media change resolve into established practices, they end up ordering the world into genres, discourse, disciplines, markets—all separated by clear boundaries. What does not fit within such boundaries can end up lost in the shadows of better-known publications, genres, and writers—dwarfed by the monuments that have been built to their contributions, as the immense statue of Ben Franklin, which still stands outside 41 Park Row, reminds us.

This chapter thus also models the methodology required to recover the overlooked network and innovations of Nueva York, whose material remains sometimes contrast sharply with the seemingly monumental solidity of the city's Anglophone publishing history. The textual evidence lingers in fragmented archives, some available digitally and others captured in decades-old microfiche or persisting precariously in brittle newsprint. Surrounding such fragile archival remains are numerous gaps—in newspaper issues or sometimes entire print runs, as well as in records from the Hispanophone publishing community's print shops and editorial offices. They add to the difficulty of reanimating past ideas, some of which never reached their full potential, and many of which align uneasily with notions of journalistic and literary value that took shape afterward and that still influence many scholarly approaches to print cultural history. Finding footing in such territory requires a combination of close and contextual reading, along with a willingness to traverse disciplinary and linguistic boundaries in search of juxtapositions and suggestions that can help rekindle the brilliance of promising ideas that burned on unfamiliar fuel.

Print Shops and Publications of 1870s Nueva York

The construction of Nueva York as an idea centered on facilitating broad-based involvement and dialogue through print to advocate for Cuban and Puerto Rican independence and for equality started with its print shops—both the physical ones that concentrated in Lower Manhattan and the representations of them that appeared in editorial notes, advertisements, and articles in the 1870s Spanish-language illustrated press. This was the decade when the illustrated press expanded in both the city's Hispanophone and Anglophone communities of print.[9] It was also a short-lived period in which the small- to mid-sized publications of the Hispanophone press and the increasingly larger operations of the Anglophone press still occupied some common ground. That territory comes into view starting with a consideration of a single site—a print shop at 40 and 42 Broadway—followed by an analysis of the representations of Nueva York's publishing community that circulated in *El Mundo Nuevo* during its short-lived partnership with Frank Leslie's Publishing House.

In the spring of 1869, Cuban writer and publisher Néstor Ponce de León set up an office in room 59 of a multiuse office building at 40 and 42 Broadway, which had previously been occupied by Juan Manuel Macías, who served as the editor in the late 1860s of the quarterly magazine *Ambas Américas: Revista de Educación, Bibliografía y Agricultura* (Both Americas: Magazine of Education, Bibliography and Agriculture).[10] When he arrived at his new work space, Ponce de León was two months into establishing a new life in New York City, after having fled Cuba in February of that same year to escape an arrest warrant issued by Spanish colonial authorities for his publishing of revolutionary pamphlets there. Soon after his escape to New York (where he would live for nearly thirty years until Spain withdrew from Cuba in 1898), Ponce de León accepted a role as secretary of the Junta Revolucionaria, dedicated to the Cuban separatist movement. His previous work as a publisher in Cuba made him well-qualified for the position, whose duties included publishing the organization's newspaper, *La Revolución* (which would soon employ Piñeyro on its editorial team, in the role that he would eventually leave to direct *El Mundo Nuevo*).[11] As Ponce de León prepared to launch the publication in April 1869, he replaced the printing press that Macías had offered to leave behind with a new one, funded by two thousand dollars in contributions raised through the Junta Revolucionaria.[12]

The range of presses that Ponce de León likely would have encountered when he set up his first print shop in New York City helps to situate the Spanish-language illustrated press within a changing media landscape that offered new technological possibilities across a spectrum that accommodated small- to large-scale publishing endeavors. The largest, best-known presses included Hoe and Company's six-cylinder rotary press, patented in 1847, which supported the largest newspapers and magazines (the *New York Tribune* was the first in the United States to purchase Hoe's six-cylinder Web Perfecting Press) that were pushing to surpass new limits of audience size at the time.[13] But such presses represented only a small fraction of the new print technologies that became available in the nineteenth century, especially during its final decades. As Elizabeth M. Harris has argued, "The whole population of printing presses formed a pyramid . . . with the few, huge, and famous presses at the top, backed up by the respectable and more numerous classes of cylinder presses and platen jobbers, and at the bottom even smaller presses in greater numbers, an underclass almost too common and trivial to be noticed at the time."[14] The smallest presses described here included a fascinating proliferation of portable presses marketed for home or office use (and sometimes as toys for children). Meant for those unfamiliar with the printing trade, the portable presses were advertised in some of the city's English- and Spanish-language illustrated magazines— offering the promise of making "every man his own printer."[15] While such presses pursued a market made up of amateurs, an increasing number of cylinder presses powered by hand or by steam provided professional printers of small- to mid-size newspapers like *La Revolución* with a range of options.

An 1872 advertisement for Hoe and Co. Presses in *El Mundo Nuevo* offers another view of the increased availability of print technology that helped to enable more collaborative models of publication. Addressed to "impresores, encuadernadores y editores" (printers, bookbinders, and publishers), the advertisement lists "prensas de mano, de carrilera, para periódicos de corta circulación, que dan á mano ochocicutas [*sic*] impresiones por hora" (hand presses, rail presses, for small-circulation periodicals, that deliver by hand eight hundred impressions per hour), as well as "nuevas prensas de cilindro . . . para periódicos con finas ilustraciones y toda clase de impresión y grabado en madera" (new cylinder presses . . . for newspapers with high-quality illustrations and all kinds of printing and wood engraving).[16] "Small-circulation," in this context, did not exclude editors and writers from high-quality printing—or, much less, from grand ambitions.

Although no circulation records exist for *La Revolución* (or for any of the illustrated magazines considered in this chapter), circulation data for a few other New York-based Spanish-language newspapers are included in George P. Rowell's *American Newspaper Directory* later in the 1870s, offering additional insight into the scale and reach of the city's Spanish-language press. For example, *El Educador Popular* (The Popular Educator), an illustrated magazine that Ponce de León edited starting in 1873, appears in the 1879 edition of Rowell's *Directory* with a circulation of 5,000.[17] Another illustrated magazine from that decade, *El Ateneo*, edited by José de Armas y Céspedes, was published just a few doors down from *La América Ilustrada* (at 31 Park Row) starting in 1874, and reached a circulation of 4,500 by 1877.[18] Among the daily and weekly Hispanophone newspapers published in New York, *El Espejo*, where Cirilio Villaverde's novel *Cecilia Valdés* first appeared in serial in 1879, is listed in the 1877 directory with a circulation of 3,000—the same rate reported for another weekly newspaper, *Las Novedades*, in the 1879 directory.[19] *El Cronista*, published from 1867 to 1877 at 53 Franklin Street and later 64 and 66 Broadway, had a circulation of 4,800 in 1871, which grew to 6,000 in the 1877 directory.[20] For comparison, the *New York Tribune's* circulation when it became the first to employ a Hoe Web Perfecting Press in 1871 was 45,000 for its daily paper and 150,000 for its weekly paper, according to the directory from that year.[21] Its closest competitors at the time included the *New York Sun*, with a circulation of 100,000 for its daily paper, and the daily *New York Herald*, which reported a circulation of 85,000.[22] Among Anglophone illustrated publications, *Frank Leslie's* claimed a circulation of 75,000, while its competitor *Harper's Weekly* circulated 100,000 copies and the newly launched *Scribner's Monthly* reached 55,000 readers.[23]

While their modest circulation rates seem to indicate vast differences between the Hispanophone community of print and its Anglophone counterparts, these numbers also convey something of the very different context in which illustrated magazines thrived during the 1870s. The estimates included here for Spanish- and English-language publications are much closer than they would become by the late 1890s, when the widest-circulating Anglophone newspapers in the city sometimes reached audiences of one million or more, while many Spanish-language publishers in the city turned to increasingly grassroots efforts to make print a vehicle for supporting the Cuban cause.[24] In the 1870s, while some Anglophone newspapers and magazines began using new (expensive) presses, smaller shops remained competitive and vital by harnessing their own forms of cutting-edge technology and effectively managing revenue from advertising, subscriptions, and job printing. For example, in an 1874 notice announcing the incorporation of *La América Ilustrada* into a new joint stock company, owner J. C. Rodrigues projects the publication's profit for 1874 as $33,746 (or about $930,000 in 2025), resulting from a combination of all three types of income.[25] It was in this context that Frank Leslie's Publishing House (probably guided by his business-minded, multilingual wife, Miriam Florence Follin) forged a partnership with *El Mundo Nuevo*.[26]

Even at a time when the emerging mass press had not yet created significant barriers to entry for smaller operations, it is not difficult to see the advantage in terms of resources that the partnership with Frank Leslie's must have provided to *El Mundo Nuevo*. An editorial note in the magazine's first issue promises that it will become "un periódico, de grandes proporciones" (a major newspaper) that features "artistas eminentes y . . . una numerosa redaccion compuesta de escritores de talento y nombradía" (eminent artists and . . . a large editorial staff composed of talented and renowned writers).[27] The note exhibits exceptional confidence even for a genre known for its tendency toward self-promotion. At a time when most of the city's Hispanophone periodicals employed a single editor or a small staff, the description of its own editorial team as "numerosa" speaks of *El Mundo Nuevo*'s unique position within an enterprise that at the time employed "between three and four hundred people, including seventy engravers."[28] And yet, although *El Mundo Nuevo* appeared to embrace the benefits provided by the size of Frank Leslie's Publishing House, its subsequent output shows that a periodical "de grandes proporciones" meant something very different to *El Mundo Nuevo*'s editors than it did to Frank Leslie's Publishing House.[29] While Frank Leslie's pursued the largest possible audience, *El Mundo Nuevo* offers another view of the power of circulation, rooted in the close-knit publishing community of Nueva York.

El Mundo Nuevo both followed and diverged from the model provided by Leslie's flagship publication, *Frank Leslie's Illustrated Newspaper*. In some ways, *El Mundo Nuevo* set itself apart among Spanish-language illustrated newspapers, as a result of the resources that Frank Leslie's Publishing House provided. The partnership made it cost-effective to include large numbers of illustrations and reproductions of news items in each issue. At the same time, *El Mundo Nuevo* also included far fewer illustrations of current US events—such as strikes, depictions of the urban poor and working classes, and official political proceedings—which had given *Frank Leslie's* a reputation for sensationalism. *El Mundo Nuevo*'s original news, which included frequent updates on the war for independence in Cuba, appeared in articles rarely accompanied by illustrations. Illustrations created specifically for *El Mundo Nuevo* tended to privilege less timely content, such as portraits of featured authors and political figures, or illustrations of cultural texts. One issue included an image of the "estatua de Benjamin Franklin recientemente erigida en la Plaza de los Impresores, Nueva York" (statue of Benjamin Franklin recently erected in the Printing House Square, New York), giving readers a glimpse of the statue with no other commentary beyond the caption.[30]

To some degree, the illustrations combined with the magazine's content made *El Mundo Nuevo* more closely resemble *Harper's Weekly*, which competed with *Frank Leslie's* by appealing to an audience that Gib Prettyman has described as having "a certain refinement that was beginning to be thought of as middle class."[31] In the editors' own words, *El Mundo Nuevo* sought to keep "siempre al corriente a nuestros lectores" (our readers always up to date) on "la industria, la agricultura, las grandes invenciones que cada día mejoran y corrijen los procedimientos en todas las artes útiles" (industry, agriculture, great inventions that improve and correct procedures every day in all useful arts), in addition to being "un periódico esencialmente artístico y literario" (an essentially artistic and literary periodical).[32] In light of such content, Kirsten Silva Gruesz has argued that "like *Harper's*, the *Atlantic*, or the *Century*, *El Mundo Nuevo/La América Ilustrada* turned culture into a marketable commodity for a designated segment of the middle-class readership."[33] Similarly, Laura Lomas has described *El Mundo Nuevo* as a purveyor of a "New Worldist discourse" that offered "scant sympathy with revolutionary remedies for working-class miseries."[34] These attentive observations help to explain why these magazines have received considerably less scholarly attention than later Hispanophone publications. As magazines that stopped short of achieving the alliances across class and racial divisions that would appear later in writings by José Martí, Sotero Figueroa, Rafael Serra, and others, the New York-based Spanish-language periodicals of the 1870s largely adhered to a White, middle-class worldview. Yet competing currents ran through these publications. Valdés has argued that a notable exception after the merger is Eugenio María de Hostos's 1874 essay "The Problem of Cuba," which criticized "members of the white Cuban upper class, such as Piñeyro himself, who feared the increased participation of Afro-Cubans in the war as soldiers as much as, or perhaps more than, they did their Spanish colonizers."[35] It is in these moments that we might locate the magazine's construction of a Nueva York that ran counter to the evident aspirations of Frank Leslie's Publishing House to extend its reach into the Spanish-language market.

Perhaps because of its internal tensions, *El Mundo Nuevo*'s sense of purpose is unusually murky in comparison to later magazines and newspapers of Nueva York. As the editors confess in their introductory editorial note, "No puede espresar cabalmente nuestro propósito este número inicial del MUNDO NUEVO. . . . Las dificultades y complicaciones, que forzosamente trae consigo la aparición de un periódico por vez primera, nos han impedido realizar por completo nuestro pensamiento." (This initial number of EL MUNDO NUEVO cannot fully express our purpose. . . . The difficulties and complications that inevitably accompany the appearance of a newspaper for the first time, have prevented us from fully realizing our thinking.)[36] Subsequent issues reveal varying and, at times, contradictory purposes. A self-promotional note "To Advertisers" published in the May 25, 1871, issue boasts that "no better means, than the columns of this paper, is offered to advertisers desirous of making their business known in Spanish countries."[37] This pitch for new advertising is the only English-language content in the issue, suggesting that the editorial team sought to sell advertising space to US-based exporters who did not speak Spanish. By contrast, the same advertisement for *El Mundo Nuevo* also includes a call for subscriptions in Spanish that promotes the magazine as "una publicación de valor escepcional, que aspira á servir de vínculo de union y progreso entre todos los paises Americanos donde se habla la lengua castellana" (a publication of exceptional value, which aspires to serve as a link of union and progress among all the American countries where the Spanish language is spoken).[38] The description of the magazine in Spanish makes hemispheric unity, rather than marketing US products, the central goal. As Silva Gruesz has noted, these two competing purposes generated contradictions within the magazine. In one of *El Mundo Nuevo*'s "most pointedly political moments," she writes, the publication of a series of poems by Juan Clemente Zenea y Fornaris while he was imprisoned (and later executed) in Cuba by Spanish colonial authorities for his revolutionary activities "sits uneasily with the advertisements from sugar and tobacco merchants—the very forces who were pressuring the U.S. government not to interfere with Spanish colonial affairs—on the back page."[39] At the same time, many of the publication's most frequent advertisers signaled the importance of the Hispanophone publishing community that produced the magazine.

The community of print represented by these advertisements suggests that the resources of Frank Leslie's Publishing House were not the only ones that powered *El Mundo Nuevo*. One advertisement reveals that *El Mundo Nuevo* was not printed at Frank Leslie's Publishing House, but rather at the "imprenta poliglota" (polyglot press) run by M. M. Zarzamendi.[40] The advertisement notes that Zarzamendi had worked previously at "la delicada tarea de corrector de pruebas en la [imprenta] del difunto Sr. Esteban Hallet, y despues en la de sus sucesores 'Hallet y Breen'" (the delicate task of proofreader in the [print shop] of the late Mr. Stephen Hallet, and afterward in that of his successors "Hallet and Breen").[41] Those familiar with the city's Spanish-language publishing community likely would have recognized the name Hallet y Breen, which printed, among other things, Macías's *Ambas Américas*. Readers might also have noted the address of M. M. Zarzamendi's press, at 40 and 42 Broadway—the same building where Macías published *Ambas Américas* before Ponce de León took over the space to publish *La Revolución*.[42] Another advertisement in *El Mundo Nuevo* shows how far Ponce de León had come in setting up a new life in New York City by this point—just two years after his arrival in New York. Starting with the first issue, *El Mundo Nuevo* included regularly occurring advertisements for Ponce de León's Spanish-language bookstore, located during *El Mundo Nuevo*'s first year at 23 Union Square and then at 17 East 16th Street. (Ponce de León moved the bookstore to 40 and 42 Broadway in 1873.) These advertisements reveal the established presence of the physical Nueva York.

By the 1870s, as scholars have noted in the Anglophone context, New York was gaining ground over Boston and Philadelphia as a publishing center.[43] The city was also becoming an increasingly important center for Spanish-language publishing because New York City had become a primary location (along with Tampa and Key West) where Cubans fleeing Spanish colonialism rebuilt their lives and planned for a future Cuban republic. In the early nineteenth century, Philadelphia had served as both a publishing center and a symbol of possibility for Latin American writers and editors, but New York took on its own revolutionary significance as increased suppression of Cuban nationalist ideas by Spanish colonial authorities followed the start of Cuba's first independence war with Spain in 1868.[44] The city's towering status as a site of Cuban revolutionary activity and of innovation in print technology (and of sugar production reaching back even earlier in the century) made it an ideal center and source of inspiration for new ideas about how a hemispheric, Hispanophone print culture might shape the future of modern media.[45] Silva Gruesz has noted that among those who noticed this opportunity for New York in the 1870s was Colombian Rafael Pombo, a contributor to *El Mundo Nuevo* as well as a diplomat and translator for the *New York Herald*, who "would make a continued effort to recenter the locus of Hispanophone literary exile from Paris to New York."[46] As Silva Gruesz points out, Pombo's writing offers "perhaps the first call for a transnational association within U.S. space based on the shared cultural and political displacement of Latinos."[47]

El Mundo Nuevo depicts New York as a city defined by the transnational communities in which it participates. An article in the August 25, 1871, issue of *El Mundo Nuevo* reflects on the diversity of the population of New York City revealed by the previous year's census. The anonymous article, probably written by a member of the editorial team, explains that the city's reported population of 419,153 born outside the United States—compared to 523,198 born in the country—made New York "la ciudad que contiene mayor número de extranjeros naturalizados" (the city that contains the greatest number of naturalized foreigners).[48] In contemplating these numbers, the article concludes, "A nadie debe ocurrírsele la idea de estudiar el carácter del pueblo americano en Nueva York, porque es la ménos americana de todas sus ciudades" (No one should have the idea of studying the character of the American people in New York, because it is the least American of all its cities).[49] While this sentence employs the adjectives *americano* and *americana* to refer to the United States, it also insists that New York City represents communities that reach beyond those borders. The language leaves open the possibility of the city's Americanness in another sense articulated far more frequently throughout the publication. For example, an editorial note reflecting on the magazine's first year of publication commits to "concediendo particular atencion . . . al progreso y bienestar inmediato de todos los países americanos donde se habla esta hermosa lengua castellana" (paying particular attention . . . to the progress and immediate well-being of all the American countries where this beautiful Spanish language is spoken).[50] In this description of the magazine's priorities, *americanos* unambiguously describes all of the Spanish-speaking hemisphere to which Nueva York belonged.

This Nueva York of *El Mundo Nuevo* takes fuller form in *La América Ilustrada*—the publication with which *El Mundo Nuevo* would merge in 1874, after its relationship with Frank Leslie's Publishing House ended.

Networking América Through *La América Ilustrada*'s Nueva York

In 1874, for reasons that remain murky, *La América Ilustrada* and *El Mundo Nuevo* merged into one publication, which continued under the name of the former. Scholarship on these magazines and cataloging practices thus tend to treat *El Mundo Nuevo* and *La América Ilustrada* as being one and the same publication. In the years leading up to the merger, however, the differences between the two publications were notable and revealing. *El Mundo Nuevo*'s frequent appeals in English to potential advertisers make clear that any revolutionary impulse expressed in the magazine competed with its role as a vehicle for advertising US products to a readership made up of potential consumers. By contrast, *La América Ilustrada* provided a platform for countering suggestions of the dominance of Anglo-American culture circulated by the Anglophone illustrated press.

One illustrative article in *La América Ilustrada* by Antonio Bachiller y Morales takes issue with a claim made in Fredric Hudson's *Journalism in the United States, from 1690–1872* (published by Harper and Brothers and promoted in the firm's news weekly, *Harper's Weekly*). Bachiller y Morales responds to the book's assertion that the first newspaper in the New World appeared in Boston: "Nosotros los de otra raza habríamos dicho, que por *meterse en Honduras*. El supuesto de esa prioridad no es exacto: Méjico precedió a Boston i no solo Méjico, Puebla publicó *relaciones* antes que la Atenas del mundo nuevo sus *ocurrencias*." (We of another race would have said that you are out of your depth. That assumed priority is not accurate: Mexico City preceded Boston and not only Mexico City, Puebla published *accounts* before the Athens of the new world its *occurrences*.)[51] It is worth noting that the phrase *meterse en Honduras* literally means "interfering in Honduras"—possibly also evoking the 1855 filibustering expedition of American William Walker, who installed himself as president of Nicaragua in 1856 and was pushed out by an alliance of Central American countries the following year. The reference links the ignorance displayed in Hudson's book to the history of US overreach in Latin America, as Bachiller y Morales sets the record straight about Boston, the so-called Athens of America. Mexico takes its rightful place in Bachiller y Morales's account as the home of the hemisphere's first printing press and newspapers. This article appears in the same issue in which the editorial team reveals its location in the New York Times Building in Printing House Square, reinforcing the hemispheric perspective envisioned and circulated from Nueva York.

By 1872, *La América Ilustrada*'s approach appeared to be gaining ground in the Spanish-language illustrated press in New York City, as indicated when *El Mundo Nuevo*, still affiliated with Frank Leslie's Publishing House, emulated its rival in both form and content. *La América Ilustrada*'s November 15, 1872, issue took notice: "Nos complacen las mejoras materiales efectuadas últimamente por *El Mundo Nuevo*. Esta publicacion parece haber tomado por norma imitar a LA AMÉRICA ILUSTRADA hasta en los mas minuciosos detalles tipográficos." (We are pleased with the material improvements made recently by *El Mundo Nuevo*. This publication seems to have taken it as a rule to imitate LA AMÉRICA ILUSTRADA up to the most minute typographical details.)[52] Another reference to this alleged copying in the December 15 issue claims that *El Mundo Nuevo* "introdujo en sus columnas una seccion de notas jenerales, que antes no publicaba, dándole la misma forma, carácter, i hasta el mismo órden tipográfico de nuestro *Mosaico*" (introduced in its columns a section of general notes, which it did not publish before, giving it the same form, character, and even the same typographical character of our *Mosaic*), in addition to switching to the same paper, a printing press of the same model, and adding "una seccion semejante a nuestra *Revista de la Quincena*" (a section similar to our *Journal of the Fortnight*).[53] Responding to an apparent defense offered by *El Mundo Nuevo* that they were actually modeling their updates on *Harper's Weekly*, the editorial team of *La América Ilustrada* demonstrates their intimate knowledge of the latter publication: "*Harper's* no dedica a sus noticias mas de un cuarto de columna, no las separa con el nombre de las diversas naciones, ni dedica a cada país un párrafo largo i único, dividiendo en él unas de otras las noticias, por medio de rayas cortas." (*Harper's* does not devote more than a quarter of a column to its news, does not separate them with the names of the various nations, nor does it devote to each country a long and unique paragraph, dividing one and another news item within it, by short stripes.)[54] *La América Ilustrada* responds as a magazine that is accustomed to setting its own standards. *Harper's* serves as a point of reference here, not as a model to be copied—but rather as a variation on *La América Ilustrada*'s own approach.

A hallmark of that approach was *La América Ilustrada*'s stated commitment to written content from contributors throughout Latin America. The magazine's first issue includes a note entitled "Colaboradores" (Contributors), which announces, "En este primer número de LA AMERICA ILUSTRADA presentamos al lector trabajos orijinales de cuatro de los mejores escritores de nuestra idioma en este continente." (In this first issue of LA AMERICA ILUSTRADA, we introduce to the reader original work from four of the best writers in our language on this continent.)[55] Although the notice includes the names of the contributors (Juana Manso, Antonio Flores, Luis Felipe Mantilla, and José Antonio Calcaño), it promotes the combined effect of their contributions by presenting them as multiple *colaboradores* and touting their collective originality. This emphasis on the quantity and quality of original contributions also appears in the introductory editorial note in this issue, which promises that the magazine will feature "la cooperacion de muchos entre los mas distinguidos escritores de Hispano América" (the cooperation of many of the most distinguished writers of Hispano América).[56] *La América Ilustrada* appeals to readers on the strength of its network of contributors.

In addition, readers play a key role in *La América Ilustrada*, especially to join through the magazine a popular movement in support of Cuban independence—a topic that provides another point of contrast with *El Mundo Nuevo*, in which expressions of support for the Cuban cause before its merger with *La América Ilustrada* conflicted with an editorial strategy to avoid hemispheric controversy rather than mobilizing a movement. As one article published in the July 30, 1872, issue of *La América Ilustrada* explained, "El honor i el interés aconsejan a la vez a los pueblos hispano-americanos, que presten su ayuda a los combatientes de Cuba." (Honor and interest both make advisable to the

Spanish American people that they render their aid to the combatants of Cuba.)[57] The article specifies that by "los pueblos hispano-americanos" the editors mean the people, not just their governments. As Cuban organizers of the independence movement knew all too well, governments "por su posicion i responsabilidad se ven muchas veces obligados a anteponer las conveniencias diplomáticas a la realización de sus deseos" (by their position and responsibility are often forced to put diplomatic conveniences before the realization of their wishes).[58] By contrast, for a popular movement, "No hai limite alguno en la libre espresion de sus simpatias por los otros pueblos que defienden una causa idéntica." (There is no limit to the free expression of their sympathies for the other peoples who defend an identical cause.)[59]

The article describes such a movement as already underway:

> Cuba goza de las simpatias de todos los pueblos hispano-americanos. Hijos de Venezuela, de Colombia i de Méjico han regado con su sangre el suelo cubano; ofrendas jenerosas del Perú han ayudado a enviar armas a los combatientes. Solo falta que esos nobles sentimientos de los pueblos se trasmitan a sus gobiernos respectivos; que se inicie un movimiento organizado i jeneral en apoyo de la libertad de Cuba.

> (Cuba enjoys the sympathies of all Hispano-American peoples. Children of Venezuela, Colombia and Mexico have watered the Cuban soil with their blood; the generous offerings of Peru have helped to send weapons to the combatants. It is only necessary that these noble sentiments of the peoples be conveyed to their respective governments; that an organized and general movement be initiated in support of the freedom of Cuba.)[60]

People, weapons, and supportive sentiments have already traveled from "los pueblos hispano-americanos" to support Cuba. Print, the article suggests, has the ability to accelerate this movement's progress: "Traten los periódicos un dia i otro dia de esta cuestion tan vital; hablen los oradores a las masas; hagan los diputados en las Cámaras proposiciones que tiendan a ese fin; haya, en una palabra, movimiento popular, movimiento a favor de la causa cubana que es la causa de toda la América." (Let the newspapers treat from one day to another this vital issue; let the orators speak to the masses; make the Members of the House make proposals to that end; let there be, in a word, a popular movement, a movement in favor of the Cuban cause that is the cause of the whole of America.)[61] Newspapers lead the charge in bringing together the people of an America that is united in its collective activity to realize Cuban independence.

La América Ilustrada's Cuban editors were also well aware that governments did not always follow the will of the people as expressed in print. When *La América Ilustrada* was banned in Cuba, the magazine's editorial team reflected in an article in the April 15, 1872, issue, "Siendo obvio que si la causa del decreto es la simple publicacion de un artículo contrario a la conducta seguida en Cuba por España, ningun periódico estranjero podrá en lo adelante circular en la isla. Pues eso es lo que ellos quieren." (It is obvious that if the cause of the decree is the mere publication of an article opposing the conduct followed in Cuba by Spain, no foreign newspaper will be able to circulate in the island in the future. That is what they want.)[62] Reading becomes a powerful act of resistance against Spanish colonial authorities that "quieren que no se lea, que no se estudie, que no se aprenda" (want you not to read, not to study, not to learn).[63] Like printing and circulating newspapers, reading is a way to participate in revolutionary change.

The magazine's illustrations also participate in *La America Ilustrada*'s efforts to mobilize its network for hemispheric unity and Cuban independence. The cover of the first issue features a portrait of Bartolomé Mitre, the former Argentine president, who was at the time director of the daily newspaper *La Nación* of Buenos Aires. Founded two years earlier in 1870, the paper was on its way to earning a reputation as one of the leading daily newspapers in Latin America. In 1877 *La Nación* would become the first newspaper in Latin America to introduce telegraph service (through a contract with the French Havas news agency), and around that time it would also achieve prominence as a leading venue for prominent writers from the region—including José Martí, who would sign on as a New York correspondent for the paper in the 1880s.[64] In the 1872 issue of *La América Ilustrada*, the note accompanying the portrait of Mitre highlights his roles as the founder of "uno de los periódicos mejor redactados de Buenos Aires" (one of the best-edited newspapers of Buenos Aires) and as a poet and translator whose accomplishments "le aseguran un lugar prominente entre los poetas hispano americanos contemporáneos" (assure him a prominent place among contemporary Hispano-American poets).[65] This brief profile emphasizes the Argentine writer, military officer, and statesman's literary accomplishments, aligning Mitre and his newspaper with the type of writer that *La América Ilustrada* also preferred to hire and feature. A closing detail in the publisher's note explains how the magazine's use of print and illustration technology complements its networked approach. The narrative notes that "el retrato con que acompañamos esta breve reseña está tomado de una fotografía del distinguido artista brasilero Christiano Jr., la cual nos ha sido facilitada por el capitan Carranza, secretario privado del jeneral Mitre durante la campaña del Paraguai." (The engraving with which we accompany this brief review is taken from a photograph by the distinguished Brazilian artist Christiano Jr., which has been provided to us by Captain Carranza, private secretary of General Mitre during the Paraguayan campaign.)[66] Technology and personal connections enable *La América Ilustrada* to circulate its vision for Hispanophone America.

An article titled "Atado el mundo" (The world tied together) indicates that the idea of a technology-enabled network resided within the imaginative horizon of *La América Ilustrada*'s editors and writers. Published in the January 30, 1872, issue, the anonymous article, most likely written by a member of the editorial team, describes plans that were then underway to expand undersea telegraph cables and "completar la banda en torno al mundo" (complete the band around the world).[67] The article introduces this initiative—led by undersea telegraph cable inventor Cyrus Field—by employing the superlatives typical of the period's widely published articles on great inventors and inventions, describing the recent advances in undersea cables as "pasos jigantescos" (giant steps) that are "verdaderamente maravillosos" (truly marvelous).[68] Yet the article concludes with a consideration of the possibilities of the increased speed of communication that extends beyond technological innovation:

> Cuando los trabajos mencionados esten concluidos, podra hacerse dar a un mensaje la vuelta entera del mundo en pocas horas. Si no fuera por las detenciones inevitables en las diversas estaciones, el mensaje que espidiésemos con la mano derecha podriamos recibirlo en la izquierda, despues de haber rodeado a la tierra en el espacio de 40 segundos.

(When the above-mentioned works are completed, a message may be made to go around the whole world in a few hours. If it were not for inevitable delays in the various stations, the message that we send with the right hand, could be received in the left, after having encircled the earth in the space of 40 seconds.)[63]

The speculation liberates the narrative from its previous focus on technological progress to consider what global connectivity through the telegraph cables could mean on a more personal or interpersonal level. The use of the metaphor of sending and receiving messages from one hand to the other enacts a subtle shift that assigns agency to the writer to imagine possibilities—and to see past practical limitations like those presented by the inefficiencies of the world's telegraph stations. Moreover, the use of "we" in this reflection suggests an ambiguous collective that may well reach beyond the editorial team. At the same time, the notion of tying up the world highlights the potentially dangerous implications of nineteenth-century media change, which also had the potential to reinforce existing hierarchies and facilitate subjugation and control. As its editorial team paid close attention to the period's new media and other technologies, *La América Ilustrada* invited its network of printers, editors, writers, and readers to see these potentialities and risks in their changing world of print—and to share in a mission of making the magazine a means of advancing Latin American culture and democracy.

Painting, Reporting, and Networking Modern Life in the Illustrated Magazine

La América Ilustrada represents the possibility that magazines might become points of connection and vehicles for action that rely on the combined efforts of printers, editors, writers, and readers. It was an idea that diverged sharply from two competing models—centered on reporting and artistic observation—that also got their start in the illustrated press of the late nineteenth century. Turning now to Charles Baudelaire's 1863 essay "Le Peintre de la vie moderne," and to the ways in which editors and writers referenced and remixed that essay's ideas—in the Anglophone illustrated press of the 1870s, including *Frank Leslie's Illustrated Newspaper*, and in Latin American *crónicas* of the 1880s and 1890s, such as those written for the Havana-based *La Habana Elegante*—shows how these models became foils to the incipient collaborative model of the 1870s illustrated press of Nueva York. In turn, a return to *La América Ilustrada* by way of a consideration of the 1876 guidebook *Guía de la ciudad de Nueva York y sus alrededores*, written by Antonio Bachiller y Morales and published by Ponce de León, brings the *taller* magazine collaborative ideal more fully into view.[70]

Scholars of literature and visual culture have long cited Baudelaire's essay as an early, possibly the first, articulation of a self-consciously aesthetic and representational strand of modernity—one that often critiques but also coincides with modernity in its economic and structural form. Baudelaire's representation centers on an artist called M.G., who was modeled on illustrator Constantin Guys of the *Illustrated London News*.[71] By casting his quintessential modern artist as a newspaper illustrator, Baudelaire defines an approach to representing "le transitoire, le fugitif, le contingent" (the transient, the fleeting, the contingent) through a combination of observation and imagination.[72] M.G.'s "faculté de voir" (ability to see) along with a "puissance d'exprimer" (power of expression) enables him to translate "fidèlement ses propres impressions" (faithfully his own impressions) and to capture "la fantastique réel de la vie" (the fantastic reality of life).[73] Through that artistic process, undertaken as he observes the city's daily spectacles, he becomes "un kaléidoscope doué de conscience, qui, à chacun de ses mouvements, représente la vie multiple et la grâce mouvante de tous les éléments de la vie" (a kaleidoscope gifted with consciousness, which, with each movement, represents the multiple life and moving grace of all of life's elements).[74] With a way of seeing that represents and embellishes reality like a kaleidoscope, M.G. constitutes a new kind of artist fashioned in Baudelaire's own image. As his own identity converges with M.G. throughout "Le Peintre de la vie moderne," Baudelaire elevates this new kind of artist to the status of the privileged seer of modern life. For his own purposes, Baudelaire's idea helped to promote his innovations as a modern poet. He also articulated a role claimed by a wide variety of writers and editors during the period, including many who led or contributed to illustrated newspapers—some in direct reference to Baudelaire and others on their own terms.

In New York City, *Frank Leslie's Illustrated Newspaper* helped to fashion what might be considered a distant cousin to Baudelaire's M.G.

(although the magazine itself never made such a claim). The flagship publication of Frank Leslie's Publishing House, *Frank Leslie's Illustrated Newspaper* became one of the first in the United States to make reporters, especially reporter-illustrators who sketched events as they occurred, central to their appeal to readers. According to Andrea C. Pearson, Leslie "began the myth of the 'on the spot' reporter, who chose to put aside his own well-being in order to have access to and sketch the most pertinent news."[75] These artists were some of the first reporters to be identified by name in print. Joshua Brown argues that, as illustrated magazines sought to assert the authenticity of their illustrations of timely events, they "increasingly ascribed authorship of their pictures to individual artists, a strategy simultaneously adopted by the daily press in the *Herald*'s innovation of reporter's 'by lines' in 1863."[76] These reporter-artists represented their publications' exclusive access to the news.

Reporters did not command much attention from the Hispanophone illustrated press of the 1870s, but by the 1880s and 1890s, editors and writers began to characterize reporters as rivals and foils to a brand of writing often associated with the Latin American literary movement of *modernismo*, and specifically, the genre of the *crónica*, which often took the form of foreign correspondence or a local newspaper column offering reflections on a timely topic.[77] Prominent *cronista* (or *crónica* writer) Mexican Manuel Gutiérrez Nájera famously characterized the reporter as a mortal enemy in 1893: "La crónica ha muerto á manos del reporter" (The chronicle has died at the hands of the reporter).[78] Gutiérrez Nájera describes what he considers the loss of a kind of artistic freedom in writing for newspapers and magazines that served as one of the defining characteristics of the genre. That articulation of outrage and loss helped *cronistas* like Gutiérrez Nájera to articulate the literary value of their writing.

At times, Baudelaire's "Le Peintre" provided a point of reference for *cronistas* as they promoted their writing. An 1885 article from the Havana-based *La Habana Elegante* demonstrates how the *crónica* genre provided a vehicle for promoting the artistic sensibilities of its authors— while also introducing Enrique Hernández Miyares, *La Habana Elegante*'s editor and a supporter of Cuban independence, who, like so many of his compatriots, would later move to New York City to escape Spanish colonial authorities.[79] Hernández Miyares's article, called "Crónica," ex-

hibits the characteristic self-referentiality of the genre, while also echoing Baudelaire's essay. The first-person narrator describes the process of
writing a *crónica* while sitting in a train station waiting to "ser testigo del
animadísimo trasiego de pasajeros que regresan á la ciudad" (witness the
lively movement of passengers returning to the city).[80] As he observes
the scene, the *cronista* "toma apuntes, traza rasgos, esboza tipos, subraya
palabras" (takes notes, draws traits, sketches types, underlines words),
all of which serve as "los colores distintos que han de combinarse en el
cuadro" (the different colors to be combined in his painting).[81] This "cu-
rioso investigador" (curious investigator) shares M.G.'s "*curiosité* [que]
peut être considérée le point de départ de son génie" (curiosity [which]
may be considered the starting point of his genius) and his method of
starting his illustrations with "dessins improvisés sur les lieux mêmes"
(drawings improvised on the spot).[82] The recognizable references to "Le
Peintre" signal the *cronista's*—as well as *La Habana Elegante's*—unique
ability to provide readers with privileged glimpses of modern life.

Given the prevalence by the mid-1880s and well into the 1890s of reporters and *cronistas* in their respective communities of print, it is striking that *La América Ilustrada* diverges from the individualized model
of painting modern life that, as we have seen, also has its roots in illustrated magazines. The absence of such figures in the Hispanophone
illustrated press of the 1870s suggests that neither the reporter nor the
flaneur model of the *crónica* is compatible with the collectivist vision
of the illustrated press of Nueva York. To glimpse that Nueva York, we
should consider the *Guía de la ciudad de Nueva York*, a guidebook for
Hispanophone travelers to New York City, which presents an Anglophone New York City for an audience already familiar with the Nueva
York of the city's Spanish-language illustrated press, where the guidebook was widely publicized.[83]

In his analysis of the 1876 edition of the *Guía*, Lisandro Pérez captures
something of the surprise that the guidebook provides to twenty-first-
century readers who are familiar with the views of city life provided by
modernista writing (like that of *La Habana Elegante* considered above)
in the decades that followed: "This is not a whimsical guidebook. It does
not dispense lighthearted practical advice to tourists. In fact, it is not really a guidebook at all. . . . Its 238 pages are full of observations, facts, fig-

ures, and illustrations."[84] Pérez describes a text that, much like *El Mundo Nuevo* and *La América Ilustrada*, rarely provides the point of view of an individual observer strolling through an urban scene.

The guide represents the city through the perspective of Nueva York print culture rather than through the individual perspective of the Baudelairian observer. References to the city's illustrated press appear throughout its pages. The narrative cites *El Mundo Nuevo* in a description of a staircase made of artificial stone—a novelty at the time and the first such construction in New York City: "En el numero 1 del *Mundo Nuevo* se ha publicado una curiosa noticia sobre el particular." (The first issue of *El Mundo Nuevo* has published a curious article on the subject.)[85] This aside appears without further explanation, suggesting that Bachiller y Morales expected many of his readers to be familiar with the magazine. Elsewhere, Bachiller y Morales asserts that the illustrated press leads the production of news in the city: "*La Gaceta de la Policía* reproduce todas las escenas que persiguen las leyes; y las modas y las novedades y las nuevas construcciones y las escenas del mundo elegante y cotidiano, exigen un empleo permanente del buril del artista como de la pluma del escritor." (The *Police Gazette* reproduces all the scenes pertaining to the law; and fashion and novelties and new constructions and scenes of the elegant and everyday world demand constant use of the artist's chisel in addition to the writer's pen.)[86] Emphasizing the significance of the illustrated press, the engraver assumes an equally important role to the writer in this account. Moreover, the reference to the *Police Gazette* (also known as the *National Police Gazette*), another competitor of *Frank Leslie's* known for its sensational coverage of murders, helps to show the range of topics that demanded the engraver's incessant work. Such topics included the crime journalism on which the *Police Gazette* built its reputation, as well as subjects that would likely have been more familiar to readers of Hispanophone illustrated newspapers, including fashion, high society, and, increasingly, representations of an emerging idea of everyday life.

As the *Guía de la ciudad de Nueva York* turns toward Broadway, Bachiller y Morales zooms in on the bustling part of Lower Manhattan pictured in *La América Ilustrada*'s panorama discussed at the outset of this chapter. The guidebook's Broadway offers a chaotic scene:

Broadway es una de las grandes arterias de la vida circulante, y acaso la
que caracteriza el movimiento de la ciudad: 18,000 carruajes la cruzan
incesantemente y el concurso de gente que acude á pié, á cada momento
la corta y obstruye, y los *policías* se ven obligados á acompañar á las señoras y despejar el tránsito en los cruceros de las calles.

(Broadway is one of the largest arteries of circulating life, and perhaps the
one that characterizes the movement of the city: 18,000 carriages cross
it ceaselessly, and the competition of people who come on foot, cut and
obstruct it at every moment, and the police are forced to accompany the
ladies and clear the traffic on the street crossings.)[87]

Horse-drawn carriages dominate this thoroughfare while pedestrians
continually compete with them—at their own peril. Here, walking poses
disorientation—or even danger—rather than mastery over city life.
This is not the urban setting of the "Hispanophone writers" that Lazo
locates in early nineteenth-century Philadelphia, who "like walkers . . .
appropriated the space of Philadelphia, using it for their own purposes
while tapping into the city's conception of itself as the birthplace of independence."[88] Nor is it the scene of the sophisticated urban wanderer
(built on images of the Baudelairian flaneur) with unique abilities of
imagination and observation who would emerge in the *crónicas* of the
Spanish-language magazines of the 1880s and 1890s.[89] This unwalkable
cityscape marks a significant departure from the individualized perspectives, particularly those of their own artists and reporters, featured in
New York City's English-language press—and also later in the Spanish-
language magazines of the 1880s and 1890s.

An alternative figure to the painter of modern life appears in an article called "El obrero moderno" (The modern worker) in the April 20,
1873, issue of *La América Ilustrada*. The article takes as its point of departure an illustration called "El taller del obrero" (The worker's workshop),
which depicts a man surrounded by tools leaning over a workbench. In
La América Ilustrada the image of the worker is presented as an alternative to the flaneur, representing the collective and the idea of democracy,
which the authors assert has been established in the United States "de
una manera tan firme que no han bastado todo jénero de influencias ni
a ponerla siquiera en peligro" (in such a firm way that all kinds of influ-

ences have not been enough, not even to endanger it).⁹⁰ Within that hopeful new reality, "el obrero ocupa lugar mui distinguido entre sus conciudadanos" (the worker occupies a very distinguished place among his fellow citizens). Much like the illustration printed with this article, which leaves ambiguous the specific trade to which the workshop is dedicated, this worker symbolizes "el trabajo en toda su dignidad bajo cualquiera forma que revista" (work in all its dignity in whatever form it takes). That work completed in the *taller*—with its dual meanings that bring together the creativity of the artist's studio with the industry of the workshop—prepares the worker to become the foundation on which democracy thrives:

> El obrero que antes era poco mas que un instrumento manejado por el dinero de los ricos, hoi cuando deja su taller toma participacion en esa cosa pública que se llama gobierno, i como no ha perdido al calor de la fragua, la conciencia de que piensa, siente i quiere, lleva su voto a la urna electoral i pesa con marcada influencia en los destinos de la patria.

> (The worker who was previously little more than an instrument manipulated by the money of the rich, when he leaves his workshop today takes part in that public thing that is called government, and since he has not lost to the heat of the forge the awareness of what he thinks, feels and wants, he takes his vote to the electoral ballot box and weighs in on the fate of the homeland with marked influence.)

The worker appears transformed from the object of oppression to a subject whose thoughts, desires, and feelings inform active participation in democracy.

This workshop that prepares the worker for the larger purpose of participation in democracy offers a different kind of model for cultural production. In the reporting and Baudelaire-influenced *cronista* models of the Anglophone and Hispanophone press, an individual brings unique sensibilities to a scene or event for the purpose of producing a finished printed product: a news story or a literary masterpiece. In the case of the modern worker, who also brings unique skills to the creation of a product that might take a variety of forms, the product created with those skills is not the point. The worker's role, in other words,

Figure 1.2. "El taller del obrero," *La América Ilustrada*, April 20, 1873, 124.

is to participate in a movement through which "se hace la luz para las masas, i sube el pueblo a la superficie, i reconquista sus derechos ahogados por tanto tiempo bajo la planta de los tiranos" (light is made for the masses, and the people rise to the surface, and their rights suffocated for so long under the plant of tyrants are recaptured). The masses here are not sights of modernity gazed upon by an aloof observer, but rather collaborative actors whose potentiality is unleashed in sites like the *taller* magazines of Nueva York. Those actors, rather than any one individual worker, become the creators of the future of democracy—in much the same way that *La America Ilustrada*'s network of writers, editors, print-ers, and readers is more important to that paper's identity than any one individual. From that perspective, print matters not so much as a means of educating a select class of citizens with cultivated content, but rather as a vehicle for engaging more people in the activities that prepare them to be the best possible participants in democracy.

In this way, *La América Ilustrada* demonstrates the beginnings of the "alternative to the modernity that serves imperial expansion" that Lomas has located in the "bodegas, tobacco workshops, Spanish-language newspapers, volumes of poetry, boarding-house foyers, po-litical speeches, and *veladas*" of the Nueva York of the 1880s and 1890s, where "the labor and culture of Latino/a migrants have transformed the metropolitan cityscape."[91] *La América Ilustrada*'s idealized image of the workshop from the 1870s anticipates the role those spaces would play in the formation of the alternative modernity that Lomas locates in Martí's writing from New York City and in the building of the coalition that ultimately led to Cuba's 1895 war with Spain. At the same time, *La América Ilustrada*'s illustration makes clear that the workshop was far from a truly inclusive space. The "obrero moderno" pictured in the il-lustration provides a reminder that—even as the workshop represented new opportunities for participation in governing from the perspective of class—it remained the domain of White men. It would not be until the 1880s and 1890s that Afro-Cuban and Afro-Puerto Rican leaders of the Cuban and Puerto Rican revolutionary movement—including Juan Bonilla, Sotero Figueroa, Francisco Gonzalo "Pachín" Marín, and Rafael Serra, who worked in partnership with Martí until his death in 1895—would revise the notion of the workshop of democracy to push for racial equality. According to Silva Gruesz, "Martí would go on to complicate the basic binary of *El Mundo Nuevo*—the two Americas, antagonistic yet inextricably bound to each other—and supply it with its missing compo-nents: racial consciousness, in the form of an insistence on the mestizo identity of Our America, and political consciousness in the form of a critique of economic imperialism."[92] During that same period, María de la Torriente and her team of collaborators, who published *Revista de Cuba Libre* (Free Cuba Magazine) from 1897 to 1898 through their women's club dedicated to fundraising for the war effort, would represent the print shop and the editorial office as spaces for women within a movement that relegated women to auxiliary roles. The collaborative form of networking modern life that preceded these efforts in the 1870s was imperfect and provisional. However, as its editorial team formulated unique ideas about the possibilities of print that they observed in Nueva York, *La America Ilustrada* put in place a piece of the foundation that these and other editors and writers built upon in subsequent decades.

This networked approach appeared in *La América Ilustrada* early enough that it may be more accurately described in the context of 1870s print culture not as an alternative, but rather as an idea that could have become a dominant media practice throughout the hemisphere. It was an idea that might have constituted modernity itself as a great collective project—an ongoing process of creativity and experimentation, as well as of participation and redistribution—in contrast to the individualist model of modernity that emphasized consumerism, exclusivity, and extraction of resources.

Rewiring the Magazine

The workshops of this 1870s Nueva York differ from another metaphorical workshop that appears in studies of the Latin American literary genre of the *crónica*, or chronicle, which emerged in the 1880s along with the movement known as *modernismo*. Considering the genre as a key site for witnessing the emergence of notions of the literary associated with distinction that would solidify in the twentieth century, Julio Ramos has argued that the *crónica* genre served as "a kind of experimental workshop" where "literature began to insistently announce the project of autonomy."[93] In Ramos's conceptualization of the *crónica* as workshop, the individual artist is able to enact "a strategy of legitimation for intellectuals who had become estranged from the utopia of progress and modernity."[94] In this type of workshop, an individual author envisions literary autonomy. By contrast, the workshop of the 1870s illustrated press pursued a different goal—one that did not empower individual artists, but rather a collective, or multiple collectives. Not limited to a particular genre, it is a way of envisioning the work of the magazine as a whole, as a virtual space for sharing and shaping ideas about democracy and hemispheric Hispanophone identity. Also, importantly, this notion of the workshop made the magazine a means rather than an end. As the publications of Nueva York built on that idea in subsequent decades, they would find themselves increasingly at odds with Anglophone models that also often claimed democratic ambitions, but always in service of circulation numbers and profits. By the 1890s, most of the publications of the Cuban separatist press, as well as the Spanish-language anarchist press, would no longer appear as viable a business as did the publications of the 1870s illustrated press. Rather, they would be shoestring operations produced with volunteer labor in the off-hours of Nueva York's print shops for the purpose of realizing their writers' and editors' dreams for the future of Cuba, Puerto Rico, and Latin America. In that context, the notion of the *taller* as a space in which to facilitate collaboration and collective action through print would return in revised, but also fuller, form.

One of the changes that took place between these decades, which will continue to surface in the chapters that follow, was the emergence of a more specialized literary discourse, which became influential to later nineteenth-century experimentation with methods of capturing the present in print. Returning to *La Habana Elegante*, for example, editor Hernández Miyares increasingly found opportunities to insist on the literary nature of the writing featured there. A humorous example appears in a *crónica* entitled "Una nevada en la Habana" (A snowfall in Havana). Attributed to "un redactor" (an editor), possibly Hernández Miyares, the article features an Ecuadorian foreign correspondent freshly arrived in Havana, who has lost his glasses in his travels and, without them, "era muy miope" (was very nearsighted).[95] In a reversal of the Baudelairian formula, "Una nevada en la Habana" assigns the Ecuadorian correspondent with acute myopia rather than an "œil d'aigle" (eagle eye).[96] Following the familiar path forged by Baudelaire's M.G., the Ecuadorian correspondent starts his tour of Havana with his notepad in hand. Once he arrives in the center of the city, the correspondent makes "una observación á pesar de su maldita miopía" (an observation despite his wretched nearsightedness) that leads him to mistake the dust covering Havana's streets for snow: "¡Nevaba en la Habana! ¡No le quedaba duda!" (It was snowing in Havana! He had no doubt!)[97] Like a good painter of modern life, he turns his observations into a thing of beauty: "Oh! Mi querido director" (Oh, my dear editor!), he writes, "no hay cosa más bella que esas nevadas en los parques y calles principales de la Habana" (there is nothing more beautiful than this snow in the parks and main streets of Havana).[98] Myopia transforms mere dust into snowy art. The clear references to Baudelaire also carefully reshape his idea, in order to serve another purpose.

With *La Habana Elegante*'s characteristic humor, "Una nevada en la Habana" turns the correspondent's confusion into an opportunity for literary creation. After sending his editor the article and a sample of the snow that, miraculously, "no se derrite con el sol" (did not melt in the sun), he receives a reproachful letter in return.[99] Back in Ecuador, it turns out, "los químicos después de un análisis detenido dijeron que la tal nieve era polvo calizo" (the chemists after a careful analysis said that the snow was limestone powder).[100] The chemist and the newspaper editor work together to deliver a "fuerte regaño al miope corresponsal" (strong scolding of the myopic correspondent).[101] In rejecting the correspondent's transformation of the dust into snow, the chemist and the newspaper editor draw a boundary between their specializations and the correspondent's art—with the result that personal impressions are interpreted as failed observation rather than artistic genius. Despite this embarrassment, however, the correspondent still manages to get the last laugh. For, by earning the disdain of the scientifically minded newspaper editor and chemist, the correspondent ends up in precisely the position that *La Habana Elegante* wanted for him, as a publication that sought to claim the terrain of modern life for literature. The correspondent's imaginative portrayal of Havana stands a world apart from the kind of newspaper writing required by the editor and the chemist. As a result, *La Habana Elegante*'s revision of Baudelaire's formula for painting modern life claims some of the vast terrain of nineteenth-century print culture as the domain of its own literary brand of writing. In the 1880s, this, too, was an emerging idea that competed with other possible futures of writing about the present, and of notions of the literary.

Before *cronistas* helped to mobilize literature as a specialized discourse within hemispheric print culture, illustrated Hispanophone magazines of the 1870s contained different possible futures for modern media—including one that made magazines into collaborative spaces for pursuing an emerging (and imperfect) democratic vision. While the illustrated magazines of the 1870s published poetry and serial fiction, they have received far less scholarly attention than the illustrated magazines associated with *modernismo* that came afterward—likely because those later magazines offer more opportunities to study texts that are recognizable from the perspective of more recent notions of literary value. From such a vantage point, *El Mundo Nuevo* and *La América Ilustrada* can seem like flatter, less interesting sources for literary analysis. And yet, as this chapter has demonstrated, entire worlds of possibility are contained in these magazines' editorial notes, explanations of illustrations, articles, poetry, and advertising copy. In this class of publication, editorial notes, especially, serve as sites of the democratic literary imagination where the hopes and ambitions of editorial teams take flight—at least briefly. When we start with the question of how editors, writers, and publishers responded to their changing world of print, those explorations come into focus in rich detail.

In the *taller* magazines of the illustrated press of the 1870s, Nueva York emerged as a place that writers and editors of Latin American descent could define on their own terms. As a site where writers and editors accessed press freedom that was unavailable in many parts of Latin America at the time, Nueva York showcased how the United States could represent the promise of democracy—even as it was also actively threatening democracy's future through its imperialist designs. It also provided a space for imagining a reversal of such designs: a hemisphere dominated by Hispano-American values, or one made stronger by good-faith collaboration across linguistic and national divides for the purpose of achieving a democratic vision that included Cuban and Puerto Rican independence from Spain. In turn, for scholars today, it also provides a foundation on which to rethink literary and media history outside its familiar formations within the magazine and beyond.

2

Heroic Reporters and Networked Authors

INNOVATIONS FROM NEW JOURNALISM AND ITS
COLLABORATIVE LITERARY ALTERNATIVES

"She's Broken Every Record!" announced the *New York World*'s lead story on January 26, 1890. The headline referred to the race around the globe successfully completed by *World* reporter Nellie Bly (the journalistic pseudonym of Elizabeth Cochran), which pitted Bly against Phileas Fogg, the fictional hero of Jules Verne's bestselling 1872 novel *Le tour du monde en quatre-vingts jours* (published in English as *Around the World in Eighty Days*). The *World* billed Bly's journey as a demonstration of "how far in this last quarter century the facilities for travel and communication have advanced."[1] The trains and steamboats on which Bly completed much of her trip—as well as the telegraph wires that carried updates on her location back to the *World*—offered a dazzling display of how much faster travel and communication had become in the not-quite two decades since the publication of Verne's novel.[2] Telegraphic communication from Bly's trip relied on an undersea cable network that ran around the globe, just as *La América Ilustrada* had predicted in 1872, eighteen years earlier (and coincidentally, the same year as the release of *Le tour du monde en quatre-vingts jours* in France). Bly's record-breaking feat exhibited the realization of these technological possibilities; it also rendered earlier print innovations as limited and stale in contrast to the unique blend of narrative and visual elements that the *World* employed.

Throughout Bly's journey, the dispatches about Bly's progress—which were written by anonymous staff reporters back in New York—made explicit the idea of a contest between Verne's fiction and the *World*'s news stories. As Karen Roggenkamp has argued,

> Pulitzer anticipated that the race around the world and against time would become a race against the very idea of fictionality as well. . . . Nel-

lie Bly's tale would be as electric as Phileas Fogg's, with an equal number of hair-raising adventures and mad dashes, but in the end its thrill would in fact surpass the thrill of the novel, because it would be real.[3]

Indeed, Bly provided a striking contrast, not only to the elder Verne, but also to the special correspondent, a newspaper illustrator, whom Verne's novel dispatched as part of the adventure. By 1889, the special correspondent, who had been the very picture of innovation in modern media of the early 1870s, signaled that the media landscape in which Verne's novel had achieved phenomenal success had since become outmoded. According to the *World*'s article that announced Bly's triumphant return, "She has turned the wild dream of a French fiction-master into sober truth and Bly's fact of to-day has made the fancy of a quarter of a century ago seem like a twice-told tale."[4] At first glance, the emphasis on truth and factuality aligns the paper with journalistic standards that would arrive in the twentieth century. Yet the *World*'s insistence on the dominance of journalism over a novel in the realm of imaginative storytelling indicates that the paper circulated within a very different context—one in which Pulitzer and other newspaper editors sought larger audiences by using appeals that popular literature seemed unique in possessing.

In 1892 an anonymous contributor to *The Journalist*, a New York-based trade journal for the newspaper and magazine industry, commented, "It may be true, as some writers still insist, that journalism and literature have little in common. I do not believe this. . . . The newspaper of tomorrow is bound to absorb all that is good in literature."[5] For Pulitzer, the good in literature centered on its ability, in its most popular forms, to achieve widespread circulation in the fast-changing media landscape of his day. However, that view—which relied on making reporters like Bly into heroes within their stories and celebrities outside them—faced competition. Like Bly's race, which traversed the genres of the news article and the novel to locate her competitor, the contest over whose stories would influence the future of storytelling about recent events reached far beyond the *World* and its most direct rivals in New York City's Anglophone mass-circulation press.

This chapter explores emergent ideas of participation and collaboration in Nueva York's publications by examining how experimentation with authorship flourished in Anglophone and Hispanophone print communities during the 1880s and 1890s. I argue that, as a "new journalism" in publications like the *World* and the *Sun* elevated reporters as central figures in news stories, this focus influenced contemporaneous texts.[6] Key examples that attempted, in varying ways, to model new forms of authorship through social networks brought together to address contemporary labor issues include Henry James's *The Princess Casamassima*, serialized in the *Atlantic Monthly* (1885–1886); William Dean Howells's *A Hazard of New Fortunes*, serialized in *Harper's Weekly* (March–November 1889); and José Martí's *crónicas* "Nueva York bajo la nieve" (New York under snow) and "Un drama terrible" (A terrible drama) published in Buenos Aires's *La Nación* (1888). James reimagines the reporter through his princess's role in London's anarchist movement; Howells experiments with collaborative authorship in *Every Other Week*, disrupted by a streetcar strike; Martí foregrounds workers over reporters in narratives on the 1888 blizzard and the Haymarket Affair. This analysis contextualizes less familiar publications like *El Despertar*, an anarchist newspaper founded in 1890 by Luis Barcia and José Cayetano Campos, which critiqued the *World* and envisioned participatory, reader-centered news.

My analysis identifies what I am calling "networked authors" in these texts to reveal their reflections on and divergences from the phenomenon of the reporter. Ryan Cordell has used the term "network author" in a US Anglophone antebellum context to describe how practices of reprinting drove "a model of authorship that is communal rather than individual, distributed rather than centralized."[7] The texts considered in this chapter explored methods of creating their own communal models of authorship that were specific to their own late nineteenth-century media moment. While the network author model in antebellum newspapers resulted from editors' "acts of circulation and aggregation" of texts written by individual, if unknown, authors, those considered in this chapter attempted to reshape storytelling itself as a collective act.[8] As new journalism made reporters entertaining foils to the telegraphed news on their front pages, James, Howells, Martí, and *El Despertar*'s editorial team explored what kinds of collaborative storytelling a faster-paced and telegraph-wired world of print might support: James linked a princess-turned-reporter to an underground network of activists rather than leaving the action to the reporter alone in *The Princess Casamassima*; Howells envisioned a new kind of publication run by its contributors, who represented differing political viewpoints, in *A Hazard of New Fortunes*; and Martí and the editorial team of *El Despertar* identified and connected oppressed groups of workers, albeit for somewhat different ends. Together, these texts lay the foundation for understanding the most powerful visions of a participatory future of print that would emerge from Nueva York, as both a center of printing and an ideal of a more communitarian approach to print culture.

By contrast, the reporters of New York City's leading English-language daily newspapers built on the success of earlier illustrated newspaper reporters and special artists in achieving broad appeal through stunts and the promotion of progressive causes. A select few of those reporters were women, like Bly, whose very presence in the journalistic profession became part of her newspaper's appeal. Many more were men whose editors fashioned them into heroes—or modern knights errant—who took it upon themselves to make the news, sometimes while they also set out to save the day.[9] That brand of reporter provides the context for understanding the collaborative alternatives offered by Howells, James, Martí, and the editorial team of *El Despertar*. As we will see, all of these networked authors were attentive readers and critics of the reporting that was emerging in Anglophone mass-circulation newspapers; their insightful observations bring into sharper focus the visionary alternatives that they modeled through their own publications.

Reporting Modern Life

The contest between fact and fiction enacted in the stories printed during Bly's race around the globe constituted an attempt to redefine authorship within the newspaper. Pulitzer's approach built on the idea of the reporter or special artist from the Anglophone illustrated press of the 1860s and 1870s to make reporters like Bly into—as the subtitle of one *World* article put it—the "Subject of a New Story."[10] Bly tracks this transformation in her own account, published after her return, of the final leg of her journey: a cross-country train ride from San Francisco back to New York, which the *World* had arranged especially for her.

As the train rushes eastward, Bly notices a change brought about by her imminent triumph over Verne's protagonist. At an early stop on her trip, she reports, "I saw a great crowd of people dressed in their best

Sunday clothes gathered at the station. I supposed they were having a picnic and made some such remark, to be told in reply that the people had come there to see me."[11] This passage shows observational skills that Bly had employed throughout her trip; even though she had completed her assignment, she continued to "keep her eyes and ears open . . . [and] note this, that, and everything."[12] In keeping with the *World*'s use of French print culture as a point of reference for this stunt, she exhibits the qualities of the keen observer of modern life of Charles Baudelaire's 1863 "Le Peintre de la vie moderne" (The painter of modern life), centered on a newspaper illustrator who exhibits similar observational skills and feels most at home "derrière la vitre d'un café . . . contemplant la foule avec jouissance" (behind a café window . . . contemplating the crowd with pleasure).[13] But as the passage ends, and Bly looks out the train window, the crowd turns the gaze toward her. As the woman "who had been the first to make a record of a . . . trip around the world," Bly becomes the news, a spectacle of the *World*'s own making.[14] This reversal signals another kind of triumph—of a new kind of author, who is both a celebrity outside the newspaper and a hero within its stories.

As Bly raced from San Francisco back to New York, another example of the *World*'s new brand of authorship appeared in a review of Howells's new novel *A Hazard of New Fortunes* by *World* reporter and critic Nym Crinkle. Crinkle offers a scathing assessment of Howells's endeavor to bring attention to working-class New Yorkers, arguing that the novel showed Howells seeking to access "a side of New York life with which [he] is entirely unfamiliar."[15] By finding "Howells Out of His Sphere," as the headline announces, Crinkle claims territory for new journalism:

> The reader who is at all familiar with the palpitant and distinctive characteristics of the metropolis will, I think, acknowledge that the author in his particularity has made an accurate study of door-knobs and bric-á-brac without perceiving the great vital currents of purpose and endeavor that throb and surge in crossing but ever-distinct channels and give an awful meaning to our complex life.[16]

As a network of currents whose pulsing movements emphasize the city's human side, the real New York evokes the notion of romance that Howells famously rejected. Amy Kaplan helpfully defines romance in the context of late nineteenth-century US debates about realism as "a protean category which encompasses subjects as diverse as classical art, the Romantic movement, and popular fiction."[17] In subtle references throughout his review, Crinkle evokes this composite category of romance to dismiss Howells's experiment. For example, in a play on the idea of the knight errant, Crinkle reports that the novel requires the reader to "plod wearily on page after page, with a superstitious and inherent notion that something will happen."[18] Only through his own perseverance and imagination does Crinkle finally succeed in "heroically reading this book."[19] This critique offers another glimpse of the emerging reporting practices of the 1880s and early 1890s. In Crinkle's humorous application of the new journalistic formula, the reporter becomes a hero—if only for managing to read Howells's meandering text.

The *New York Sun* employed a similar, if less flamboyant, approach through articles that featured, as the title of a regular front-page column put it, "Life in the Metropolis Dashes Here and There by the Sun's Ubiquitous Reporters."[20] One article, called "To Coney Island at Last," sent an unnamed reporter to the iconic beach resort during New York's Great Blizzard of 1888; his errand takes the form of a quest through a deserted city made dangerous and unfamiliar by the storm. The reporter arrives at Coney Island to receive a hero's welcome from residents, who receive him "like a strange being from a far land."[21] The city's telegraph lines, the article notes, "were as good as useless" during the storm.[22] "One or two telegraph lines were working at intervals all the while, but the blizzard happened to catch all the operators out of town."[23] The article emphasizes the importance of the reporter's role in making news: the main currents of this news are not the electric ones running through the telegraph wires, but rather the romantic ones brought into view by the *Sun*'s intrepid reporter.

The New York-based trade journal *The Journalist* printed numerous articles in the 1880s and 1890s that recognized the reporting practices of leading newspapers like the *Sun* and the *World* as promising directions for the future of news. An 1891 piece described how a reporter should approach a murder story: "He plays detective and unearths many things that are news to the police. He reports to them and keeps the public waiting a day or two that the ends of justice be not defeated. He is ubiquitous. He works on every clue."[24] In that role, reporters face danger, act spontaneously, and ultimately become the heroes of their own stories.

Such an approach to news writing did not preclude the idea that newspapers needed to remain faithful to the truth or the so-called facts of a story. However, as Michael Schudson has shown, "Reporters believed strongly that it was their job both to get the facts and to be colorful. . . . In their desire to tell stories, reporters were less interested in facts than in creating personally distinctive and popular styles of writing."[25] In alignment with this view, one instructional book for journalists from the period supported the practice of "filling in the missing details from your imagination," as long as the key points of the story could be supported by fact.[26] The idea that reporters could apply creative license as they struck a balance between facts and imaginative storytelling also appears in commentary made by Joseph Pulitzer and *New York Sun* editor Charles Dana. According to Dana, "The invariable law of a newspaper is to be interesting. Suppose you tell all the truths of science in a way that bores the reader; what is the good? The truths don't stay in the mind, and nobody thinks any better of you because you have told him the truth tediously. The telling must be vivid and animating."[27] Pulitzer also demanded that his writers enhance the factual parts of their stories with imaginative writing. He insisted that his reporters produce "what is original, distinctive, dramatic, romantic, thrilling, unique, curious, quaint, humorous, odd, apt to be talked about . . . without impairing the confidence of the people in the truth of the stories or the character of the paper for reliability and scrupulous cleanness."[28] Through the *Sun's* literary leanings and the *World's* fast-paced sensationalism, both papers employed a new journalistic approach that turned city life into daily dramas featuring their own reporters.

It was not until the late 1890s that this view of reporting received widespread criticism within the US Anglophone press. The *New York Times*, in particular, sought to marginalize the practice of imaginative embellishment within newspapers that had accompanied the rise of the new journalistic reporter, and those efforts would succeed by the first few decades of the twentieth century.[29] As journalism shifted to require reporters to remove their creativity and passions from the stories they wrote, some became nostalgic for an era of reporting that provided greater artistic freedom. In his 1902 short story "A Derelict," Richard

Harding Davis, a leading reporter for the *Sun* and the *Journal* in the 1880s and 1890s, offered such a view. The story features a talented reporter named Charlie Chanring who can no longer succeed in a field increasingly dominated by a news agency called the Consolidated Press Syndicate. The syndicate demands a different kind of prose: "We do not want descriptive writing. . . . We do not pay you to send us pen-pictures or prose-poems. We want the facts, all the facts, and nothing but the facts."[30] In this new world of "machine-made" news, new journalism's signature style no longer qualifies as news.[31] Even the fictional form through which Davis delivered his critique shows that by the turn of the century, print culture had been carved up into more distinct regions. By then, the intrepid reporter of late nineteenth-century news had become the stuff of fiction.

At the turn of the 1890s, such a fate for the new journalistic reporter would have been difficult to imagine. The *World*'s and the *Sun*'s attempts to redefine authorship through the news—and to absorb the future of literature along with it—appeared to be winning a race whose contestants wrote varying forms of news and timely literary prose. As a writer whose living depended on a literary market increasingly centered in New York City, Henry James must have recognized the stakes of that contest well before the *World* made it explicit in Bly's race around the globe. In that context, he developed an unlikely competitor to the new journalistic reporter in his novel *The Princess Casamassima*, which first appeared in serial in the *Atlantic Monthly* from 1885 to 1886.

James's Revolutionary Reporter

James's novels of the 1880s and 1890s teem with examples of his dismissive attitude toward reporters. The ever-nagging Henrietta Stackpole of *A Portrait of a Lady* is absolutely unable to comprehend privacy.[32] In *The Reverberator*, George Flack, a US foreign correspondent based in Paris, torments a French aristocratic family in his pursuit of a story for a New York gossip column. The link between newspapers and the invasion of privacy also figures prominently in *The Bostonians* and *The Aspern Papers*. In contrast, *The Princess Casamassima* offers a more subtle consideration of reporting, which refuses to discard it altogether. While the novel rejects the bravado and individualism of the heroic reporter of new journalism, it also seeks to articulate an alternative centered on self-reflection and, at times, collaboration through London's underground anarchist network, which leaves intact the idea of narrating the news through an individual reporter's perspective. This incipient form of reporting also rejects placing literary writing in its own, exclusive sphere, suggesting that James might have been exploring his own ambivalence at the time about the very notion of the literary with which scholars have since associated him.

The Princess Casamassima's version of the reporter is the Italian American princess Christina Light, who arrives alone in London to find "something fresh in other walks of life."[33] Echoing characterizations of reporting from within newspapers and trade journals at the time, the novel sets its princess on a quest to find a new vantage point on city life. Describing her decision to sell her aristocratic trappings, move from one of London's most exclusive neighborhoods to the modest Madeira Crescent, and engage with the city's anarchist underworld, Christina explains, "I want so much to know London—the real London" (PC, 348). The meaning of the "real London" becomes apparent through the contrast that the novel establishes between the princess, who has "thrown herself with passion into being 'modern,'" and Hyacinth, who shares Christina's love for walking through the city but also represents an elitist perspective that Christina rejects (PC, 211). Characterized as a "true artist," Hyacinth is a bookbinder and, as such, is linked to artisanship and an older, more exclusive realm of the period's rapidly changing media system (PC, 340). Christina is quite clear about her position on the system of representation embodied by Hyacinth: "I don't care about the artists!," she declares (PC, 348). Throughout the novel, Christina enacts a shift away from the world of artistic sensibilities to which Hyacinth belongs toward a form of reporting that replaces heroism with self-reflection. This was an idea of reporting born of its early 1880s context, in which the future direction of news writing (and its relationship to literature) was under debate.

To excavate those ideas and their engagement with late nineteenth-century media change, we need to consider why they have been so difficult to recognize in scholarship on The Princess Casamassima. Notwithstanding Christina's unambiguous dismissal of Hyacinth, interpretations of the novel have tended to privilege Hyacinth's perspective over

Christina's, thus contributing to the difficulty of recognizing in hindsight the revolutionary alternative that Christina represented. In 1950, for example, Lionel Trilling described Hyacinth as an exemplar of what he called "the liberal imagination." In Trilling's view, Hyacinth suggests "that the man of art may be close to the secret center of things when the man of action is quite apart from it."[34] Scholars have continued to center Hyacinth in readings focused on the representational issues raised by the novel, while others have elaborated the links between the novel's fictional anarchist movement and the political unrest that occurred in London while James wrote the novel there.[35] By establishing such a parallel, these readings encourage the recognition of another similarity— between Hyacinth's impressionistic observations of London and James's own artistic sensibilities. Even as late twentieth-century scholars began to reconsider the relationship between text and context, their analyses of *The Princess Casamassima* have typically looked to Hyacinth to make sense of James's views and his literary career as a whole. Mark Seltzer has argued influentially that the young artist's sensibilities enact a critique of the rationalizing, discursive practices—from politics to sociology to criminology—that were then constructing modern society. From that perspective, the realist novel's signature omniscient narrator represents a kind of rationalizing order that James undermines through the character of Hyacinth. His individual, impressionist viewpoint, which again recalls the painter of modern life, embodies a "technique of 'central recording consciousness'" that "displaces the authority of the narrative voice and disavows any direct interpretive authority over the action."[36] In this way, Seltzer interprets *The Princess Casamassima* not as a critique of contemporary politics, as Trilling suggested, but rather as a demonstration of the role of the literary in revealing and reinforcing the discursive practices that shape social reality.

The fascination with Hyacinth throughout the criticism on *The Princess Casamassima* points to a commonality shared by arguments as different as Trilling's and Seltzer's. Although they convey contrasting ideas about how the text engages with social reality, the readings rest on similar foundations. For both, the literary—and a corresponding notion of authorship modeled in Hyacinth's image—provides the foundation from which to interpret the novel. Informed by notions of literary autonomy and critical distance that solidified in the twentieth century, these influential readings take the ultimate triumph of Hyacinth's point of view as a foregone conclusion. Yet, in the 1880s, Hyacinth did not necessarily represent the most promising direction for storytelling to engage the modern world, suggesting that James himself was ambivalent about Hyacinth's approach to seeing and representation and used his novel to attempt to articulate an alternative. The novel constitutes James's boldest experiment with another kind of storytelling.

James expressed an awareness of the fluid boundaries between news and literary writing as early as the 1870s, when he wrote a column from Paris for the *New York Tribune*, which he described as "a sort of *chronique* of the events and interests of the day."[37] After James had contributed about twenty such articles, *Tribune* editor Whitelaw Reid wrote James a letter asking that future submissions "be rather more 'newsy' in character."[38] James's response mixes defiant sarcasm with sincere relief: "I quite appreciate what you say about the character of my letters, and about their not being the right sort of thing for a newspaper."[39] As he explains,

> It would cost me really more trouble than to write as I have been doing (which comes tolerably easy to me) and it would be poor economy for me to try and become "newsy" and gossipy. I am too finical a writer and I should be constantly becoming more "literary" than is desirable. . . . If my letters have been "too good" I am honestly afraid that they are the poorest I can do, especially for the money![40]

This passage demonstrates James's commitment to the literary, but it also reveals the negotiation of terms that was then underway. At a time when new approaches to writing news stories had not yet drawn clear lines between "newsy" and "literary" writing, his savvy response to his editor's complaint aligns the literary character of his writing with quality.[41] At this early stage in his career, James clearly grasps the transition that was taking place in the news industry, and he attempts to influence its future direction.

As experimentation with news writing intensified among New York newspapers in the 1880s, James continued to engage debates about the future of news. By then, the *Tribune*, which cultivated a reputation for cultural and intellectual sophistication, must have appeared far less objectionable to James than the newspapers that made reporters into the stars of dramatic news stories. *A Portrait of a Lady*, which first appeared in serial in the *Atlantic Monthly* and *Macmillan's Magazine* from 1880 to 1881, speaks to that emerging context. The sharp critique embedded in the novel's account of the reporting practices of Henrietta Stackpole suggests that James had noticed what papers like the *Sun* sought to achieve, even before Pulitzer entered onto the scene in New York in 1883. While Reid had been content to simply exclude James's so-called literary writing from the *Tribune*, Dana set out to incorporate the literary to give mass appeal to his own style of news. As Pulitzer's *World* was achieving unprecedented circulation numbers by employing a similar approach, James was working more urgently to secure a place for literary prose in this new world of news.[42] It was during this period that he provided his unusual consideration of possible new directions for literary prose in *The Princess Casamassima*.

In the context of the debates about the future of news with which it conversed, *The Princess Casamassima* assigns potentiality to the point of view represented by Christina. She is, after all, the novel's namesake, and she exhibits several striking similarities to the new journalistic reporting of New York newspapers during the period.[43] Like the modern knights errant of those newspapers, the novel's modern princess perceives the city through a mix of scientific exploration and individual passion. As she wanders through the streets of London, the princess pursues "discoveries" that she "pretended to be sounding in a scientific spirit" (*PC*, 354), following in the footsteps of reporters whose editors demanded that their writing reveal the so-called "facts" of city life. At the same time, she also shares "the energy of feeling, the high free, reckless spirit" that appears in the heroic tales that appeared in newspapers like the *Sun* and the *World* during the 1880s (*PC*, 354). In the context of the mid-1880s, Christina serves as James's answer to the rising status of the form of authorship represented by the reporter. As leading editors like Dana and Pulitzer advertised the "literary" qualities of their news as a way of making their papers more appealing to readers, James reverses that relationship, bringing the new forms of journalistic reporting into the novel. *The Princess Casamassima*, then, constitutes a literary reflection on narrating the news.

Transplanted into James's literary world, the reporter takes on new qualities. In contrast to the *Sun*'s and the *World*'s unambiguously heroic depictions of reporters, Christina is not always worthy of admiration. Her connection to the urban poor and the underground anarchist movement remains ambiguous throughout the text. As numerous critics have noted, the impoverished residents who represent for Christina the "real" London rarely come into view; even on her walks with Hyacinth through the neighborhoods that she believes will gratify her quest, London appears primarily through Hyacinth's perspective. In addition, for all her desire to contribute to revolutionary activities, even Christina does not seem to know whether she has succeeded in gaining the confidence of its leader, "the right man . . . the real thing," Hoffendahl (PC, 245). Her uncertainty becomes apparent when she asks Hyacinth's friend Paul Muniment, who seems to have close ties to the movement, "Do you consider that I'm in—really far?" (PC, 427). Hoffendahl's decision to bypass the princess when he sends Hyacinth his top-secret orders at the end of the novel suggests that she has not managed to become as involved with this underground network as she had hoped. In the novel's form of reporting, Christina can only reveal part of a larger story populated by a wide array of (sometimes invisible) actors. These are not her own personal shortcomings, but rather guaranteed constraints of the reporter's activities. Through Christina, the novel suggests it is simply not possible for the reporter to know everything or to be the hero of anything.

In a world where heroic reporting proves impossible, Christina embodies a consciously provisional alternative—informed by James's own connections to New York's publishing market of the late nineteenth century. The novel's form of reporting holds onto authorship as an individual activity while highlighting the limitations of any one individual's ability to see the full picture. This model of authorship includes self-reflection—even doubt—and, while not fully collaborative, it requires additional points of view. It is a form of authorship that contrasts starkly with that of Hyacinth, who appears not as the enduring hero he would become in many twentieth-century interpretations of the novel, but rather as a relic of an earlier era of print culture centered in Britain and France. In this way, James makes a move similar to Pulitzer's use of Verne as a contrast to Bly in her race around the globe: He positions a figure representing an earlier phase of print culture as the foil to a new form of authorship of his own making.

Indeed, descriptions of Hyacinth throughout the novel recall Baudelaire's painter of modern life, M.G., depicted more than two decades before. Like M.G., Hyacinth frequently engages in "interminable, restless, melancholy, moody, yet all-observant strolls" (*PC*, 67). The "fantastic, erratic way of seeing things" that Hyacinth exhibits on his walks through London echoes M.G.'s ability to transform what he sees into "le fantastique réel de la vie" (fantastic reality of life) (*PC*, 122).[44] During his trip to Paris, Hyacinth's manner of seeing produces such a spectacle of modern life:

> The boulevard was alive, brilliant with illuminations, with the variety and gaiety of the crowd, the dazzle of shops and cafés seen through uncovered fronts or immense lucid places, the flamboyant porches of theatres and the flashing lamps of carriages, the far-spreading murmur of talkers and strollers, the uproar of pleasure and prosperity, the general magnificence of Paris on a perfect evening in June. (*PC*, 318)

The Parisian boulevard appears illuminated and transformed by lights that show the mark of the artist's passion. Yet although this artistic perspective may seem well aligned with James's own signature style, the novel itself displays a different attitude toward Hyacinth.

From the outset, the "exceedingly diminutive" young man occupies a vulnerable position (*PC*, 32). The narrative foreshadows his eventual demise during one of his many strolls through the city with Christina: "She affected him at this moment as playing with life so audaciously and defiantly that the end of it all would inevitably be some violent catastrophe" (*PC*, 354). Hyacinth's suicide brings his way of understanding the city to a dead end, as it were, but his demise already has been all but guaranteed. The young artist's death reinforces the idea, evident throughout the novel, that he represents an outmoded print cultural tradition demonstrated and inspired by the illustrated newspaper—which by then had become a widely adopted form on both sides of the Atlantic, in Anglophone and Hispanophone communities of print.

James's experiment with reporting through his novel's protagonist, Christina, appears especially bold in the context of the *Atlantic Monthly Magazine*, which published the novel in serial. Beyond its reviews of recent book releases, little of what appeared in the *Atlantic* could be con-

sidered news. Instead, as a so-called quality monthly, the *Atlantic* provided an exclusive venue for essays, poetry, and serialized novels from
the most respected literary writers. In a sense, the novel's presence in
the magazine performs an act that parallels the secret undertakings of
the underground anarchist movement in the novel. Perhaps more successfully than the novel's anarchists, who seek to overthrow the political
establishment, James's version of the reporter infiltrates the very center of the US Anglophone literary establishment. While still embracing
the literary as a privileged site for individual expression, the novel also
suggests the need to update literary writing by including precisely the
content that the *Atlantic* excluded: news stories, in general, and those
featuring reporters, in particular.

That suggestion of a possible intermingling of literary writing and a
more self-reflective form of reporting modeled by Cristina Light must
have become far more difficult to explain once the period's questions
about the future of news had found a resolution within the twentieth-
century journalistic profession. James's own 1908 preface to the New York
edition of *The Princess Casamassima* offers a different interpretation of
his experimental novel through the lens of the twentieth-century literary
field. There, a retrospective James insists, "This fiction proceeded quite
directly, during the first year of a long residence in London, from the
habit and the interest of walking the streets."[45] Drawing an evident parallel with the novel's "sensitive hero," James assigns himself the role of "the
habitual observer, the preoccupied painter, the pedestrian prowler."[46] By
painting himself in the image of Hyacinth, James resurrects his artist and
reshapes the novel to fit within the boundaries of a field that had begun
to understand the literary as a separate space of critique—much like the
cronistas considered in the preceding chapter, Enrique Hernández Miyares and Manuel Gutiérrez Nájera, had also begun to do by the 1880s.
This portrait of himself as the artist would ultimately guide subsequent
readings of *The Princess Casamassima* and influence James's own legacy
within the US literary field. From that vantage point, James's consideration of a novelistic form for the new journalistic reporter became difficult to recognize as a reflection on the news. Instead, it began to appear
as a text that pursued purely literary ends.

The Princess Casamassima contemplated possibilities of authorship
in the age of the new journalistic reporter that Howells would explore a

few years later in *A Hazard of New Fortunes*. There, Howells provided his
own vision that strayed farther than *The Princess Casamassima* from the
realm of the new journalistic reporter. While James sought to revise and
limit the new journalistic reporter's sovereignty over the news, *A Hazard
of New Fortunes* contemplates storytelling about the modern world that
picks up where Christina left off in building a network of collaborators.

Howells's Editorial Community

As he wrote *A Hazard of New Fortunes* and serialized the novel in *Harper's Weekly* in 1889, Howells was well positioned to participate in the
debate over the future of news and literary writing. Recently installed
in New York with an impressive new contract from Harper and Brothers, he had reached the height of his influence in the world of print.
With that context in mind, we can read *A Hazard of New Fortunes* as
a vehicle for promoting alternatives to the period's emerging reporting
practices. The novel's plot revolves around the creation of a biweekly
periodical, called *Every Other Week*; throughout, Howells emphasizes
the magazine's experimental nature through conversations between
the characters that provide an insider's view of the publishing industry
of the late 1880s. The publisher, Fulkerson, and his newly hired editor,
Basil March, carefully design *Every Other Week* to "invade no other field,
. . . prosper on no ground but its own."[47] Even the format of the paper
signifies March's ambitions to create a new type of periodical: "We've
cut loose from the old traditional quarto literary newspaper size, and
we've cut loose from the old two-column big page magazine size" (*HNF*,
86). *Every Other Week* becomes a "new departure in literary journalism,"
as well as a "new departure in magazines" (*HNF*, 60, 137). Within this
liminal space, the magazine provides the answer for those who "begin
to look round and ask what's new" (*HNF*, 75). As it follows this singular magazine's quest to reach the vanguard of periodical literature, the
novel lingers on the questions and possibilities of that search, exploring two main approaches to storytelling: collaborative authorship and
impersonal narration.

The motivation for the novel's experiment becomes evident in the
apartment search conducted by March and his wife as they prepare to
relocate from Boston to New York City, where Fulkerson has chosen

to locate *Every Other Week*. Scholars have noted that the painstaking evaluation of each apartment visited by the Marches exemplifies novelistic realism, especially the unit that the couple eventually chooses, where "every shelf and dressing-case and mantel was littered with gimcracks" (*HNF*, 27). Such imagery at first seems to support the claim in Crinkle's review for the *World* that the novel overflows with bourgeois domestic detail. Less noted is Howells's accompanying critique of the city's leading newspapers. After making "March buy her the *Herald* and the *World*," Mrs. March puts together a collection of advertisements that showcase New York City as it appears in the popular press: "She read the new advertisements aloud with ardor and with faith to believe that the apartments described in them were every one truthfully represented. . . . 'Elegant, light, large, single and outside flats' were offered with 'all improvements—bath, ice box, etc.'—for twenty-five to thirty dollars a month. The cheapness was amazing" (*HNF*, 31). The couple's subsequent visits to the apartments advertised reveal the exaggerations and embellishments of the newspaper listings: "Flattering advertisements took them to numbers of huge apartment-houses chiefly distinguishable from tenement-houses by the absence of fire-escapes on their facades" (*HNF*, 34). Through such "reiterated disappointments," the advertisements exhaust the Marches with "useless information in a degree unequaled in their experience" (*HNF*, 33). The flood of information provided by the newspapers—both the old guard represented by the *Herald* and the new journalism of the *World*—proves entirely unreliable.[48]

Like the information provided by the newspapers, the street-level perspective of the reporters they featured also proves inadequate. On foot, Mr. and Mrs. March find New York to be "no longer impressive, no longer characteristic" (*HNF*, 31). March faces similar difficulties when he wanders the streets on his own. Although he frequently encounters picturesque scenes that he would like to depict in articles for *Every Other Week*, the editor never finds time to turn them into inspired prose. His tours of the city produce only fleeting glimpses that "remained mere material in his memorandum-book" (*HNF*, 196). The failure of these walks to lead to stories in print casts as outmoded both new journalism's reporting and the model of the Baudelairian observer inspired by the illustrated press that preceded it. Indeed, March's inability to write emphasizes that he is not an author at all.[49] He is an editor, rather than

a contributor or a reporter, whose publication thrives on bringing together a collection of viewpoints. In this role, he sets the stage for the
novel's exploration of its primary alternative to the reporting of the time.

Every Other Week's "co-operative character" rests on its business
model, which pays contributors a share of the profits generated by the
issue in which their work appears (HNF, 2). According to Fulkerson, the
idea represents a "beautiful vision of a lot of literary fellows breaking
loose from the bondage of publishers and playing it alone" (HNF, 3). Cooperation at the financial level provides the foundation for collaboration
among contributors, who represent a range of interests and opinions. As
March observes,

> I don't believe there's another publication in New York that could bring
> together . . . a fraternity and equality crank like poor old Lindau, a belated
> sociological crank like Woodburn, and a truculent speculator like Dry-
> foos, and a humanitarian dreamer like young Dryfoos, and a sentimental-
> ist like me, and a nondescript like Beaton, and a pure advertising essence
> like Fulkerson. (HNF, 208)

The unique quality of Every Other Week celebrated by the editor proves
especially significant in light of the novel's treatment of labor conflict:
the magazine proves able, at least initially, to accommodate a range of
differing positions on economic issues. Lindau's interest in "fraternity
and equality" fuels his passionate support of unions and his concern
for the poor, in addition to reflecting his own class position. The young
Conrad Dryfoos brings his religious convictions to the labor question,
as he dedicates himself to service among the poor. At the other end of
the political spectrum, Conrad's father (the farmer-turned-speculator
who serves as Every Other Week's sole investor) represents the interests of capital. These "heterogeneous forces . . . co-operate to a reality
which March could not deny" (HNF, 125). Indeed, by the time the first
issue goes to print, the endeavor appears validated by Fulkerson's declaration that the publication is "going to a hundred thousand before
it stops" (HNF, 129). Fulkerson's prediction puts Every Other Week on
par with the most successful literary and cultural magazines of the
period—including Harper's Weekly, where A Hazard of New Fortunes
first appeared in print.

This "initial success," however, reveals itself to be unsustainable (*HNF*, 137). The dinner at which March admires the heterogeneous forces brought together by *Every Other Week* ends in a heated argument between Lindau and the older Dryfoos. Lindau's subsequent resignation from his position as a translator for the publication suggests that "the violence of Lindau's sentiments concerning the whole political and social fabric" makes him too radical to cooperate with the others brought together by the experiment (*HNF*, 189). Moreover, March's and Fulkerson's failure to decide on a means of writing about the strike that takes place in the novel—even after they both express a desire to do so—leaves unresolved the question of whether their magazine could improve upon the newspaper accounts of the event. If the publication promises an approach to writing about current affairs that could be more inclusive than other news of the day, it never delivers a complete picture of the alternative it envisions—not even within the limited range of political diversity explicitly delineated, and notably not racial diversity, which it altogether fails to address.

As *Every Other Week*'s experiment with collaborative authorship begins to fall apart, the novel introduces impersonal narrative as another alternative. The elevated train, which makes frequent appearances in the backdrop of the novel, introduces this approach that anticipates omniscient narration. On the L train, March and his wife find an escape from the trials of their apartment search, as they glimpse the interiors of apartments visible from the train: "It was better than the theatre, of which it reminded him, to see those people through their windows: a family party of work-folk at a late tea, some of the men in their shirtsleeves; a woman sewing by a lamp; a mother laying her child in its cradle" (*HNF*, 45). In contrast to the hazy, unimpressive scenes that greeted March and his wife in the street, the glimpses of the tenements provided by the train make the city accessible: "What suggestion! What drama! What infinite interest!" (*HNF*, 45). The distance provided by the train supplies the intensity and excitement that the couple fail to experience on their walks through the streets. But it is no longer their gaze that taps into these exciting currents of city life. Rather, the train pulls these scenes of city life into view for them—performing a function here not unlike the telegraph wires that also traversed the city carrying stories of the news. Yet, while the telegraph carries words originated by human authors, the train's role in storytelling here assigns a bigger role to technology—making the train the source of the story.

The scene's suggestion of a technologically authored viewpoint comes further into view when considered in light of the striking contrast between the Marches' experience on the train and Bly's narration of her own train ride at the conclusion of her race around the globe, which was published in the *World* a few months after Howells's novel debuted in *Harper's Weekly*. From the train, Bly sees a crowd that returns her gaze, ultimately making Bly herself into a new kind of subject matter for the *World*'s news. For the Marches, in contrast, the city's "work-folk" become the story as they "see those people through their windows" (*HNF*, 45).

The passage offers an intriguing variation on a pattern that Barbara Hochman has identified in her analysis of the emergence of omniscient narration in US novels associated with realism and naturalism in the 1880s and 1890s. Noting that "the self-consciously impersonal realist or naturalist narrator was a controversial phenomenon when it first appeared," Hochman identifies portrayals of the author as a public performer in novels of the 1890s and 1900s as one way in which writers grappled with this transformation.[50] She explains, "When the author was no longer represented as a personable storyteller, he or she was often imagined as a public performer," especially as a woman on stage.[51] By contrast, back on the train in *A Hazard of New Fortunes*, the Marches are the audience. They are not the agents of a new perspective. The performers here are those at home in the tenement house, but their performances would not be visible without the presence of the train. If there is an authorial agent here, it is somewhere between the train, without which tenement house residents would simply be engaging in the activities of their home lives, and the residents themselves without whom the train would not be able to reveal the scenes that the Marches find so exciting. Such a form of narration is impersonal because no one individual selects these scenes; it is also incomplete as an approach to storytelling, as it only works with an audience, like the Marches on the train. We see the novel grasping here for a method of using technology to find an alternative to the reporter's gaze—and also to that of the Baudelairian artist.

Near the end of the novel, March's attempt to see the strike for himself offers another reflection on a more impersonal style of writing that rejects new journalistic reporting and ultimately signals the need for a more collaborative approach. Walking toward the strikers, March "interested himself in the apparent indifference of the mighty city, which kept on about its business" (*HNF*, 267). The unusual wording offers a hint of the experimentation in which the novel is engaging here; March seems to be drawing his own attention outside himself into the city's larger, impersonal form. The city's dispassionate backdrop accompanies March's first glimpse of the strikers as he "watched them at a safe distance" (*HNF*, 267). March attempts to maintain this distance as he continues his journey in a streetcar (apparently not affected by the strike) that takes him "to one of the farthermost tracks westward, where so much of the fighting was reported to have taken place" (*HNF*, 268). From inside, March finds a way to contain the emotions that the scene inspires: "He began to feel like the populace; but he struggled with himself and regained the character of the philosophical observer" (*HNF*, 268). In contrast to his and his wife's experience on the elevated train, March manages to form impressions as a keen but also aloof observer—although they are not the result of sincere inward feeling or impulse (per Romanticism). Instead, March feels compelled to involve himself, at least emotionally, in the scene by some outside force. While that force is never fully articulated, it is linked to the distance associated with the streetcar.

As the tragedy of the streetcar strike unfolds, the narrative returns to the street-level view that we saw much earlier in the novel during the Marches' apartment search. This time, however, we see things from the perspective of the publication's young idealist, Conrad. Conrad watches the strike in an "exalted mood" through which "all events had a dreamlike simultaneity" (*HNF*, 274). In Conrad's personal reverie, he witnesses "a little way off . . . a street-car, and around the car a tumult of shouting, cursing, struggling men" (*HNF*, 274). The scene finally allows the city to appear from the perspective of an individual observer, but the exaltation it produces for Conrad is short-lived. Indeed, Conrad quickly slips into a role that looks more like that of the new journalistic reporter. He sees his own friend and colleague from *Every Other Week*, Lindau, as he is attacked by a police officer in the crowd. At that moment, Conrad's connection with the scene from an aesthetic point of view turns into recognition of his own involvement in what is unfolding. Before he can act, however, he gets hit by a stray bullet: "Conrad fell forward, pierced through the heart by that shot fired from the car" (*HNF*, 274). Conrad's fate provides a nightmarish variation on the reporter's heroism (one that anticipates the war correspondents of the yellow press considered in chapter 4). In the context of a streetcar strike in New York City in 1889, Conrad's fatal shot to the heart—as well as the narrator's unembellished description of it—suggests that the future of news that it considers unviable is the very one so hotly pursued by the new journalistic reporters of the city's leading newspapers.

While both Conrad's and March's parts in the streetcar strike scene clearly reject new journalistic reporting—as well as an earlier individual impressionism that recalls Baudelaire—the novel never fully embraces the impersonal narration that intermingles with both characters' experiences. The fatal shot issues from a streetcar, thus belying the suggestion of impersonal or critical distance that the novel had previously located in the city's modern forms of transportation—as in the Marches' experience on the elevated train. Instead, the streetcar enables a shot to be fired anonymously, becoming in a sense an accomplice to the crime—and also suggesting the power and privilege of the anonymous observer. Moreover, the streetcar offers no neutral footing in a scene brought about by a strike of the laborers whose working conditions in such vehicles provided the motivation behind the entire drama. Like *Every Other Week*'s collaborative aspirations, the novel's explorations of a more distanced, impersonal point of view never reveal a clear path forward. By the end of the novel, the path that appears most possible is a kind of authorship explored in *Every Other Week* that arises out of a collective experience of urban modernity.

The novel's incompleteness, in this sense, offers a chance to reconsider a widespread idea within studies of the US realist novel, which provides another example of the way in which twentieth-century notions of literary value have obscured late nineteenth-century innovations. Starting in the 1940s, scholars took an interest in evaluating US realism in terms of its success (or, more often, failure) in establishing a "relation between American fiction and American society."[52] As Amy Kaplan has noted, this line of inquiry resulted in the view that the genre never entirely succeeded in its effort to forge a new literary form in opposition to what Howells called "romance." Realist novels told stories from the distant perspective of an omniscient narrator in contrast to the more personal and impassioned points of view embodied by individual characters. Yet the effort to overwrite the world of personal experience with a more objective point of view ends up undermined by characters who impose their own designs on the narratives. In this way, the genre ultimately "failed case by case by refusing to renounce romance."[53] Failure, however, came with an important consolation—as the inability to tame a romantic element became the mark of an author's literary prowess. For example, Eric Sundquist celebrates James, Stephen Crane, and Mark Twain because "their reckless, imaginative selves refused to yield to the literalizing demands of a strict realism."[54] By portraying realist writers as rebels who defended literature's distinction from other rationalizing discourses, such a reading ultimately defines the value of realism in twentieth-century literary terms.

If we remove the notion of the literary that underpinned twentieth-century assessments of realist writing, we might reread its so-called failures instead as the inchoate or emergent results of experimentation with the literary imagination. As we have seen, Hochman has shown that omniscient narration, itself an innovation of the period, never provided a fully formed model for writers at the time. In addition, another strain of scholarship has zoomed out from the "high realism" that circulated in the late nineteenth century in leading literary publications (including those in which *A Hazard of New Fortunes* and *The Princess Casamassima* debuted) to situate realism and its negotiation of class differences within a longer history of public debate about the role of literary writing in US culture.[55] This perspective has incorporated a more diverse range of voices—from Charles Chesnutt to Zitkala-Sa to Kate Chopin—whose convergences with and divergences from previously recognized realist strategies bring into view another notion of the literary, which, according to Nancy Bentley, "begins to look like an unstable compound molecule."[56] In this view, realist texts make sense not as a set of similar designs implemented imperfectly by each author (as it may have seemed from the perspective of the twentieth-century literary field), but rather as a heterogeneous collection of competing responses to a shifting cultural and media context—attempts to create an innovation that might take hold.[57] *A Hazard of New Fortunes* revels in this exploration of inchoate possibilities.

In his essays, Howells exhibits an appreciation of the instability that accompanies artistic experimentation: "In the beginning of any art, even the most gifted worker must be crude in his methods."[58] In another article, he elaborates, "Sometimes it has seemed to me that the crudest expression of any creative art is better than the finest comment upon it."[59] Howells's words describe the very challenge that he undertook with *A Hazard of New Fortunes*. In the context of a period of media transition when the very idea of news and its relationship to literary prose had been called into question, the novel offers an emerging, provisional reflection on what the literary might become—and perhaps also a view of the way in which magazines of the period themselves engaged in such experimentation. Considering *A Hazard of New Fortunes* in the context of *Harper's* magazine in 1889 provides further insight into the media change of that moment.

Like *Harper's*, the novel's experimental periodical, *Every Other Week*, constitutes an attempt to keep pace with trends within the magazine industry while maintaining an identity as a literary periodical. As Gib Prettyman has noted, "The fictional magazine venture that forms the plot of the novel, is itself an attempt to capitalize on trends in the magazine marketplace, not the least of which is the overwhelming popularity of illustration."[60] Further details signal *Every Other Week*'s similar position to that of *Harper's* within the magazine industry of 1889. For example, like *Harper's*, Fulkerson places an emphasis on continuing to update approaches to illustration as a means of occupying the cutting edge of a periodical press in transition. His hiring of Angus Beaton as art director—a new role in the publishing profession at the time—puts further distance between *Every Other Week* and the special artists of the earlier illustrated press.

Moreover, *Every Other Week* exhibits a commitment to combining literary refinement with attention to current affairs that echoes *Harper's*. Tellingly, Fulkerson cites an interest in cultivating female readers, thus tapping into a trend within newspapers and popular magazines at the time: "We want to make a magazine that will go for the women's fancy every time. I don't mean with recipes for cooking and fashions and personal gossip about authors and society, but real high-tone literature that will show women triumphing in all the stories, or else suffering tremendously" (*HNF*, 88). The types of articles that Fulkerson rejects here had recently found a home in the *World*'s Sunday edition, and the new *Cosmopolitan* magazine (of which Howells would later briefly become an editor) had also begun cultivating a female audience with similar content. Fulkerson's insistence that his own publication's pursuit of this audience would take the form of "real high-tone literature" distinguishes *Every Other Week* from those endeavors, while recalling the editorial strategies of *Harper's* and other so-called genteel magazines of the period (*HNF*, 88).

Howells's novel aligns with the depiction of social class that scholars have identified with *Harper's*. According to Prettyman, the novel, like the magazine, offers a space where middle-class readers can familiarize themselves with (and differentiate themselves from) "stories on immigrants, industries, industrial leaders, labor disputes, and technological changes."[61] Although Kaplan does not draw explicit comparisons with *Harper's*, her attentive reading of *A Hazard of New Fortunes* aligns with Prettyman's characterization of the fictional magazine and its historical point of reference. She contends that the novel "forges an urban community out of the debris of social conflict, and molds a common language" while also producing what gets called at one point in the novel "knowledge of the line" that separates classes within the city.[62] Consequently, *A Hazard of New Fortunes* "divides the city into two separate but unequal camps and veils the antagonism between them so that the social nature of this division fades from view."[63] In Kaplan's reading, as in Prettyman's, the novel reproduces "the spectacle of industrialization" in ways that ultimately serve middle-class readers.[64] Like the news articles of *Harper's*, the novel acknowledges social difference while enabling readers to distance themselves from its causes through categories such as crudeness and respectability, radicalism and reason, and newspapers and literature. Yet *A Hazard of New Fortunes* also strives to reach beyond *Harper's* brand of literary distinction and consequent social containment. The novel itself represents a departure from the original idea with which *Harper's* approached Howells: to write a series of sketches about the city. That March considers a similar idea within the narrative and finds it impossible to achieve highlights the novel's daring experiment. Moreover, the streetcar strike that brings about the novel's conclusion showcases an important difference. Unlike *Harper's*, *Every Other Week* never publishes a story about the strike.

Instead, the presence of the strike within the novel sparks an extraordinary conversation between March and Conrad, in which they articulate the new possibilities that they see in their literary experiment. Conrad starts the conversation by remarking to March that he believes *Every Other Week* "will succeed. I think we can do some good in it" (*HNF*, 93). March responds thoughtfully with a series of questions: "What do you mean by good? Improve the public taste? Elevate the standard of literature? Give young authors and artists a chance?" (*HNF*, 93). March and Conrad explore a series of different possible meanings of the same word employed by the commentator in *The Journalist* who predicted that "the newspaper of tomorrow is bound to absorb all that is good in literature."[65] While March's first two suggestions appear to uphold ideas of taste and cultural distinction, his third question about "giv[ing] young authors and artists a chance" indicates the novel's ambition to do some serious and groundbreaking thinking about how literary value might be redefined to reflect democratic values of access and equality (*HNF*, 93).

In turn, Conrad responds to March's vision of success for their magazine with another proposal: "If you can make the comfortable people understand how the uncomfortable people live, it would be a very good thing, Mr. March. Sometimes it seems to me that the only trouble is that we don't know one another well enough; and that the first thing to do is this" (*HNF*, 93). While middle-class markers of distinction make the working class appear, according to Kaplan, "as background, as cityscape, [which] becomes invisible as an arena for social agency," Conrad's choice of words refuses to perform the same erasure of responsibility.[66] Describing those on either side of the line in similar terms, he makes the suffering of those who are "uncomfortable" more relatable, familiar. This exchange between March and Conrad sheds new light on the detailed depictions that the novel provides of the publishing industry of its day. In its most hopeful and unique moments, the novel sets up the possibility of a new kind of writing that has the potential to bridge some of the very social divisions that its narrative showcases.

In one of the novel's most revealing moments, Fulkerson considers whether *Every Other Week* could offer an alternative to the newspapers' "noisy typography about yesterday's troubles on the surface lines" (*HNF*, 270). With March, he brainstorms various perspectives that the periodical could offer—from the "aesthetic aspects" that might be treated by March and Beaton, to the "literary part" that the aspiring novelist Kendrick might play, to the version that might be provided by the strikers themselves: "What's the reason we couldn't get one of the strikers to write it up for us?" (*HNF*, 267). Unlike other discussions that take place in the editorial room, this one does not lead to a decision. Yet, by raising questions about who should represent the strike, the conversation emphasizes the need for an approach that can accommodate multiple points of view. In Fulkerson's words, "It takes all kinds to make a world" (*HNF*, 267).

Howells's exploration of such inclusiveness ran into the limits of its own media moment. The strike that tests *Every Other Week*'s ambitions to provide a multi-perspectival point of view proves that the publication cannot escape its own Anglo-American, White, middle-class, male boundaries (and only ever tries to push those boundaries by including but later rejecting the German former professor Lindau). The publication's collaborators who visit the site of the strike all fail to cross the line that separates them from the strikers—let alone find a way to give them a voice within its pages. In such a context, the emerging impersonal viewpoint through which March experiences the strike might have appeared as the more viable of the novel's alternatives. Perhaps this explains why March survives his attempt to experience the strike, while Conrad and Lindau, who insist most earnestly on greater inclusivity, do not. His editor's role represents the greatest possibility—which the novel's ending suggests that he will continue to explore after he manages to buy Conrad's bereaved father's shares of *Every Other Week*.

By the time the news industry stabilized in the early twentieth century, *A Hazard of New Fortunes*' remarkable insights had faded from view. US writers and scholars who reflected on Howells's legacy disassociated him from the context provided by the media change of his day. As they defined their own contributions to the literary field, some of them echoed Crinkle's accusations that Howells belonged to a sphere outside the real world of news. Their reflections, exemplified by Crinkle's review, buried the connections between *A Hazard of New Fortunes* and contemporary debates about news.

Tellingly, however, the news industry of the early 1890s recognized Howells's publishing acumen. An 1892 issue of *The Journalist* devoted an article to Howells following his decision to take a position as the editor of *Cosmopolitan*, through which he enacted his own short-lived experiment with the magazine form. That Howells's position would be newsworthy to a trade journal dedicated to journalism provides another indication of the breadth and diversity of the news industry during the period. Indeed, the article describes *Cosmopolitan* as "the most interesting and suggestive of the current publications. It has achieved success in what is practically a new field by bold and original methods."[67] Howells's brief stint as editor at the magazine may have turned out to be another unrealizable attempt to influence the direction of literary writing with his own revolutionary alternatives. But the attention that his position received in *The Journalist* demonstrates a clear contrast with the kind of criticism that would follow in the twentieth century: "The fact that his opinions as expressed in his essays and criticisms are widely discussed, and that certain of his methods as a writer of fiction are severely criticized, are proof of his leadership—the world does not talk about little men."[68] As a leader in the publishing industry who recognized how news and literary prose could intersect, Howells made *A Hazard of New Fortunes* an exploration of literary writing that might improve upon the social conditions of his day.

In the mid- to late 1880s, both Howells and James saw a moment of opportunity in their changing world of print. Again, James's reflections from *The Art of Fiction* prove illuminating: "The novel and the romance, the novel of incident and the novel of character—these clumsy separations appear to me to have been made by critics and readers for their occasional queer predicaments, but to have little reality or interest for the producer."[69] James's words differentiate his ideas from the debates of his day about the major categories of the novel form. His commitment to shifting away from "clumsy separations" to the challenges faced by "the producer" enable him to engage in a set of reflections about how, why, and what novelists write—and they also apply to this chapter's reading of *The Princess Casamassima* and *A Hazard of New Fortunes* as incipient and incomplete, but nonetheless insightful literary alternatives. Narrated from the perspective of "the producer" who had a front-row seat to the period's media change, James's and Howells's novels demonstrate that literature itself constituted an unstable category, whose characteristics and future had been called into question. In that context, it was experimentation with authorship in the age of the new journalistic reporter that provided the inspiration for James's and Howells's reflections on the potential for literature to mediate new realities. That ambition enters James and Howells into a conversation that extended well beyond the boundaries of the US realist genre—and indeed, found fuller expression in the contemporaneous Spanish-language press of Nueva York.

Martí's Foreign Correspondences

When Martí arrived in New York City in 1880, he joined a Spanish-language publishing community that had flourished for decades, while also finding opportunities in the Anglophone press. Famously, he befriended Charles Dana of the *Sun*, whose newspaper had a long history of collaboration with New York's Cuban community.[70] Dana helped Martí commission some of his first articles in New York City at the English-language magazine *The Hour*, a publication that likely had connections with other Cubans in New York City given the *Hour*'s location in the same building at 40 and 42 Broadway where Néstor Ponce de León ran a print shop, as well as the largest Spanish-language bookstore in the US Northeast. Martí subsequently became an editor at the Spanish-language illustrated magazine *La América*, founded in 1882. He was still active in the city's Hispanophone press nearly a decade later, when his 1891 essay "Nuestra América" (Our America) appeared in *La Revista Ilustrada de Nueva York* (New York Illustrated Magazine).

Martí also worked as a New York correspondent for a variety of Spanish-language newspapers published throughout Latin America, including *La Nación* of Buenos Aires. By the time Martí joined the contributor list, *La Nación* had earned a reputation as one of the leading dailies in Latin America. Martí drew on topics covered in New York's leading English-language newspapers throughout his correspondence for *La Nación*, and scholars have compared Martí's prose with articles from New York's newspapers to understand the formation of the *crónica* genre. The foundational study on this topic is Susana Rotker's 1992 *Fundación de una escritura: Las crónicas de José Martí* (translated into English in a 2000 edition as *The American Chronicles of José Martí*), in which she argues that, although Martí drew inspiration from leading New York newspapers, "he did not say the same things about those topics. As a writer and mediator, he tells a different story about the same episode."[71] As part of that approach, Martí crafted his own challenges and alternatives to the new journalistic reporter.

Martí's interest in revising the reporting practices of new journalism appears in his *crónica* "Nueva York bajo la nieve" (New York under snow), first published in *La Nación* of Buenos Aires in 1888, which describes the Great Blizzard also depicted in the *Sun*'s "To Coney Island at Last," considered earlier in this chapter. Initially, the *crónica* paints a similar scene. New York appears "muda, desierta, amortajada, hundida bajo la nieve" (shrouded, mute, empty, buried in snow).[72] The snow overwrites the streets: "ya no se veían las aceras. Ya no se veían las esquinas" (sidewalks and street corners were no longer visible) (NY, 11:419; 227). Yet while the city's infrastructure for navigating the street on foot disappear beneath the snow, its residents do not: "Entre los montes blancos, hay leguas de hombres" (Between the white mountains, there are leagues of men) (NY, 11:418; 226). Rather than presenting a story of the lone, intrepid reporter's dangerous trek across the city, Martí highlights the trials and triumphs of the city's residents: "¡Y por Broadway y las Avenidas, levantándose y cayendo bajaban al trabajo, ancianos, mozos, niños, mujeres!" (And down Broadway and the avenues, falling and picking themselves up again, came old men, youths, children, and women—going to work!) (NY, 11:419; 227). At every turn, Martí's snowbound New York offers scenes of resilience and kindness: "El dependiente toma de brazos a la trabajadora: la obrera joven lleva por la cintura a la amiga cansada" (The salesclerk takes the working woman by the arm; the young factory girl supports her tired friend with an arm around the waist) (NY, 11:419; 228). Martí admires the spirit of these workers: "¡Qué bravos los niños, qué puntuales los trabajadores!" (How brave the children, how conscientious the workmen!) (NY, 11:422; 230). But he also launches a critique: hearing "una voz de niño a quien la nieve impide ver" (the voice of a small boy who can hardly be seen for the snow), Martí remarks, "Es un mensajero, que una empresa vil ha permitido salir con esta tormenta a llevar un recado." (He is a messenger boy, and some villainous company has allowed him to go out in this tempest and deliver a message) (NY, 11:420–21; 229). The *crónica* celebrates the heroism of the city's workers while suggesting that the true villain of the story is not the snow, but rather the employers who carelessly demand that their workers—including children—put their lives at risk in the snow-filled streets. Ultimately, "Nueva York bajo la nieve" relocates the heroism assigned to reporters in newspapers like the *Sun* to the realm of what we might call the essential workers of the nineteenth century.

"Nueva York bajo la nieve" puts Martí in the company of Howells and James—as a reader of the city's leading dailies who offered unique insights about their approach to reporting through his own writing. Like Howells, Martí pursues the stories of people who have been left out by the reporting practices that had become popular within the city's leading newspapers. At the same time, when Martí's writing takes the form of foreign correspondence, its value still derives from his own unique insights and style. From that perspective, Martí's narrative falls somewhere in between James's and Howells's novels. If James models in Christina a kind of reporterly authorship that is self-doubting and incomplete without others, and if Howells envisions multivalent narration produced by a collaborative editorial team rather than an individual author, Martí authors stories that put the working poor at the center of the action.

There are good reasons why Martí might have been more successful than Howells or James in crafting a method of giving voice to those who had been left out of—or stereotyped by—the dominant narratives within New York's print culture. As an outsider to US culture with his own experiences of political oppression and economic exploitation, Martí was rarely included within conversations among elite US writers about the future of news and literary prose, even though his writing concerned those very topics. Indeed, Martí's own commentary on Howells seems to preview the kinds of disciplinary and cultural divisions that would become more pronounced in literary scholarship of the twentieth century.[73] Although he praised Howells for his political views (especially for Howells's support for the anarchists accused in the Haymarket Affair), Martí called the author's novels "burdas" (crude) for their adherence to a "falso código literario" (false literary code).[74] From the perspective of their representational strategies, Howells and Martí, especially, appear a world apart. Martí responded more favorably to another contemporary writer from the period, Mark Twain, who engaged with reporting in his literary writing, and whose *Connecticut Yankee in King Arthur's Court* won Martí's admiration. But the apparent differences between James's and Howells's approaches, compared to Martí's, even as they all contemplated the labor question of the period, prove particularly instructive.

Martí's reflections on the status of literature at the end of the nineteenth century reveal some common ground between James, Howells, and Martí. His widely read prologue to poet Juan Antonio Pérez Bonalde's "Poema del Niágara" (Poem of Niagara), which Martí published in New York in 1882, locates his ideas about literature within a context that recalls the "bewildering change of ideals and criterions" that Howells notes in *A Hazard of New Fortunes* (*HNF*, 143). In Martí's words, "todo es expansión, comunicación, florescencia, contagio, esparcimiento" (all is expansion, communication, florescence, contagion, diffusion), and this leaves "alarmado a cada instante el concepto literario por un evangelio nuevo; desprestigiadas y desnudas todas las imágenes que antes se reverenciaban; desconocidas aún las imágenes futuras" (the concept of literature shaken at every moment by some new gospel, with all the images that were once revered now naked and discredited while the future's images are as yet unknown).[75] This world of change renders the forms once revered by previous ages as unholy, as well as misleading: "Las convenciones creadas deforman la existencia verdadera, y la verdadera vida viene a ser como corriente silenciosa que se desliza invisible bajo la vida aparente." (Established conventions deform true existence, and true life comes to be like a silent current that slips invisible between the life that is apparent.)[76] Martí's suggestion that casting off older forms provides a means of tapping into the electricity of "la verdadera vida" (true life) recalls Howells's own frustration with "wearisomely reproducing the models of former ages."[77] Both writers believed that the changes unfolding within the social, political, and media systems of their day required a visionary new kind of literature that could mediate new levels of human understanding. For Martí, that new territory included his journalistic experiments in *crónicas* like "Nueva York bajo la nieve," in which he saw the possibility of achieving what Rotker has described as "the democratization of writing."[78] According to Rotker, Martí's preface to Pérez Bonalde's poem "concludes . . . that the place for ideas is in journalism, the space of what is non-permanent, of communication, of new facts, of a public majority, a place to inquire and not to establish."[79]

In this light, the seemingly irreconcilable differences between Howells's and Martí's literary styles—as well as the differences that have made it so difficult to accept that Howells and James belong to the same brand of realism—may constitute the kinds of "clumsy separations" that James rejected. Considered as responses to the reporting practices that Howells, James, and Martí all carefully observed, their texts constitute relevant and insightful—if also imperfect and incomplete—collaborative literary alternatives. They all adhere to the belief that, borrowing James's words, "art lives upon discussion, upon experiment, upon curiosity, upon variety of attempt, upon the exchange of views and the comparison of standpoints."[80] Each of these texts constitutes a self-conscious effort to construct a role for literature that was incomplete and provisional, but also—at the time at least—full of potential that we might associate with the democratic literary imagination.

For Martí, that potential rests on his own concerns with those who are in danger of being left behind by the sweeping changes of his day—from the workers of New York City whom he sees repeatedly oppressed by the city's more privileged residents, to his readers from throughout Latin America whose way of life appears to him as endangered by the growing imperialist interest that the United States exhibits toward the region, to Cubans like himself, whose own independence movement he hopes will be respected rather than exploited by the island's closest neighbor to the north. In this way, "Nueva York bajo la nieve" demonstrates one of the defining characteristics of Martí's crónicas. His images of the streets of New York City frequently feature crowds of workers, soldiers, mothers, and immigrants: "ríos de gente" (rivers of people), as he puts it in a crónica on the "Fiesta de la estatua de la libertad" (Statue of Liberty festivities).[81] Even his most famous crónicas that showcase the major icons of New York City's modernity surround those images with people—from the bustling beaches of the fashionable Coney Island, to the crowds walking across the newly opened Brooklyn Bridge, to the explosive celebration that marked the inauguration of the Statue of Liberty—and highlight ordinary people's trials and triumphs. Writing from his perspective as a New York correspondent with an audience throughout Latin America, Martí combines an outsider's critical distance with a sense of solidarity with the city's working classes.

That perspective both recalls and diverges from earlier models founded on walking in the city. According to Laura Lomas, as "a non-Anglo working migrant" in New York City, Martí is "unlike Edgar Allan

Poe's 'man in the crowd,' and Charles Baudelaire's flâneur, who studied with fascination and sometimes terror an urban crowd from a café window" because his vantage point tended to originate outside such privileged spaces.[82] Instead, Martí "observed the imperial project in the guise of a democratic republic from the perspective of the streetcar passenger, a participant in a demonstration for the eight-hour workday, or a person amid the throngs watching a burning building from the street."[83] One might say that Martí's street-level perspective provided the very vantage point that Howells tried to provide in *A Hazard of New Fortunes*. A key difference that contributed to Martí's success is that, while Howells's novel never gets past its obsession with exploring and selecting ways of seeing, Martí's writing investigates and invents ways of being and belonging. From that perspective, the question is not so much who can see or write a story about a strike—or a child worker struggling to survive in the snow—but rather what communities might be mediated to recognize and act on their plight.

Another *crónica* by Martí published in *La Nación* proves illuminating here. The January 1, 1888, edition included Martí's "Un drama terrible" (A terrible drama), which describes the execution of four anarchists who were convicted on slim evidence of conspiring to throw the bomb that killed several police offers at a demonstration in support of the eight-hour workday on May 4, 1886, in Chicago's Haymarket Square. This *crónica*, in which Martí recognizes Howells for his courage as one of "tres voces nada más [que] habían osado hasta entonces interceder" (only three voices [that] had dared to intercede), includes some of Martí's most beautiful and incisive observations about US politics.[84] Immediately after the trial, Martí had praised the guilty verdict, but "Un drama terrible" shows a transformation in his understanding of US labor issues.[85] A believer in the promise of democratic institutions—if only the United States and the nations of "Nuestra América" could live up to democracy's ideals—Martí never embraced anarchism; he remained committed throughout his life to the nation-state as the primary vehicle for anticolonialism. Yet his analysis of the sentenced men and their beliefs that led to their conviction demonstrates that he had given a great deal of consideration to the roots of their political ideology and the dreams that they pursued. In Martí's view, understanding their ideas started with recognizing that "esta república, por el culto desmedido a la riqueza, ha caído, sin ninguna de las trabas de la tradición, en la desigualdad, injusticia y violencia de los países monárquicos" (this republic, in its excessive worship of wealth, has fallen, without any of the restraints of tradition, into the inequality, injustice, and violence of the monarchies) (DT, 11:335;197). Associating the United States with the violence of absolute monarchies, Martí shows the vast distance that separated the nation in reality from its democratic ideals.

Martí understands anarchism's appeal to workers as the result of a "sistema que castiga al más laboroso con el hambre, al más generoso con la persecución, al padre útil con la miseria de sus hijos" (system that punishes the hardest workers with hunger, the most generous with persecution, and the laboring father with the poverty of his children) (DT, 11:336; 198). He describes the convicted men as

> las cabezas vivas de esta masa colérica, educadas en tierras donde el voto, apenas nace, no se salen de lo presente, no osan parecer débiles ante los que les siguen, no ven que el único obstáculo en este pueblo libre para un cambio social sinceramente deseado está en la falta de acuerdo de los que lo solicitan, no creen, cansados ya de sufrir, y con la visión del falansterio universal en la mente, que por la paz pueda llegarse jamás en el mundo a hacer triunfar la justicia.

> (the keen minds at the head of this angry mass, educated in lands where the vote is still in its cradle, [who] do not step back from the present moment, do not dare to appear weak to their followers, do not see that in this free country the only obstacle to a sincerely desired social change is disunity among those who demand it, do not believe . . . that justice can ever triumph in this world by peaceful means.) (DT, 11:337; 200)

As the great unifier of the coalition that would launch Cuba's third war for independence in 1895, Martí sees unity and use of the vote as the means of overcoming oppression. While he is clearly critical of what he considers the anarchists' misunderstanding of what is possible in the United States, as well as their claims that violence was necessary to achieve their goals, Martí is also quick to point out, "Pero todo era verba, juntas por los rincones, ejercicios de armas en uno que otro sótano, circulación de tres periódicos rivales entre dos mil lectores desperados."

(But it was all words, backstreet meetings, drilling with weapons in some cellar, three rival newspapers circulating among two thousand desperate readers" (DT, 11:338–339; 201). Martí asserts that the discussion of violence was just that, a conversation that circulated, as ideas do, through the streets, homes, and newspapers of a community.

He also painstakingly elaborates the desperation and exasperation driving Chicago's anarchist community. The workers faced incredible cruelty and violence in response to the simplest of requests—"alguna hora de sol en que ayudar a su mujer a sembrar un rosal en el patio de la casa" (an hour or two of sunlight to help his wife plant a rosebush in the yard) (DT, 11:339; 201). In this context, Martí asks,

> ¿Qué querían ellos, puesto que es claro a sus ojos que se vive bajo abyecto despotismo, que cumplir el deber que aconseja la declaración de independencia derribándolo, y sustituirlo con una asociación libre de comunidades que cambien entre sí sus productos equivalentes, se rijan sin guerra por acuerdos mutuos y se eduquen conforme a ciencia sin distinción de raza, iglesia o sexo?

> (What else could they do but their duty, as set forth in the Declaration of Independence, and overthrow it [the government] to replace it with a free alliance of communities that exchange equivalent products among themselves, govern themselves without war by mutual agreement, and educate themselves by scientific methods without distinction of race, creed or gender?) (DT 11:342; 205)

Martí recognizes the brutal conditions that motivate the anarchists, as well as the lofty ideals they pursue, even as his summary of their beliefs in the form of a question suggests that he himself sees another alternative.

Martí's attentiveness also contrasts with the coverage of the anarchists' trial, as he describes it, in the Anglophone mass press: "La prensa entera, de San Francisco a Nueva York, falseando el proceso, pinta a los siete condenados como bestias dañinas, pone todas las mañanas sobre la mesa de almorzar, la imagen de los policías despedazados por la bomba; describe sus hogares desiertos, sus niños rubios como el oro, sus desoladas viudas." [Every newspaper from San Francisco to New York misrepresents the trial, depicting the seven accused men as noxious beasts, putting the image of the policemen ripped apart on every break-fast table, describing their empty homes, their golden-haired children, their grieving widows) (DT, 11:349; 212). The press appears here as a ve-hicle of spreading disinformation in service of protecting the interests of capital on a massive scale. Martí depicts a conspiracy against the an-archists repeated in the homes of every reader of the newspaper, as they consume—along with their daily breakfast—emotionally manipulative images of the accused and the impact of their alleged crime.

In the prison on the eve of the execution, that power of the press appears in "el golpeo incesante del telégrafo que el 'Sun' de Nueva York tenía en el mismo corredor establecido, y culebreaba, reñía, se desbo-caba, imitando, como una dentadura de calavera, las inflexiones de la voz del hombre" (the chatter of the telegraph that the *New York Sun* set up right there in the corridor—which meandered endlessly on, scold-ing and ranting, imitating with its skull's teeth all the inflections of a human voice) (DT, 11:351; 214). In contrast to the telegraph wires that fall useless in the snow of "Nueva York bajo la nieve," the telegraph in "Un drama terrible" aids the mindless, but still dangerous, repetition of lies about the anarchists and the workers' cause in the mass press. The tap-ping of its signals back to the *Sun's* office in Lower Manhattan blends in the corridors of the prison with "los últimos martillazos del carpintero en el cadalso" (the final taps of the carpenter's hammer on the gallows being erected at the end of that corridor) (11:351; 214). In rhythm with the hammers used in constructing the platform from which they would be hanged, the telegraph aids in the unjust end brought to these men following a trial that convicted them "en virtud de un cargo especial de conspiración de homicidio de ningún modo probado" (under a spe-cial charge of conspiracy to commit homicide which was by no means proven)" (11:348; 211). This chilling account of the anarchists' final hours makes the telegraph a haunting accomplice to carrying out the sentence brought about by unjust trial.

"Un drama terrible" offers a powerful demonstration of Rotker's ob-servation that Martí "tells a different story about the same episode" in comparison to Anglophone newspapers.[86] In "Un drama terrible," we see the story about the working class that mass-circulation newspa-pers and middle-class Anglophone magazines like *Harper's* refused to tell—and that the fictional *Every Other Week* did not possess enough understanding to access. At the end of the *crónica*, Martí incorporates the voices of the anarchists themselves, including a poem by Henrich Heine recited by George Engel before he was taken to the gallows and Albert Parson's final words, which formed the beginning of a sentence he never completed because he was cut off by the noose. As Christopher Conway has argued, "The diminishment of Martí's authorial voice in the final section of the chronicle . . . enables the voices of the anarchists to be poignantly sanctioned."[87] The *crónica* concludes by giving the anarchists a voice denied to them by the penal system.

Similarly, consider Martí's description of the worker who, "fusilado en granel por pedir una hora libre para ver a la luz del sol a sus hijos, se levanta del charco mortal apartándose de la frente, como dos cortinas rojas" (shot down in wholesale numbers for having asked for one hour of freedom in which to see their children by the light of day, and he rises from the fatal puddle and pushes his bloodied locks like two red curtains back from his forehead) (TD, 11:342; 205). Martí's lurid metaphors animate the feverish desperation that, he suggests, follows from the violent repression of workers' request for a better life. But unlike the sensational depictions of violence and scandal that would become the norm by the 1890s in the Anglophone yellow press, Martí's bloodstained imagery here is not meant to entertain through shock value. It is about achieving understanding, even empathy, in addition to inviting participation from his readers in imagining another way forward. Here, as in many of his *crónicas*, Martí addresses his readers directly, asking them to envision the conditions of the workers who made the eight-hour workday one of their primary demands:

> ¡Quien quiera saber si lo que pedían era justo, venga aquí; véalos volver, como bueyes tundidos, a sus moradas inmundas, ya negra la noche; véalos venir de sus tugurios distantes, tiritando los hombres, despeinadas y lívidas las mujeres, cuando aún no ha cesado de reposar el mismo sol!

> (If you want to know whether the demand was fair, come here: watch them going back like flogged oxen to their squalid dwellings with the night already dark around them; watch them come from those distant slums, their shoulders shivering, the women unkempt and ashen, when the sun itself has not risen from its repose.) (TD, 11:344; 206)

Martí parades these images of suffering and squalor in front of his readers, asking them to watch and try to understand. In addition, he shares his ideas and wisdom, posed as questions that invite reflection: "¿Quién que anda con ideas no sabe que la armonía de todas ellas, en que el amor preside a la pasión, se revela apenas a las mentes sumas . . . ? ¿Quién que trata con hombres no sabe que, siendo en ellos más la carne que la luz?" (Is there anyone who deals in ideas but does not know that the harmony among them all, in which love takes precedence over passion, hardly reveals itself even to the finest minds . . . ? Is there anyone who deals with men and does not know that there is more flesh in them than light?) (TD: 337; 199). Martí acknowledges the difficulty of enabling collaboration for the purpose of the common good. His questions invite consideration of the challenges and possibilities of organizing for a better future.

Here we might revisit some of the most astute—although seemingly contradictory—observations about the *crónica*. The genre is known for articulating what Ramos has called "a new individuality that presupposes the progressive dissolution of public, communitarian spaces in the modern city."[88] At the same time, it also serves as a site for envisioning and mobilizing new forms of collective organizing. As Ramos has argued, the Latin American *crónica* in general, and Martí's writing in particular, provided a space for developing "strategies for representing capitalist everyday life."[89] This genre, whose subject matter is almost always, in one way or another, the modern city, employs personal impressions to "mediate between modernity and areas that modernity has excluded or run over."[90] In that context, he argues, the street-level gaze of the chronicler takes on a somewhat surprising role. Even as the author offers personal impressions, they create a new sense of community: By strolling through the city, the chronicler "reinvents a collective space."[91] In Martí's *crónicas*, that collective space populated with forgotten workers always faces danger and oppression as a result of "fragmented and privatized social experience."[92] At the same time, the very act of representing such collective spaces in print creates new possibilities, which Ramos describes as an opportunity within the *crónica* to create "simulacra, images of an organic and healthy community."[93] Or, in the case of "Un drama terrible," the *crónica* identifies the barriers to creating such a healthy community and invites reflection on what it would take to get there.

It is worth noting here that some of Martí's most powerful critiques of the US mass press and of US politics appeared in Spanish-language publications outside the United States. In addition to critical analysis of US capitalism, media, and democracy in "Un drama terrible," published in *La Nación*, he published several articles exposing the horrors of lynching and mob rule, including "El asesinato de los italianos" (The lynching of the Italians), about a mob that broke into a New Orleans jail and lynched eleven of seventeen Sicilians who had been acquitted of having participated in the murder of the city's police chief; and his *crónica* published in the March 5, 1892, issue of *La Nación*, "El negro en los Estados Unidos" (The Black man in the United States), about a mob that lynched a Black man accused of offending a White woman. Martí was certainly well aware of the distortions and lies disseminated through the US mass press, as well as the deliberate omissions that refused to acknowledge the violent suppression of Black rights and Black lives during the period, as well as the rampant xenophobia of the period. He used his *crónicas* to tell those stories for a Latin American audience. The fact that Martí had relocated to the United States in search of the freedom to publish his views on Cuban independence, but also learned how to navigate the ways in which the US Anglophone press did indeed suppress stories of racially motivated violence, is another example of the dual role (as a source of hope for the future of democracy and as a site of oppression and potential danger) that the United States played for many participants in Nueva York.

Martí's innovations in print were not limited to the *crónica* genre. He brought his vision of the transformative possibilities of language not only to his work as a foreign correspondent but also to his work as an editor. As the editor of the New York-based *La América*, for example, he transformed the magazine into a vehicle to serve and unite "la mente de los Estados Unidos del Norte ante la mente de aquellos que son en espíritu, y serán algún día en forma, los Estados Unidos de la América del Sur" (the mind of those who are in spirit, and will someday be in form, the United States of South America).[94] Jorge Camacho has argued that Martí played a similar role through the *crónicas* that he contributed to another New York-based publication, *El Economista Americano*, from 1885 to 1888, arguing that it was another venue where Martí "alaba la florescencia de las ideas, la libertad de crear y el poder trasmitir los conocimientos de un lugar y de una persona a otra, independientemente de la clase social a la que perteneciera" (praises the flowering of ideas, the freedom to create and the ability to transmit knowledge from one place and from one person to another, regardless of the social class to which they belonged).[95] Moreover, as he focused on mobilizing support for Cuban and Puerto Rican independence, he gave up the role as a foreign correspondent that resulted in his most acclaimed *crónicas*, but he never stopped seeing the newspaper as a primary means of mediating change. Even more than his *crónicas* published in *La Nación* and elsewhere, his newspaper, *Patria*, which represented the Partido Revolucionario Cubano, mobilized a hemispheric community and created a space for debating and modeling the form that a future Cuban republic would take. *Patria* was not "fragmented and privatized," in other words, but rather a primary means of mediating change through collective efforts.[96]

It follows from such a perspective that the collective space and possibility first envisioned in *crónicas* like "Nueva York bajo la nieve" and "Un drama terrible" might lead to broader experiments with reader engagement and participation—including with the *crónica* genre itself. Both *crónicas* might be understood as attempts to bring into his writing the very readers whom the *World* sought to engage in its own most participatory moments. They also anticipate the social network that Martí would work to produce more deliberately by the 1890s, identified in his appeal to "Nuestra América" in 1891. These are roles for the *crónica* that diverge from the more widely recognized version of the *crónica* associated with literary professionalization and automatization.

The difference comes to light through a comparison with another text with which "Nueva York bajo la nieve" converses: *La Habana Elegante*'s "Una nevada en la Habana" (A snowfall in Havana), considered in chapter 1. Martí described himself as a regular reader of *La Habana Elegante* in a letter to the editor: "No tiene la semana para mi día más grato que el lunes cuando encuentro en mi mesa, entre los periódicos de Cuba, *La Habana Elegante*" (There is no more pleasant day of the week for me than Monday when I find on my table, among the newspapers from Cuba, *La Habana Elegante*).[97] It is not unlikely that he read Hernández Miyares's humorous *crónica* about a nearsighted correspondent from Ecuador who, without his glasses, mistakes all of the dust in Havana's streets for snow, which appeared in *La Habana Elegante* about a year before Martí penned "Nueva York bajo la nieve." If the snow in "Una nevada en la Habana" provides an opportunity to reverse the Baudelairian formula of impressionistic observation by replacing a keen observer of modern life with one whose impressions are the result of his blurry vision, Martí makes New York City's massive storm into a chance to offer another viewpoint centered on the plight of the working class. In other words, Martí is less interested in individualized artistic expression, as "Una nevada en la Habana" explores, than he is in opening up new democratic vistas—to borrow the words of another US Anglophone writer whom Martí greatly admired, Walt Whitman. The two texts show how the *crónica* contained multiple forms of literary experimentation. The better-known form that is most associated with the *crónica* and parodied in "Una nevada en la Habana" pursued literary distinction and specialization through the unique abilities of an artistic observer. The other explores ways in which print might facilitate collaboration and exchange of ideas. The pursuit of new political realities was not exclusive to either of these forms of the literary, but the idea that writing could facilitate greater participation in creating a more just world powered the democratic literary imagination of Nueva York across various publications.

El Despertar, which drew on Barcia's and Cayetano Campos's deep connections to the anarchist communities in Spain and Cuba, provides another illustrative example.

Reimagining the Newspaper

Pulitzer's successful 1884 campaign to raise money to build a pedestal for the Statue of Liberty shows a possible future direction of the changing world of print. The March 16, 1885, issue of the *New York World* included this call to action:

> We must raise the money! The World is the people's paper, and now it appeals to the people to come forward and raise the money. The $250,000 that the making of the Statue cost was paid in by the masses of the French people—by the working men, the tradesmen, the shop girls, the artisans—by all, irrespective of class or condition. Let us respond in like manner. Let us not wait for the millionaires to give us this money.[98]

The text reveals an aspect of the *World*'s effort to transform journalism that preceded the push toward heroic reporting heralded by Nellie Bly's race around the globe (which she completed in 1890). Over the course of about five months after publishing its appeal to "the people," the *World* collected more than $100,000, nearly all of it in donations of one dollar or less. In advertisements throughout the campaign, the *World* published the names of those who donated. It was an exploration of the power of print to mobilize people to come together for a cause in the public interest.

The Brooklyn-based *El Despertar* (The Awakening) closely followed the *World*'s efforts to become "the people's paper." The biweekly newspaper was one of the few New York-based Hispanophone periodicals to persist into the twentieth century. In its early years, the paper supported the Cuban and Puerto Rican separatist movement while also pushing for greater prioritization of workers' issues. Following the end of the war in 1898, when many editors, printers, and writers of periodicals dedicated to the Cuban cause ended their exile to start the work of nation building on the island, *El Despertar* remained in the environs of New York City for four more years, until 1902, and became a voice of the global anarchist movement. The collaborative that made up the editorial team of *El Despertar* provided candid commentary on the possibilities it saw for print, as well as the failures to reach that potential that they saw exemplified in the *World*.

El Despertar's editorial team appeared to view the *World* as both a paper with a worthy aspiration to serve the people of New York City— and as one that often fell short of realizing that vision of journalism in service of the public interest. An article in the June 1, 1892, issue, "El remedio" (The Remedy), reprints an excerpt of what *El Despertar*'s editors call "un interesante artículo" (interesting article) from the *World*.[99] The anonymous author calls attention to the failure of current laws to prevent the accumulation of vast concentrations of wealth. Despite laws in the United States meant to prevent "el establecimiento de una aristocracia hereditaria del dinero" (the establishment of a hereditary monied aristocracy), the *World* article argues, "las familias que poseen grandes fortunas han sabido manejarse de tal modo que han hecho ineficaces todos los esfuerzos de la ley" (families who possess great fortunes have learned to manage in such a way that they have made ineffective all the efforts of the law).[100] *El Despertar*'s reprinting of the *World*'s article provides an opportunity to raise a key issue of concern for the anarchist movement: the accumulation of wealth across generations. Presenting the problem of wealth concentration in the *World*'s words also enables *El Despertar* to show a contrast between the *World*'s "remedio" and the anarchist solution that *El Despertar* represented. While demonstrating clear agreement on the problem, *El Despertar*'s editorial team argues that the *World*'s solution does not go far enough: "El remedio que propone el *World* para impedir el establecimiento de esta aristocracia hereditaria del dinero, es la creación de una renta sobre las grandes fortunas. Este remedio es ineficaz." (The remedy that the *World* proposes to prevent the establishment of this monied aristocracy is the creation of an income tax on great fortunes. This remedy is ineffective.)[101] The critique provides an opportunity for *El Despertar* to advocate for its own "remedio más decisivo y enérgico: con la Revolución Social" (more energetic and decisive remedy: with social revolution).[102] It also represents a pattern in *El Despertar*'s ongoing critique of the *World*.

In *El Despertar*'s assessment, the *World* never goes far enough in pursuing its mission for the people. An 1895 article titled "El divorcio de Vanderbilt" (Vanderbilt's divorce) finds another opportunity to promote an anarchist talking point by reprinting the *World*'s words from an article that addresses the favoritism before the law received by the Vanderbilts when they pursued a divorce. During a period when the law limited access to divorce, the Vanderbilts easily secured one: "Todo el caso se ha arreglado tras cortinas y la misión del tribunal se ha limitado á dar sanción legal á los términos del arreglo." (The whole case has been settled behind curtains and the court's mission has been limited to giving legal sanction to the terms of the settlement.)[103] The *World*'s article argues that no such quick and quiet process is available to poor couples who seek a divorce: "Mientras el divorcio por consentimiento mutuo es formalmente rechazado por el tribunal cuando se trata de personas pobres, un hombre . . . [quien es] milionario y su mujer pueden combinar entre sí un divorcio de este género, con la certeza ha de ser sancionado por los tribunales." (While divorce by mutual consent is formally rejected by the court when it comes to poor people, a man . . . [who is a] millionaire and his wife may agree on such a divorce with the certainty of being sanctioned by the courts.)[104] This time, *El Despertar* gives the *World* little credit for speaking such a truth.

The introduction to the reprinted excerpt of the *World*'s article mocks the newspaper's mission, by describing it as "engañar incautos" (deceiving the unwary).[105] *El Despertar*'s editorial team also suggests that the *World*'s critique of the Vanderbilt divorce case resulted not from a sense of justice but rather because the paper was "despechado de no haber podido husmear la podedumbre [*sic*] de los Vanderbilt" (disdainful of not having been able to sniff up the rottenness of the Vanderbilts).[106] Thus, in spite of, not because of, what the *World* has come to represent, the article happens to "echa[r] por los suelos la tan decantada 'igualdad ante la ley,' proporcionándonos un dato más para poder sostener con brillantez que es una solemne farsa la Ley" (tear down the much praised 'equality before the law,' providing us with one more data point to back up brilliantly that the Law is a solemn farce).[107] Indeed, the closing commentary on the article from *El Despertar*'s editorial team suggests that journalists cannot be trusted to reveal such injustices: "Injusticias tamañas se realizan todos los días; sino que se cuidan muy mucho de velarlas los asalariados periodistas." (Such injustices happen every day; but salaried journalists take great care to veil them.)[108] From that perspective, the problem is not just new journalism, but rather the profession of journalism more broadly, in which employees protect their jobs rather than tell the truth about the inequality of the existing order.

Another article from the December 1, 1891, issue offers further insight into *El Despertar*'s critique of the period's growing journalistic profession. There, an anonymous author who signed the article as "un asalariado" (a salaried employee), reflects on the possibilities of journalism: "La imprenta: he ahí el recurso de que se quieren valer todos los oprimidos para hacer públicas y oíbles sus quejas." (Print: there is the resource all the oppressed want to use to make their grievances public and heard.)[109] As a potential tool for the oppressed, print holds the promise of the "astro solar, que debiera alumbrar á la humanidad con los divinos destellos de la verdad y de la ciencia" (heavenly body, which should enlighten humanity with divine flashes of truth and science).[110] Interestingly, the writer connects print's power here to the sun, in contrast to the electricity of the telegraph wires or the steam power of the trains that have appeared throughout experiments with reporting and its literary alternatives considered in this chapter. From this more organic perspective, the journalism that the *World* represents fails to achieve "su sagrada misión" (its sacred mission) because "la ambición de gloria y de riquezas ha invadido también la imprenta" (ambition for glory and wealth have also invaded print).[111] The article's examples are newspapers from Spain, but this 1891 observation also offers timely insight into the problem with making reporters into heroes of the news. Especially in the context of a newspaper like the *World*—which at least claimed to represent the idea that print could empower people and advance democratic institutions— new journalistic reporting appeared to chart a different course.

While the fundraising campaign for the pedestal of the Statue of Liberty is perhaps the best example of the *World*'s efforts to define a participatory role for readers (as consumers or donors)—whose small donations added up to make it possible to construct a home for a monument to the promise of democracy—the *World*'s experiments with reader participation often took on more self-serving projects. Contests—such as one that invited readers to guess how many days it would take Bly to complete her trip around the world—encouraged reader engagement, but they were actually thinly veiled advertisements for the *World*'s own news stunts. The stunts themselves provided the stage on which the *World* pursued the other current of its journalism, which made reporters into heroes who performed fantastic feats, solved crimes, and exposed corruption. As this list suggests, new journalistic reporting did not abandon the public interest altogether. However, it made reporters into heroes who no longer needed the public to act on the causes they deemed worthy. In such a context, the newspaper served not as a resource for the oppressed, as *El Despertar* characterized it, but rather as a stage on which reporters starred in "true stories of the news."[112] No wonder, then, that *El Despertar*, which existed to act on the liberatory potential of print, would cast a critical eye on the *World* as it perfected its approach to absorbing literature in the late 1880s and 1890s. By the time Bly completed her journey, the *World* had embraced a resource-intensive future of reporting that seemed to leave behind the ideal of reader engagement and participation—putting readers instead in a position that looked much more like passive spectatorship.

In an article that identifies "la prensa diaria y sus reporters" (the daily press and its reporters) as the greatest danger in the United States—

because the press is "dominada por el afán del *bussiness* [*sic*], no inspirada por ideal alguno" (dominated by business desires, not inspired by any ideal)—we see an alternative, anarchist view of print.[113] The newspaper is the vehicle through which anarchists "anhelan, sueñan, constituir una sociedad donde no hayan amos ni esclavos, dominadores, ni dominados, engañadores ni engañados, basada en la libertad, el trabajo y el apoyo mútuo" (yearn, dream of building a society where there are no masters or slaves, dominators or dominated, deceivers or deceived, based on freedom, work and mutual aid).[114] The words emphasize imaginative and intellectual work as key components of the effort to realize anarchist ideals centered on equality and collaboration. Such a commitment to unleashing creativity for the purpose of liberatory ideals appears most clearly in the writings of Martí, whose publishing community in Nueva York overlapped with that of the city's Spanish-language anarchist press.

The comparison with Martí helps to underscore the highly original and revolutionary nature of Howells's experiment in *A Hazard of New Fortunes* and the slightly less groundbreaking but no less original revision of reporting provided by *The Princess Casamassima*. In Howells's novel, even as the experiment in collaborative authorship enacted through *Every Other Week* rejects Lindau's anarchism, the ending, which puts the publication's business interests in the hands of its editorial team, appears to be seeking a way to run a publication that can prioritize its ideals, albeit not anarchist ones. In *The Princess Casamassima*, while James's novel shows deep understanding of the new journalism of his day, it does not exhibit the same level of engagement with the anarchist movement's critique of journalism and its own ideas of the possibilities of print. Maybe Christina—as an experimental reporter who sought to contribute to that movement—was too quick to separate the role of self-reflection from her own work in her dismissal of Hyacinth. Ironically, James's novel that is most openly sympathetic to the anarchist movement in depicting a protagonist who sought to support it might be the most distant from a commitment to equity exhibited in *El Despertar*. Yet, in the novel's effort to forge a new point of view, it participates along with Howells's and Martí's texts in enacting a departure from a new journalistic approach to reporting that employed the literary in service of selling newspapers, exploring instead different forms that the literary imagination might take, guided by ideals of collaboration, justice, or (although anarchists themselves at the time called it corrupt) democracy. Even as their novels and *crónicas* remained within the paradigm of individual authorship, they operated as networked authors in the sense that they pursued democratic ends that contrast sharply with the capitalist motivations of the period's stunt journalism, telegraphy, and urban transit systems.

3

Mobile Libraries and Telephonic Literature

PARTICIPATORY FUTURES OF PRINT FROM *LA HABANA*
ELEGANTE AND *LA REVISTA ILUSTRADA DE NUEVA YORK*

The January 1891 issue of the New York-based illustrated monthly *La Revista Ilustrada de Nueva York* (New York Illustrated Magazine) greeted the new year with a commitment to "ser la fiel depositaria de la cultura de nuestra raza y recoger en sus páginas todas las vibraciones de su alma" (be the faithful repository of the culture of our people and to collect in its pages all the vibrations of its soul).[1] Promoting the magazine's new design, this front-page editorial note depicts *La Revista Ilustrada* as a unique kind of repository, whose cultural material takes the form of "vibraciones" that represent the very soul of the magazine's "público de la América española" (Spanish American public).[2] The magazine's owner, Colombian Elías de Losada, and his editorial team, which at the time included Puerto Rican Sotero Figueroa and Nicaraguan Román Mayorga Rivas, pay tribute to "estos *Magazines* admirables" (those admirable magazines) of England and the United States that they identify as sources of inspiration for their own magazine, describing them as "verdaderas bibliotecas ambulantes . . . que sirven á los altos fines del progreso con el caudal de ideas" (true mobile libraries . . . that serve the high purpose of progress with an abundance of ideas).[3] The articulation of the magazine's cultural work as a contribution to progress echoes the English-language magazines, which saw themselves engaged in a "civilizing mission" to distinguish their own literary output.[4] At the same time, the unique metaphor of the mobile or walking library introduces something different: an interest in involving its community of writers and readers in the production and spread of ideas.

In the term *bibliotecas ambulantes*, the word *ambulante*—rooted in the verb *ambular*, to walk, and also associated with itinerant wanderers or street vendors—helps to bring what more typically symbolized an elite interior space to the street level. Scholars of *modernismo*, in which some of *La Revista Ilustrada*'s contributors participated, note that the movement constructed an idea of the *reino interior* (inner kingdom) as a site of originality and creativity often portrayed as the artist's studio or writer's study. As Gerard Aching explains, in *modernista* literature

> there are abundant descriptions of salons, drawing-rooms, cells in cas-
> tles and monasteries, alcoves, medieval or preindustrial work-rooms,
> and other private niches. It is from and through these real and imagined
> spaces that Manuel Gutiérrez Nájera and Julián del Casal, for instance,
> draw their inspiration to create sublime realms in which the mundane is
> either deemed extraneous or invoked in a disparaging fashion.[5]

Such interior spaces devoted to intellectual or artistic activity also rep-resent an elevation of literary writing to its own exclusive sphere, which is set apart from other forms of print culture. *La Revista Ilustrada*'s ambulatory library breaks off that metaphorical interior space from its foundation of exclusivity. In addition, the notion of a library fitted to walk down the street or to travel across the hemisphere represents a significant recasting of the individualistic method of painting modern life adopted by new journalistic reporters and their literary counterparts of the 1880s.[6] This new kind of interior space—perhaps still privately owned, but also constructed to bring communities together around a public mission—raises the question, What if the heralds of modern media were defined as such not because they told new kinds of sto-ries, but rather because they told stories in new kinds of collectively created spaces? Periodicals like *La Revista Ilustrada* took advantage of print culture's expanding capacity to travel more quickly across greater distances to mediate and empower communities as the collaborative authors of new designs for the present and the future. In light of that possibility, the mobile library constitutes a fitting symbol for the democ-ratizing, participatory experiment undertaken by *La Revista Ilustrada*. The image also complemented efforts by one of *La Revista Ilustrada*'s interlocutors in Havana, *La Habana Elegante*, to figure a similar demo-cratic impulse through the image of the telephone as a representation of greater exchange between writers and readers, which this chapter will also explore.

La Revista Ilustrada and *La Habana Elegante*, to which Nicanor Bolet Peraza contributed before and after his tenure as *La Revista Ilustrada*'s lead editor from 1886 to 1890, exemplify how writers and editors in Nueva York's network made intentional use of storytelling and print media in the changing media context of the 1880s and early 1890s. The chapter's analysis shows how the period's new print and electric media technologies powered both publications' efforts to "servir á la causa del progreso de las naciones hispano-americanas" (to serve the cause of the progress of Spanish American nations).[7] During the same period when popular English-language newspapers in New York City were banking their futures on mass circulation enabled by those technologies and on a clear dividing line between producers and consumers, *La Revista Ilustrada* and *La Habana Elegante* emphasized—in their own unique expression of a democratic literary imagination—quality over quantity, ideas over entertainment, and, most importantly and experimentally for the time, reader participation over passive consumption.

La Habana Elegante and *La Revista Ilustrada* participated in envisioning what I consider an emergent participatory print culture. As danah boyd has noted in her analysis with Henry Jenkins and Mizuko Ito in *Participatory Culture in a Networked Era*, "True participation requires many qualities: agency, the ability to understand a social situation well enough to engage constructively, the skills to contribute effectively, connections with others to help build an audience, emotional resilience to handle negative feedback, and enough social status to speak without consequences."[8] While these publications were limited in their ability to pursue such egalitarian standing—in that their writers and readers tended to be White, male, and privileged—in their best moments, *La Revista Ilustrada* and *La Habana Elegante* made print a vehicle for promoting greater participation in the production and circulation of ideas about the present and future of Cuba, Puerto Rico, and the hemisphere.

Both periodicals built on the participatory foundations provided in the 1870s by *El Mundo Nuevo* and *La América Ilustrada*, which constructed an idea of Nueva York powered by a hemispheric network of printers, editors, writers, and readers and offered an inchoate notion of the magazine as a workshop for facilitating idea sharing and collaboration across distances. *La Habana Elegante*'s editor, Enrique Miyares Hernández, and his contributors, including the Havana-based Julián del

Casal and the New York-based Nicanor Bolet Peraza, engaged with the period's discussions of simultaneity inspired by the telegraph and, especially, the telephone to blur the line in the publication between writer and reader, producer and consumer—by enabling a two-way flow of ideas between them. Concurrently, *La Revista Ilustrada* emphasized the significance of opening its own print shop as its editors sought to provide readers with access to the production of ideas through the world of print. That vision, in turn, sheds new light on José Martí's widely read essay "Nuestra América" (Our America), which first appeared in *La Revista Ilustrada* in January 1891, at the height of that publication's efforts to extend its own print and publishing capacity. As we will see, both *La Revista Ilustrada*'s owner/editor Losada and Martí sought, in their own ways, to transform readers into producers or creators—Losada through material means (such as printing presses and investment in his magazine) and Martí from the perspective of creating ideas within print and models of democracy outside it. The chapter's analysis will also demonstrate how Sotero Figueroa, an Afro-Puerto Rican editor and contributor to *La Revista Ilustrada* who would go on to become a leader and key collaborator with Martí in the Cuban and Puerto Rican independence movement, challenged the magazine to commit to racial equality in its participatory experiments.

Together, these publications' editors and writers demonstrate how innovators of nineteenth-century Nueva York explored a new kind of relationship between writers and readers. Moreover, those ideas accompanied an emerging notion of *latinidad*, which took shape as *La Habana Elegante* and *La Revista Ilustrada* pursued a potential future of modern media that would have established a Spanish-language hegemonic print culture throughout the hemisphere. This vision of progress looks quite different from the colonialist notion of progress through the spread of White, middle-class, Anglo-Saxon values associated with their English-language contemporaries.

La Habana Elegante, Cuban Nueva York, and Hemispheric Latinidad

Throughout its existence, *La Habana Elegante* exhibited a tension between its status as a Cuban publication, which catered its literary selections and cultural news to an elite Cuban audience, and its participation in a network of Spanish-language editors, writers, and readers united by a "hemispheric ethos."[9] One 1888 self-promotional article characterizes the magazine as a dear friend who drops by the reader's home each week around sunset: "A esa hora, os supongo, bella lectora, regando las escogidas plantas que ornan y perfuman sus pintadas flores vuestro patio, vuestro azotea ó vuestro balcón." (I imagine you at that hour, lovely reader, watering the arranged plants whose painted flowers adorn and perfume your patio, your terraced roof, or your balcony.)[10] Employing the lush imagery and invocations to an imagined female readership (*lectora*) that were characteristic of the period's *modernismo*, the article locates *La Habana Elegante* in the elite homes and private libraries of central Havana. Like a personified mobile library, the magazine enters that comfortable setting as a cultivated connoisseur, who offers "un juicio crítico concienzudo y noticias artísticas de todas partes" (a thorough review and artistic news from everywhere) to a cultural world whose center is Havana.[11]

Although Havana typically appears in the weekly as a lively literary capital, it takes on a very different form in the expressions of frustration with the Spanish colonial administration that occasionally burst through the magazine's bookish scenery. One editor laments that in Havana "todo es desorden, desidia y desaseo" (all is disorder, carelessness, and uncleanliness).[12] The article is surprisingly direct in casting blame, given the censorship laws that governed the Cuban press at the time: "Censuramos, con justicia, al Municipio" (We do censure, justly, the municipality), whose "deber de implantar en la Habana . . . puerto comercial" (duty of establishing in Havana . . . a commercial port) prioritizes Spain's economic interests over the city's well-being.[13]

Some lamentations about "las calles [que] no pueden ser peores" (the streets [that] could not be worse) seem to mimic *modernista* malaise, but others display the periodical's characteristic humor.[14] One example is the 1887 *crónica* "Una nevada en la Habana" (A snowfall in Havana). While this *crónica* tells one story (considered in chapter 1), of a nearsighted correspondent who mistakes all the dust in the city for snow, it also conveys the infrastructural neglect of one central Havana neighborhood that was the source of *La Habana Elegante*'s most privileged class of readers, in the guise of enthusiastic praise for the dust that the *cronista* mistakes as snow: "Los techos de las lindas y elevadas casas, sus barandas, vidrieras, todo estaba blanco. Los asientos de los parques, las flores, las fuentes, los árboles, ¡qué espectáculo tan hermoso! ¡blanco, blanco, todo cargado de purísima nieve!" (The rooftops of the tall and beautiful houses, their handrails, stained glass—all was white. The park benches, flowers, fountains, trees—what a beautiful spectacle! White, white, all filled with the purest snow!)[15] With bitter irony, the article turns the conditions that plague this neighborhood of influential readers into cause for celebration. When the narrative ultimately reveals that the so-called snowfall "no es más que una broma que quieren dar los Padres del pueblo á los inocentes corresponsales de las naciones extranjeras" (is nothing more than a prank that the fathers of the town want to play on the innocent correspondents of foreign nations), it becomes clear that the real joke is on the colonial administrators responsible for the city's deteriorating streets.[16]

As Havana decayed under colonial rule, the Nueva York depicted in the Hispanophone illustrated magazines of the 1870s is figured in *La Habana Elegante* as an idealized Cuban space. The periodical's correspondence from New York regularly features "lo que ocurra por acá en la colonia cubana" (what is happening here in the Cuban community), whose members included Martí, as well as the writer, publisher, and Spanish-language bookstore owner Néstor Ponce de León and the novelist Cirilio Villaverde.[17] In *La Habana Elegante*'s Cuban Nueva York, for example, "Coney Island en todo su esplendor" (Coney Island in all its splendor) is "lleno de familias cubanas" (full of Cuban families).[18] The correspondent Luis A. Baralt portrays the city's iconic modern attraction as a haven for Cubans, including two leading figures of the city's Spanish-language press: "Ayer tuve el gusto de ver allí á los amigos José Martí y Enrique Trujillo, que piensan pasar todo el verano en ese pueblo." (Yesterday I had the pleasure of seeing there José Martí and Enrique Trujillo, friends thinking of spending the whole summer in that town.)[19] (Readers likely would have recognized *La Habana Elegante*'s humor here as well, for Martí and Trujillo were known political rivals.) *La Habana Elegante*'s Nueva York becomes, as Baralt writes in another letter, the "Centro Cubano en los Estados Unidos" (Cuban center of the United States).[20]

But in Nueva York, it becomes difficult for *La Habana Elegante* to focus exclusively on "los escritores cubanos de más reputación" (the most reputable Cuban writers).[21] Reporting on the publishing activities of that city's Spanish-language press requires a more inclusive view. Announcing that Martí's children's magazine *La Edad de Oro* (The Golden Age) "debe salir de las prensas hoy mismo" (should come off the presses today), Baralt describes the periodical's intended audience as "los niños de América latina" (the children of Latin America).[22] Here, Baralt pictures a transnational rather than strictly Cuban audience, which he refers to again as that of "la América española" (Spanish America).[23] A similar notion of a Spanish-speaking transnational audience appears in an 1888 editorial note announcing the publication of Martí's translation of Helen Hunt Jackson's novel *Ramona*: "Aplaudimos la idea de su versión á un idioma que habla la mitad de América tanto más también cuanto el asunto es completamente americano." (We applaud the idea of its translation into a language spoken by half of America—even more so because its subject matter is fully American.)[24] The new translation speaks to the "half of America" for which English is a foreign language. At the same time, the language barrier that the description constructs does not prevent access to something more "fully American" that, the editors seem to hope, unites the hemisphere's parts.

Indeed, in *La Habana Elegante*, the hemisphere appears as an undivided site of circulation and exchange. One editorial notice called "Nuestros huéspedes" (Our guests) describes a visit from "ilustrados colegas" (illustrious colleagues) representing Hispanophone periodicals from "Estados Unidos, Méjico, Venezuela, Isla de Trinidad, Colombia, Santo Domingo, Rep. Argentina, Curaçao, Jamaica, Guatemala, Ecuador, Honduras."[25] On display is a hemispheric print culture that stretches from the United States (where *La Revista Ilustrada de Nueva York*, which was edited at that time by Bolet Peraza, appears first on the list), to the Caribbean, to South America—including countries that are not predominantly Spanish-speaking.

La Habana Elegante's articulations of a hemispheric, Latin American audience put the magazine in conversation with—and also set it apart from—contemporaneous efforts to envision new audiences for a changing media landscape. Along with its Hispanophone peers (including *La Revista Ilustrada*), *La Habana Elegante*'s editors and writers generated an emerging notion of *latinidad* with hemispheric dimensions. That incipient *latinidad* did not replace or even compete with the notions of identity provided by the nationalities of the writers and readers who saw themselves as part of the periodical's Spanish-language print community. As it took shape in the pages of *La Habana Elegante*, hemispheric *latinidad* represented the possibility of belonging to a common culture led by the "movimiento de la literatura hispano-americana" (Spanish American literary movement) that *La Habana Elegante* represented.[26] It was also an identity built on shared struggle for democracy and, perhaps most experimentally, to a hopeful effort to realize the potential of emerging modern media to increase opportunities for communication and connection. In *La Habana Elegante*, that latter hopefulness centered on the idea of telephonic simultaneity in ways that set the weekly apart from many of its Hispanophone and Anglophone contemporaries.

Telephonic Literature in *La Habana Elegante*

Significantly and uniquely for the period, *La Habana Elegante*'s editors and writers located their ideas about telephonic simultaneity in the world of print rather than in emerging aural or visual media. As William Uricchio has noted in the context of the late nineteenth-century origins of film, "An idea of simultaneity already defined and experienced through the telephone quickly took hold in the popular imagination as a quality that could be extended in image."[27] While some cultural producers imagined the simultaneous transmission of images associated with "the televisual" long before the emergence of television, another class of fantasies focused on the transmission of sound.[28] An illustrative example is the *Telephone Herald*, a newspaper service launched by the Hungarian Tivadar Puskás in 1893, which used telephone technology to deliver daily news in a form that anticipated radio broadcasting. What gets lost in such examples, whether centered on images or sound, is the two-way directionality that constituted one of the telephone's unique characteristics. In *La Habana Elegante* telephonic possibility does not take the form of proto-broadcasting (a one-way activity by definition) of sounds and images. Instead, the magazine explores how print might blur the line between writer and reader, producer and consumer—by enabling a two-way flow of ideas between them.[29]

A hint of a new kind of relationship between writer and reader appears in an 1888 article for *La Habana Elegante* by the Havana-based

Casal. The article, called "La prensa" (The press), assesses the city's active newspaper industry with surprising insight, especially given Casal's reputation in Latin American literary history as a poet who distanced himself from the practical concerns of a print market dominated by newspapers. Casal explains a recent proliferation of newspapers in Havana by asserting that starting a publication "no se necesita protección, ni dinero, ni se adquiere inmediata responsabilidad" (does not require protection, or money, nor does it come with immediate responsibilities).[30] From Casal's perspective, the real challenge is not launching a publication, but rather staying in business. Some publications "logran sostenerse a costa de grandes esfuerzos; otros desaparecen rápidamente por falta de lectores; siendo difícil que alguno prospere, toda vez que el público tiene sus diarios predilectos" (manage to sustain themselves at the expense of great effort; others disappear rapidly for lack of readers, since it is difficult to prosper when the public has its favorites).[31] Casal emphasizes the central role of readers in driving the content—and ultimately the sustainability—of a publication. His suggestion that a successful periodical must reflect the views of its audience, not just of its editors, lent particular cogency to his analysis of *La Lucha* (The Struggle), a pro-independence daily to which he contributed—and which also ran into trouble with Spanish censors.

No doubt with issues of censorship in mind, Casal praises *La Lucha* as a periodical that "no sirve directamente a ningún partido político, sino a los intereses generales del país" (does not directly serve any political party, but rather the general interests of the country).[32] The ideas that Spanish colonial authorities might find objectionable, he suggests, come not from the paper but from the people themselves: "Tanteando el pulso de la muchedumbre, es su primer cortesano y su más ardiente defensor. El pueblo compensa a su periódico, consumiendo diariamente numerosos ejemplares." (It [the paper] feels the pulse of the crowd, which is its first courtesan and most ardent defender. The people repay their newspaper, consuming numerous copies daily.)[33] By asserting that readers drive the paper's content, Casal reverses the direction of the flow of ideas typically associated with a periodical. Significantly, the choice of words here transforms the consumption of the newspaper into an act of repayment on the part of the readers. Reading the newspaper in this light is not just about consumption, but rather mutually beneficial exchange.

Even more surprisingly, Casal characterizes these contributing readers as a crowd. The vision he offers is not the one of refined consumption conducted within the confines of a privileged interior space (such as a personal library or study) that is typically associated with *modernismo* (and especially with Casal's brand of it). Nor does the article describe the kind of one-way transmission of print from a privileged (and increasingly professionalized) class of producers to passive consumers. Instead, Casal describes *La Lucha* as a paper that, although it does not draw content directly from readers, accesses their sentiments and passions. In hindsight, his vision of the newspaper might be considered an alternative blueprint for the mass press and its related "new category of person: the consumer."[34] Casal gestures toward a more active readership whose consumption of the paper constitutes a means of communicating with its editors, rather than an end in itself.

Another version of a two-way exchange between writers and readers appears in one of Bolet Peraza's contributions to *La Habana Elegante*'s "Carta de Nueva York" (New York letter), written as foreign correspondence for *La Habana Elegante* in the year before he took his post as the editor of *La Revista Ilustrada de Nueva York*. Bolet Peraza's July 5, 1885, letter describes the festivities that surrounded the arrival of the French steamboat carrying the disassembled Statue of Liberty to New York. His account does not situate the idea of liberty represented by France's gift in a US context (as one might expect in a piece of foreign correspondence written from New York), but rather styles it as something within reach of all humanity: "Los colores de todas las naciones del globo flotaban alegres, como si la humanidad entera hubiese querido asociarse á aquellos festejos de la Libertad." (The colors of all the nations of the globe floated happily, as if all humanity had wanted to associate itself with those festivities of Liberty.)[35] Beyond the clear reference to Cuba's own independence struggle, Bolet Peraza's reflection on the flags flown at the event offer another glimpse of a different kind of print culture: "El rasgo distintivo de esta rumbosa fiesta ha sido el de su carácter eminentemente popular." (The distinctive feature of this lavish party has been its eminently popular character.)[36] Despite the "ostentosa pompa oficial" (ostentatious official pomp), he explains, the celebration ultimately exhibits and thrives on "la efusión de almas libres" (the outpouring of free souls).[37] Like the mass of readers whose interests and beliefs determine the content of *La Lucha*, the crowd celebrating the arrival of the Statue of Liberty—and not its official planners—ultimately shapes the celebration. While Casal's readers exercise their influence as consumers, Bolet Peraza's crowd acts as a public empowered by the democracy that many of those organizing for Cuban independence—as well as other exiles from Latin America—longed to establish. One such exile was Bolet Peraza himself, who fled Venezuela in 1880 after criticizing President Antonio Guzmán Blanco's abuses of power.

Although Casal's and Bolet Peraza's articles never mention the telephone directly, a series of articles offering a variation on the periodical's weekly update on local cultural and social events indicates that the telephone resided within the imaginative horizon of *La Habana Elegante*'s editors and writers. The series narrates the city's cultural news "Por teléfono" (By telephone), through flirtatious exchanges between a female caller and a male editor. Recalling the stories of romances between female telephone operators and male callers that were popular at the time, the articles parody the magazine's typical society news and explore further what two-way exchange might look like in print.

One such article published on February 13, 1893, begins with a call to *La Habana Elegante*'s editorial office from an unnamed female reader who seeks to "darle algunas noticias para su semanario" (give you some news for your weekly paper).[38] In the exchange that follows, the caller replaces the editor as the narrator of the article's news. Speaking for "la Junta auxiliar de señoras que tiene á su cargo remitir á la Exposición de Chicago los productos de la mujer cubana" (the Ladies Auxiliary Board, which has been charged with sending products produced by Cuban women to the Chicago Exposition), the caller conveys "un llamamiento por medio de la prensa, á las señoras y las señoritas de la Isla para que si quieren presentar trabajos en la Exposición, los remitan á la morada de la presidenta, Prado 90" (a call by way of the press to the single and married ladies of the island announcing that, if they want to submit works to the exhibition, they should send them to the home of the president, at Prado 90).[39] The caller's message thus echoes the work achieved by her own narration of that message in the article—that of engaging female readers in representing themselves, in this case not just in *La Habana Elegante* but on the world stage provided by the Chicago Exposition.

Although the text was in fact written by one of the publication's male editors, the article's byline seems to uphold the potentiality signaled by its female caller; the author, who elsewhere in the magazine uses the pen name Ignotus, signs off here with an ambiguous single letter *I*. Ultimately, the lighthearted exchange depicted in the article raises the serious possibility of increasing the female voices included in the magazine's male-dominated contributor list.

In the context of a magazine whose editors sought to advance a hemispheric, Spanish-language print culture, each of these examples suggests the inseparability of *La Habana Elegante*'s hemispheric *latinidad* and the possibilities its editors saw in the world of print in the age of electricity. Even in this Cuban publication that—with its weekly updates on Havana's cultural society news—spoke to a readership largely centered on the island, the telephonic possibility explored in its most ambitious articles belongs to a larger community of people of Latin American descent throughout the hemisphere. As the magazine pursued an idea of the literary focused on its exclusivity (as in the examples considered in chapter 1), it also experimented with we might call telephonic literature.

In a sense, the telephonic literature of *La Habana Elegante* extended beyond the idea of the mobile library in *La Revista Ilustrada de Nueva York*. There, the magazine as library in motion represents a more accessible cultural repository because of its ability to travel. At the same time, that library—still enclosed in a way that makes it possible to limit who can participate in the intellectual activity that transpires inside—does not yet include an idea of how those readers would participate in creating the ideas within that mobile space. By contrast, contemplating the new medium of the telephone liberates *La Habana Elegante*'s contributors from residual imagery that associates cultural production with privileged interiors. Instead, examples like "Por teléfono" introduce a paradigm that privileges the flow of ideas from reader to writer. While one would not expect an entire newspaper to be communicated via telephone, it is emblematic of *La Habana Elegante*'s editorial strategy that included repeated reflection on increasing access to the production of print—and that circulated a proud new form of *latinidad* meant to help describe that print culture's media practices, its geographic reach, and the people whose ideas and sentiments would circulate freely within it.

La Revista Ilustrada de Nueva York's Future of Print

From an office in Lower Manhattan at the corner of Reade Street and West Broadway, *La Revista Ilustrada* reached about nine thousand subscribers throughout the Americas during the 1880s and 1890s. Its carefully designed "programa" centered on uniting Hispanophone readers throughout the hemisphere in supporting the growth of democracy in both the newly independent nations of Latin America and those still under Spanish rule and on promoting Latin American culture throughout the hemisphere.[40] A July 1887 editorial notice celebrating *La Revista Ilustrada's* second anniversary evoked the English-language daily newspapers of nearby Newspaper Row—which by this time included the *New York Sun*, the *New York Tribune*, the *New York Times*, and, following the opening of its iconic gold-domed skyscraper in 1890, the *New York World*: "No hemos querido hacer de esta publicación una mera entretenida lectura." (We have not wanted to make this publication a mere entertaining read.)[41] The claim makes "mere entertainment" a foil to what the editors suggest is a worthier class of content: "Escribimos para nuestra raza, para nuestra patria inmensa, que es toda la grande América que fué hispana, que padeció bajo el poder colonial y que sigue padeciendo bajo sistemas que proclamamos como redentores." (We write for our people, for our immense homeland, which is all of the great America that was Spanish, which suffered under colonial power and that continues to suffer under systems that we proclaim as redeemers.)[42] The candor with which these ideas were expressed would have seemed exhilarating to many readers and contributors, given the limits on press freedom in Cuba and many parts of Latin America at the time: the editors commit to redeem democracy for an entire region of former and existing Spanish colonies brought together under the banner of *nuestra raza* (our people, nation, race).[43] In the years following this reflection, the publication increasingly sought ways to involve its readers in its democratizing mission of making "nuestras prensas" (our presses) more widely available.[44]

Throughout its run, *La Revista Ilustrada's* editors promoted the publication as an elite cultural journal, while at the same time exhibiting a clear desire to engage an ever-increasing community of Spanish speakers throughout the hemisphere. Losada and his editors self-consciously and skillfully navigated the tension between these contradictory goals of exclusivity and accessibility as they engaged with three distinct communities of print: the community of Spanish-language cultural magazines of which *La Revista Ilustrada* became a leader; the English-language mass-circulating newspapers through which the periodical defined its own mission by suggesting that the emerging mass press represented nothing more than mindless entertainment; and the English-language illustrated magazines that served both as a model and as another point of departure (as we saw in the introduction to this chapter). In frequent editorial notes and self-reflective articles, *La Revista Ilustrada*'s editors triangulated these communities to articulate their own unique vision of the potential for print to create readier entry into the world of ideas for their contributors, their subscribers, and their network of representatives who sold the magazine throughout Latin America.

First and foremost, *La Revista Ilustrada* (like *La Habana Elegante*) belonged to what was by then a distinguished class of Spanish-language illustrated magazines that built on the foundations of the 1870s illustrated press. These weekly and monthly periodicals, which scholars have primarily studied for their contributions to *modernismo*, printed a mix of poetry, prose, and cultural news featuring leading Latin American writers, as well as the latest cultural developments in both the United States and Europe, especially France.[45] Many such magazines explicitly invited collaboration among editors and writers throughout this journalistic community, often circulating notices of visits from colleagues at other publications and publishing complimentary reviews of the work of their peers. One review of *La Revista Ilustrada* published by the Nicaraguan *El Independiente* (The Independent) offers further insight into what the publication represented to its typically middle- or upper-class readers:

Desde el papel magnífico lujoso y brillante como hecho para andar entre manos aristocráticas de gente de alto coturno hasta el último detalle de la impresión todo tiende á hacer de LA REVISTA ILUSTRADA un periódico de moda objeto solicitado por las personas cultas y de buen gusto.

(From its magnificent, luxurious, and brilliant paper made to circulate through the aristocratic hands of people of high station to the last detail of the printing, everything tends to make of *La Revista Ilustrada* a fashionable periodical, an object sought after by cultivated people of good taste.)[46]

El Independiente's editor Román Mayorga Rivas, who later moved to New York and became a coeditor of *La Revista Ilustrada*, captures in winning detail the sense of prestige that all such publications cultivated.[47] At the same time, the extension of his praise into the quality of the printing itself recognizes one of the primary means by which *La Revista Ilustrada* distinguished itself from its peers: by emphasizing the resources and technology made available to print publications based in New York City. It is a vision of good taste and access to print technology that situates the publications of Nueva York in a unique position to lead conversations among their peers and audiences about the future of the hemisphere.

La Revista Ilustrada's editors keenly observed the changes unfolding in New York's print culture. A November 1887 article entitled "El periodismo en América" (Journalism in America) reflects on the high-volume presses that had helped to power the rapid expansion of newspapers like the *New York World* in the neighboring English-language popular press:

> Los viejos diarios aumentan día por día sus ediciones, y nacen otros nuevos, y las fundiciones producen prensas maravillosas que luego hay que sustituir con otras más veloces, hasta inventar esos modernos aparatos, rápidos como el pensamiento . . . de los cuales salen . . . periódicos que parecen sábanas . . . hojas impresas á alimentar con ideas á un pueblo que de ellas vive.

> (The old newspapers increase their editions day by day, and other new ones are born, and foundries produce wonderful presses that then must be substituted with others that are even faster, to the point of inventing those modern apparatuses, rapid as thought itself . . . from which come newspapers that look like sheets . . . printed pages that feed ideas to a people who live off them.)[48]

The writer combines a familiarity with the capacity of the new presses with analysis that seems familiar in light of *La Revista Ilustrada*'s mission. When the writer muses that the volume of printing made possible by this new technology might "feed ideas" to its readers, one can see the imprint of the editors' own hopes of achieving widespread intellectual nourishment. From the perspective of *La Revista Ilustrada*'s editors, the value of the new presses was not simply "feeding" a rapacious demand, it was also about enabling the elevation of quality of the printing itself and of the ideas it circulated.

Amplifying a trend started in the New York-based Hispanophone magazines of the 1870s, *La Revista Ilustrada* asserted its technological sophistication, in part, through comparison to the technological achievements of English-language illustrated magazines. An October 1890 announcement, for example, boasts that "nuestros talleres se han enriquecido de nuevos útiles, hasta ponerlos á la mayor altura que en los Estados Unidos es posible" (our workshops have been enriched with new tools, putting them at the greatest height possible in the United States).[49] In contrast to their predecessors of the 1870s, Losada and company place more emphasis on their own print capacity. When a January 1890 notice in *La Revista Ilustrada* states that the issue was released late because "los trabajos del grabado han sido muchos y exquisitos" (the engravings were many and intricate), the apology is also an invitation to associate the magazine with the achievements of the English-language illustrated press.[50] By associating *La Revista Ilustrada* with technological sophistication, the editors recast familiar claims to fine taste made by many of its Spanish-language peers. Their new print capacity, the editors assert, will make *La Revista Ilustrada* "un modelo de elegancia y buen gusto tipográfico" (a model of elegance and good typographic taste).[51] The claim marks a slight difference from better-known forms of Latin American *modernismo*. While many Spanish-language illustrated magazines at the time rested such claims on the display of intimate knowledge of culture and fashion, particularly from Europe, *La Revista Ilustrada*'s editors base their sophistication on technological expertise.[52] In other words, they suggest that the modern impulse joins taste with technology. Perhaps this was the suggestion that Losada had in mind when he added the word "illustrated" to the title in 1886, thus reflecting a shift made under his leadership from the magazine's previous identity as a free review advertising North American products to Latin American readers.[53] "Illustrated" in the context of *La Revista Ilustrada* signals the print technologies in which Losada saw not just abstract possibility, but also a tactical means of distinguishing his publication and achieving its mission for Latin America.

To be clear, this association with the same new technologies as those of the Anglophone illustrated press helped to set *La Revista Ilustrada* apart from other Spanish-language periodicals by demonstrating its unique capacity to advance Latin American conceptions of culture and democracy more than it did to make the publication into "our own *Harper's* magazine," as a reprinted review by *La Revista Ilustrada de Costa Rica* suggested.[54] *La Revista Ilustrada* published far fewer illustrations than its English-language counterparts, and most were portraits of the writers or politicians featured in its articles or small supplementary drawings. The magazine never printed the more labor-intensive images, such as depictions of newsworthy events and illustrations accompanying serialized fiction, on which magazines like *Harper's Weekly* staked their reputations. In quantity and in content, *La Revista Ilustrada*'s illustrations looked more like those of a typical Spanish-language illustrated magazine. Instead of quantity, it was by emphasizing their increased quality, achieved through technological innovation, that Losada differentiated his magazine from its Spanish-language peers.

Especially after 1890, Losada and his editors began to chart a path that lay in between the mass-circulating press, which they rejected, and an exclusive high cultural sphere, which the elite Anglophone illustrated press, along with *La Revista Ilustrada*'s Spanish-language peers, were then working hard to construct. *La Revista Ilustrada*'s characterizations of its Spanish-language peers help to elucidate the collaboration that Losada and his editors envisioned through the literary imagination for a community that included contributors, other publications, and readers. In introducing the aforementioned review of *La Revista Ilustrada* by *El Independiente*, the editors praise the Nicaraguan publication as "una nueva voz que responde á la nuestra cuando desconfiando de nosotros mismos, preguntamos al público si hemos conseguido servirle con acierto" (a new voice that responds to our own when, doubting ourselves, we ask the public if we have managed to serve them successfully).[55] *La Revista Ilustrada*'s editorial notes frequently employed the term "public" to address its audience, and the term helps to define the magazine's vision compared to more familiar ways of conceiving the history of print.

The culture of discussion and debate associated with the Habermasian public sphere (also referenced in the introduction) characterizes the base level of engagement in a hemispheric, Hispanophone world of ideas that *La Revista Ilustrada* meant to inspire. Yet the editors' hopes reached further: they invited their readers to work together with other members of its network in producing them. As much as *La Revista Ilustrada* sought to become a leading voice, its rise as a new kind of "publicación colectiva" (collective publication) hinged on working with colleagues, editors, contributors, and readers not just to debate ideas but also to work together in producing them.[56]

The interest in increasing involvement in cultural production by forging a new, more collaborative relationship between the publication, its peers, and its readers was also evident in the periodical's print shop and in the publishing house that Losada opened in 1890. A notice from January 1890 advertising "Lo que ofrecemos á los lectores" (What we offer to readers) de-emphasizes the role of the magazine itself in pursuing its mission: "De hoy más, no solamente será esta publicación mensual de LA REVISTA ILUSTRADA la que ponga á prueba nuestro amor por la gran patria americana." (From today on, it will not only be this monthly publication that proves our love for the great American homeland.)[57] Instead, as a follow-up announcement in the October 1890 issue elaborates, "Los empresarios de LA REVISTA ILUSTRADA DE NUEVA YORK hemos ensanchado el campo de acción en que trabajamos para servir á la causa del progreso de las naciones hispano-americanas, estableciendo sobre sólidas bases una casa editorial" (*La Revista Ilustrada*'s entrepreneurs have widened the field of action in which we work to serve the cause of the progress of Spanish American nations, establishing on a solid basis a publishing house), which builds on its previous efforts to engage in "labores tipográficas" (typographic work).[58]

As *La Revista Ilustrada* celebrates its new publishing house and promotes its "arsenal completo del arte tipográfico" (full typographic arsenal), the periodical equates the ability to pursue its mission for Latin America with wider access to print technologies.[59] *La Revista Ilustrada*'s own editors and contributors certainly appear as primary beneficiaries of the new print shop and publishing house: "Hemos constituido un cuerpo de escritores distinguidos y de traductores de notoria competencia, para que con su incesante labor intelectual tengan siempre trabajo nuestras prensas." (We have assembled a group of distinguished writers and translators of recognized competency so that, as a result of their unceasing intellectual labor, our presses will always have work.)[60] Yet even as the magazine assigns its team a leading role in keeping the presses going with their rich arsenal of ideas, the editorial notice makes clear that *La Revista Ilustrada*'s presses will also produce "todas aquellas obras que nos pidan los gobiernos ó los particulares, y las que creamos necesarias para satisfacer los gustos del público y los intereses morales de nuestra raza" (all those works requested of us by governments or individuals, as well as those that we believe are necessary to satisfy public demand and the moral interests of our people).[61] This expansive list of those who might access the new presses traverses the very line between producer and consumer on which that advertising function relies. Individuals appear alongside governments as potential collaborators with *La Revista Ilustrada* in making use of its presses to forward their common cause. Although the language slips back into describing a more traditional role for such a journal—that of pleasing its public—it equates such work with that of advancing the interests of *nuestra raza*. As its editors invite increased access to *nuestras prensas*, *La Revista Ilustrada* appeals to its readers as allies in promoting Latin American cultural production among Latin Americans and on the world stage.

It is from that same perspective of increasing access to the production of print that *La Revista Ilustrada* takes up the cause of granting women entry into the world of ideas. As scholars of *modernismo* have long recognized, women made up a key audience of Spanish-language magazines and newspapers, most of which published sections on topics such as family and fashion designed especially for female readers. *La Revista Ilustrada* made a point of asserting that its interest in involving women did not stop at content. An article announcing a new contributor, Peruvian writer Amalia Puga (who married Losada in 1893 and is better known as Amalia Puga de Losada), explains, "Nuestra misión va más allá; hay en nuestro amor á la humanidad y en nuestra devoción por el progreso, algo que no habíamos satisfecho, y era el traer á este campo de nuestros trabajos, de una manera más activa y tangible, la colaboración de la mujer hispano-americana." (Our mission goes further; there is in our love for humanity and in our devotion to progress, something that had not satisfied us, which was to bring to this field of our work, in a more active and tangible way, contributions from Spanish American women.)[62] Although many of *La Revista Ilustrada*'s peers published the work of women writers, the description of the significance of Puga's participation seems uniquely animated by *La Revista Ilustrada*'s vision of increasing the field of those involved in the production of print.

In a poem called "La Revista Ilustrada de Nueva York" published in the same issue, Puga offers her own take on the magazine's mission. The poem makes the newspaper a site of witnessing "la ilustración, las glorias ó el talento del gran pueblo latino-americano" (the enlightenment, the glories, or the talent of the great Latin American people).[63] The poem extends an invitation to readers to reflect on the magazine itself, asserting that, should the reader begin to have any doubts, "Yo en el acto . . . / Le mostrara el periódico-portento / De nuestra joven prensa soberano" (I on the spot . . . / would show you the newspaper-wonder / of our young sovereign press).[64] As a new female contributor to the publication, Puga uses her poetry to align herself with this publication's self-reflexivity, which more commonly appears in articles and editorial notes in *La Revista Ilustrada*. By bringing this reflection into her poem, Puga brings her own style and vision for the publication to the first issue in which she participated, asserting that she, too, will be pursuing the potentiality of her changing world of print.

A series of advertisements for portable presses that appeared repeatedly in *La Revista Ilustrada* indicate that the idea of increased participation was not so far-fetched in a nineteenth-century context as it might initially appear. In one example, the Joseph Watson Company appeals to readers with the promise of simple, easily maintained portable presses "para el uso de todo el mundo" (for everyone to use).[65] Another advertisement (figure 3.1) advertises Kelsey and Company's small, simple hand presses, which come with "instrucciones completas para imprimir de manera que cualquiera persona pueda hacer sus propios trabajos" (complete instructions for printing so that anyone can do his/her own work).[66] Simplicity and ease of use provide the foundation for this advertisement's invitation to "¡Sea Usted mismo su impresor!" (Be your own printer!).[67]

Certainly, it would be a mistake to conflate such advertising slogans with *La Revista Ilustrada*'s editorial strategy. Yet the consistent presence of these advertisements in the magazine indicates that the new availabil-

Figure 3.1. Advertisement for Kelsey Press, *La Revista Ilustrada*, January 1890. Courtesy of Washington University Library microfilm collection, filmed from originals held at the Nettie Lee Benson Latin American Collection, University of Texas Libraries, University of Texas at Austin.

ity of print fell within the horizon of expectations for the publication's editors and readers. Moreover, a December 1888 editorial notice that adopts as its title the Kelsey ad's slogan, "¡Sea Usted mismo su impresor!," suggests that the editors did not miss the resonance between these ads and their own ideas. In the notice, the editors themselves recommend the hand press for "el especiero, el droguista, el vendedor de géneros, el hostelero, el comerciante, todos cual más, cual menos, se valen de la imprenta, para anunciar lo que venden, lo que ofrecen ó lo que compran" (the grocer, the drugstore owner, the seller of merchandise, the hotelier, the shopkeeper, all who make use of the printing press more or less, in order to advertise what they sell, offer, or buy).[68] The editors' embrace of the promise of portable presses gestures toward a more democratic impulse, and their interpretation of the promise of the portable presses helps to bring into focus the commitment to a participatory future of print on which La Revista Ilustrada and its accompanying print facilities were founded. While the usefulness of the portable presses for all things one might "sell, offer, or buy" remains outside the realm of ideas that was clearly so important to La Revista Ilustrada, the editorial team's approach to increasing access to print lies between the advertisers' vision of easy (if low-quality) portable printing and the capital-intensive presses that powered New York City's mass-circulating dailies. No wonder, then, that the model of high-quality printing of English-language magazines proved so appealing to La Revista Ilustrada. They gave a much-needed point of reference in the otherwise uncharted territory of a future of print that did not sacrifice quality even as it sought to increase access to production.

The presence of the portable printing ads within La Revista Ilustrada makes legible some key questions raised by the journal's unusual effort to advance a print culture in which a greater number of people would participate in the production of ideas: Would it be possible to achieve in the production of ideas the kind of universal participation that the advertisements imagine for the production of calling cards and promotional materials? Did the periodical's evident impulse toward increasing access to production really strive for full participation? Or did the notion of quality that the editors aimed to associate with their publication's participatory community still turn on some measure of elitism? And even if La

Revista Ilustrada's editors had the best intentions of universal inclusivity, could their vision hold up under the systemic conditions that then rigidly separated most of the population from a much smaller, privileged class on the basis of race, sex, and socioeconomic status? Given that such processes of exclusion operated in part by limiting access to education and cultural production itself, could print ever succeed as the great democratic vehicle for advancing Latin American sovereignty and culture?

Martí takes up these very questions in "Nuestra América," which debuted in *La Revista Ilustrada* just as its increased print and publishing activities entered their second year.

Martí's Community of Creators

Perhaps no one saw the potentiality of *La Revista Ilustrada*'s vision more clearly than Martí, who published "Nuestra América" in that magazine on January 1, 1891. It was the first printing of Martí's essay, followed closely by its appearance in the Mexico City-based *El Partido Liberal* later that same month. In the first of the four contributions that Martí made to *La Revista Ilustrada* between 1891 and 1892, he called on readers to reject and reverse the process of political subjugation of Latin America to the United States.[69] The essay's urgency and incisiveness have earned it a place in scholarship and many course syllabi as an essential source of historical insight into US-Latin American political and cultural relations.[70] At the same time, scholars have noted that Martí was not just reacting against US colonialism, but also promoting a more generative vision of a hemispheric democracy.[71] Reading "Nuestra América" in the context of *La Revista Ilustrada* and its editorial ambitions reveals that Martí's vision of such a future of democracy also depended on the future direction of the period's media change.

Scholars have previously overlooked the fact that "Nuestra América" was specifically placed and written in dialogue with the issue's lead article, "Nueva era," which characterized *La Revista Ilustrada* as a walking library. In that same article, the editors also describe the magazine as "una verdadera enciclopedia americana, en la cual se refundan las ideas de nuestros pensadores y se hagan sentir las palpitaciones de nuestra vida social" (a true American encyclopedia, in which the ideas of our thinkers merge and make felt the palpitations of our social life).[72]

While the imagery shifts here from the more idiosyncratic metaphor of the mobile library that appears earlier in the same essay, "Nueva era" maintains its emphasis on ideas as the periodical's central currency. Echoing the editors' desire to spread original Latin American ideas, "Nuestra América" converses with *La Revista Ilustrada* by contemplating how the production of print might be opened up to participation from the hemispheric public mediated by *La Revista Ilustrada* on a massive scale.

In dialogue with this editorial note, Martí's essay begins by reflecting on what makes ideas so important: "Trincheras de ideas, valen más que trincheras de piedras. No hay proa que taje una nube de ideas." (Trenches of ideas are worth more than trenches of stone. A cloud of ideas is a thing no armored prow can smash through.)[73] Ideas provide Latin Americans with a primary mechanism for coming together "para conocerse, como quienes van á pelear juntos" (to become acquainted, like men who are about to do battle together).[74] This converging interest in ideas within *La Revista Ilustrada* and "Nuestra América" makes it all the more significant that Martí both engages and revises the magazine's conviction of sustaining greater participation in cultural production.

Far more directly than any of *La Revista Ilustrada*'s editorial notes, Martí questions who should be involved in shaping Latin America's future. In praising the signs he sees that "nuestra América se está salvando de sus grandes yerros" (America is saving itself from its grave blunders), Martí notes that among those errors are the processes of exclusion that have divided the region along racial, ethnic, and economic lines:

> El indio, mudo, nos daba vueltas al rededor, y se iba al monte, á la cumbre del monte á bautizar á sus hijos. El negro, oteado, cantaba en la noche la música de su corazón, sólo y desconocido, entre las olas y las fieras. El campesino, el creador, se revolvía, ciego de indignación, contra la ciudad desdeñosa, contra su criatura.

> (The Indian circled about us, mute, and went to the mountaintop to christen his children. The Black man, pursued from afar, alone and unknown, sang his heart's music in the night, between waves and wild beasts. The campesino, the man of the land, the creator, rose up in blind indignation against the disdainful city, his own creation.)[75]

Martí's recognition of these neglected communities constitutes a rare reference to life outside Latin America's elite circles, in either this magazine or its peers. Moreover, in light of the reflections in "Nueva era" concerning the editors' ambitions to publish a vast repository of Latin American ideas throughout the hemisphere, this passage implicitly problematizes the presumption that a privileged space of cultural production such as a library or encyclopedia, however radically reimagined, could ever become truly inclusive.

How would a project that concentrates on engaging Latin Americans as producers, including speakers, singers, and writers, traverse the linguistic boundaries constructed by Latin American elites' ignorance of Indigenous languages? How would an activity that historically belonged to Latin America's elite culture tackle the racial and economic prejudices that had left Indigenous people "mute," Blacks "unknown," and *campesinos* outside the cities where political and economic power was strongest? The word *creador* (with its range of both worldly and transcendent connotations: inventor, designer, creator) that Martí introduces in the last sentence of this passage serves as the basis for a subtle shift that he makes throughout the essay: He moves from a notion of participation conceived as writing, reading, and printing to one that consists of creative acts not limited to the printed page.

Indeed, creativity becomes within "Nuestra América" the key to defining a hemispheric, Hispanophone community that might break down walls of exclusion: "Los jóvenes de América se ponen la camisa al codo, hunden las manos en la masa, y la levantan con la levadora de su sudor. Entienden que se imita demasiado y que la salvación está en crear. Crear es la palabra de pase de esta generación." (The young men of America are rolling up their sleeves and plunging their hands into the dough, and making it rise with the leavening of their sweat. They understand that there is too much imitation, and that salvation lies in creating. *Create* is this generation's password.)[76] Martí's call to his hemispheric community to get their hands dirty in the dough of Latin America's daily bread invokes the manual labor of the men and women of working classes. By thus situating his call for creativity, Martí completes the escape from privileged spaces associated with intellectual activity that *La Revista Ilustrada*'s notion of the mobile library initiated. In this way, "Nuestra América" proposes a new kind of community engagement defined by participating in creative acts—not just as the work conducted in an editor's study or even a printer's or other workshop, but also work done by those who perform the most basic and the most vital functions of daily life. One might also say that Martí shows that the power of the democratic literary imagination reaches beyond the magazine; for it is ultimately about the ability to engage creativity to produce collaborative acts of making democracy.

By imagining what it might look like to bring Latin Americans together through creativity, Martí extends the vision born of the possibilities that he and the editorial team of *La Revista Ilustrada* saw in the changing world of print beyond the printed page. His essay interpellates the community that he calls "Nuestra América" not as readers or consumers, but as producers of their own "realidad local" (local reality).[77] This is Martí's imaginative alternative to "la importación excesiva de las ideas y fórmulas ajenas" (the excessive importation of foreign ideas and formulas) he so resolutely rejects.[78] By becoming more self-sufficient and thus less reliant on Europe and the United States, "Nuestra América" can also model a different kind of modern society, casting off the materialism he criticizes in US culture and embracing creativity. In this late nineteenth-century context, the idea that everyone can be a creator was a groundbreaking way of imagining widespread participation in American—in the broadest sense of the word—democracy and culture, as well as a visionary construction of Latin American identity itself. For he articulates a notion of *latinidad* characterized by creativity. Thus, Martí improves upon the notion of making everyone a printer that *La Revista Ilustrada* had promulgated. Despite the editors' ambitions, their presses are still available only to those who could pay and those who were educated enough to be writers and readers. By contrast, Martí finds a way to envision a kind of creative production that could be open to all—although his version of this idea is still radically heteronormative and male.

Losada may have been attempting to carry out Martí's demands when he solicited investors for a scheme that would transform *La Revista Ilustrada* into a proposed new entity called the Sociedad Cooperativa Hispano-Americana (Spanish American Cooperative Society).[79] In describing the endeavor, Losada appeals to the groups whose participation the journal had appealed to all along: "Hemos resuelto dirigirnos á todos nuestros estimables colaboradores, agentes y suscritores, y á los gobiernos de los países hispanoamericanos . . . para que tomen parte en nuestra empresa." (We have resolved to go to all of our valuable contributors, agents and subscribers, and to the governments of Latin American countries . . . so that they may take part in our company.)[80] The magazines of Nueva York, at this time, did not typically seek out investors. While the impulse surely came from a growing need for funds, Losada's language shows the imprint of the magazine's long-running participatory ambitions. Choosing to call this new investment initiative a Sociedad Cooperativa Hispano-Americana over other language that was common at the time (such as the formation of a joint stock company that we saw in the consideration of *El Mundo Nuevo* and *La América Ilustrada* in chapter 1), Losada presents this new scheme as part of the magazine's strategy for achieving his mission for Latin America.

As if in answer to the earlier questions raised by the periodical's efforts to increase involvement in cultural production, the announcement expresses the editors' hopes for the new endeavor: "Deseamos hacer un periódico de todos y para todos. Más que el provecho particular, buscamos el beneficio colectivo y la satisfacción de que pueda enorgullecerse América de la obra que acometemos." (We wish to make a newspaper of all and for all. More than particular advantage, we seek collective benefit and satisfaction so that America can be proud of the work that we undertake.)[81] Interestingly, Losada's description of a newspaper "de todos y para todos" anticipates Martí's language in a famous 1891 speech in Tampa, in which he advocates for a Cuban republic designed "con todos y para el bien de todos" (with all and for the good of all).[82] While the potential of the portable presses in *La Revista Ilustrada*'s earlier editorial note never extends beyond job printing, the idea of a newspaper of and for all points to an ideal of widespread participation in the kind of print culture that circulates on ideas. Yet the kind of participation that Losada imagines—in the form of financial investment—still falls short of Martí's community of creators, which includes but is not limited to commercial activity.

Maybe Losada could understand mass participation only within the confines of his own professional experience. He was, after all, first and foremost a businessman. Or maybe he simply could not escape his financial constraints as the owner of *La Revista Ilustrada*, which clearly required considerable economic resources. As early as the February 1890 issue, which immediately followed *La Revista Ilustrada*'s launch of its new print shop, the magazine showed signs of distress. The magazine had always included frequent reminders to readers to renew their subscriptions or to pay overdue balances; now, a notice asked readers and agents who sell the magazine to pay off their delinquent accounts, a matter that it views as "la más apremiante necesidad" (the most pressing need).[83] According to the editors, "No es posible que esta empresa pueda afrontar gastos de consideración como los que tiene . . . si no cuenta con todos los recursos que deben sostenerla." (It is not possible for this company to afford considerable expenses like the ones it has . . . if it doesn't have all the resources necessary to sustain it.)[84] Anxiety over the vast amount of fiscal responsibility that the organization must have assumed to fund its expansion into print and publishing is palpable. Similar notices appeared with increasing urgency in the following two years, and, in December 1892, Losada found it necessary to sell the publication.

Even if it was a last-ditch effort to save *La Revista Ilustrada* from financial ruin, however, Losada's attempt to reinvent the magazine as a cooperative displays his characteristic visionary style. Like Martí's community of creators, the notion of a publication by all and for all (if only from the perspective of its finances) constituted an imperfect and incomplete, but also revolutionary conception of a different kind of mass engagement. Here we can also see more clearly how Martí's essay diverges from *La Revista Ilustrada*. For even in Losada's most expansive idea of mass participation, the publication itself is both a means and an end. The goal is ultimately to produce a publication, albeit one radically reimagined to enable greater collaboration in its production. In "Nuestra América," Martí reminds readers that the point, after all, was not simply to create a world of producers of print. It was to build on the era's increased capacity to communicate across vast expanses (both geographically and socially) and thus to create vital, creative democracies characterized by their widespread participation, their inclusivity, and their ability to foster originality and human understanding. From a twenty-first-century perspective, Martí's emergent and never fully realized idea of mass participation in "Nuestra América" also points to a difference with—and perhaps a key shortcoming of—twenty-first-century participatory culture. His vision takes as its end goal the creation of a vibrant, inclusive, creative democracy—rather than the success of a particular publication or platform.

Lost Connections

Soon after the heyday of *La Revista Ilustrada* and *La Habana Elegante*, the forms of mass-appeal journalism championed by newspapers like the *World*—which relied on the use of expensive, high-volume presses— solidified into a new regime of dominant media practices that brought an end to the open-ended experimentation in which *La Revista Ilustrada* participated. Along with those new media practices came high production costs and a stark dividing line between the professionals who produced content and others who consumed it. In that context, the hope represented by these publications that small-scale publishers themselves might represent a different, more predominantly Latin American future of print throughout the hemisphere began to look like a thing of the past—and eventually disappeared from view altogether. A hint of that disappearance appears in *La Habana Elegante* near the end of its run, as its editor, Hernández Miyares, escaped an increasingly volatile political situation in Havana and relocated to New York City.

An innovator poised to transform a print culture with hemispheric dimensions, Hernández Miyares recounts his "primeras impresiones" (New York—First impressions) of New York City in the magazine's June 24, 1894, issue. There, Hernández Miyares describes what at first appears as a minor miscommunication with a man he mistakes for "un *reporter del Herald* que deseaba *intervieviarme* [sic] como director de *La Habana Elegante*" (a *Herald* reporter who wished to interview me as director of *La Habana Elegante*).[85] When Hernández Miyares replies affirmatively to the North American's incomprehensible English, the man "comenzó á limpiarme los zapatos" (began to polish my shoes).[86] Like so many instances in *La Habana Elegante*, the humor of this scene—including Hernández Miyares's use of Spanglish to highlight the practice of interviewing, which was then a mistrusted innovation of the reporters of the English-language press—veils a sentiment that cuts much deeper. The would-be reporter whom Hernández Miyares considers an equal here turns out to have been a fantasy built on misunderstanding. Ultimately, Hernández Miyares finds himself unrecognizable to the US-based Anglophone press as a fellow media innovator.

Throughout 1894, *La Habana Elegante* exhibited a growing sense of the periodical's invisibility from the perspective of the US English-language press. The November 11 issue includes an article in which the North American translator Mary Elizabeth Springer observes, "Es tan poco conocida la literatura hispano-americana en los Estados-Unidos, que hasta algunas personas ignoran que existe." (Spanish American literature is so little known in the United States that some people are unaware that it exists at all.)[87] Even Springer's own laudatory comments limit *La Habana Elegante*'s lofty ambitions: "Nuestros vecinos del Sur pueden lisonjearse de poseer una literatura espléndida, digna de estudio, y muchos autores renombrados, cuya fama se ha extendido por Europa é Hispano-América." (Our neighbors to the south can delight in having a splendid literature, worthy of study, and many renowned authors, whose fame has stretched throughout Europe and Spanish America.)[88] Springer's well-meaning praise contains Spanish-language cultural writing within the southern half of the hemisphere, completely ignoring its presence on North American soil.

The sense of novelty and possibility so evident throughout most of the magazine's run gives way in its final years to frequent expressions of frustration. In another installment of "La Habana Elegante por teléfono," which appeared on February 3, 1895, another female caller asks, "Por qué no escribe ya las crónicas?" (Why don't you write *crónicas* any more?), to which the editor, signing himself as Ignotus, answers, "Es tan pesado escribir sobre el mismo tema en *El Fígaro, La Discusión, La Primavera,* de Guanabacoa y *La Habana Elegante!*" (It is so annoying to write about the same thing in *El Fígaro, La Discusión, La Primavera,* of Guanabacoa, and *La Habana Elegante!*)[89] In contrast to the active field of periodicals representing diverse interests and new possibilities evident in Casal's "La prensa," Ignotus depicts a world of repetition and excess. Moreover, the telephone's potentiality here is superficial compared to that of the earlier installment in this series. In this article, the phone call merely provides a means of venting frustration in a print landscape on the verge of becoming obsolete—and also on the verge of war. Later that February, uprisings around the country started Cuba's third independence war with Spain. *La Habana Elegante* ceased publication the following year. A few years later, in 1897, Hernández Miyares would start the New York-based newspaper *Cacara Jícara* (named after a town in Cuba that was the site of a significant battle in 1896, in which Antonio Maceo and his troops triumphed over the Spanish) to support the Cuban war effort.

La Revista Ilustrada also reached its end in the mid-1890s, although the exact end date—sometime after Losada sold the publication—is unclear. What is clear is that, by the turn of the century, the media landscape, as well as the fields of US and Latin American literature, no longer had a place for such publications. Several potential reasons help to explain why this happened. The death of Martí in 1895, at the outset of Cuba's independence war with Spain, undoubtedly dealt a major blow to the Spanish-language publishing community in New York in which *La Revista Ilustrada* once flourished. As the independence struggle wore on, US intervention in Cuba and subsequent triumph over Spain disturbed the vision of hemispheric collaboration that *La Revista Ilustrada* and its peers in New York promoted. The transitional media context that propelled *La Revista Ilustrada*'s mission and the political one in which it still was possible to imagine a different kind of relationship between Latin American nations and the United States had been irrevocably transformed in the aftermath of the 1898 US intervention in Cuba.

Alternatives of Modern Media and *Modernismo*

In differing ways, *La Habana Elegante* and *La Revista Ilustrada* envisioned what might be considered a divergent course for modern media—one that attempted to link a democratic vision to the technical affordances of the period. In *La Habana Elegante*, telephonic simultaneity inspired an incipient telephonic literature that explored how a publication might represent the ideas and hopes of its readers, not simply inform and entertain them. In *La Revista Ilustrada*'s version of that idea, centered on the magazine as mobile library, access to print production itself provided the foundation for greater participation. Both publications considered the magazine in its late nineteenth-century form as a powerful tool for facilitating the exchange and circulation of ideas. From that perspective, both the mobile library and telephonic literature models make the magazine a tool of personal empowerment and collective mobilization, rather than a form of private edification or of mass entertainment.

Maybe such ideas that centered on making a more participatory print culture came more readily to Hispanophone media innovators involved with the Cuban independence movement because mobility—through circulation of their papers, and also their own transnational migrations—characterized their own experience of print culture. Cuban Néstor Ponce de León, who by the 1880s and 1890s represented an older generation of Cubans in New York City, offers a hint of this reality in his series of articles for *La Revista Ilustrada* called "En mi biblioteca: Notas al vuelo" (In my library: Notes on the fly). Ponce de León's introductory installment describes for his readers the type of library to which his title refers: "Al oir la frase *mi Biblioteca*, no vaya á figurarte, lector amigo, un espacioso y magnífico salón, con techo de cristales, lujoso mueblaje, araquelería de maderas esquisitas, bustos de grandes escritores etc." (Upon hearing the phrase *my Library*, do not go and imagine, reader friend, a spacious and magnificent hall, with glass roof, luxurious furniture, shelves of exquisite wood, busts of great writers, etc.)[90] In place of this image of an opulent interior refuge, Ponce de León describes a more modest scene of writing: "La composición de una biblioteca, cuando no es un artículo de lujo, se resiente siempre de los estudios, las aficiones, las pasiones y hasta los caprichos de su propietario." (The composition of a library, when it is not a luxury item, always suffers from the studies, hobbies, passions and even the whims of its owner.)[91] Those passions include Ponce de León's lifelong dedication to the Cuban cause, which led him to pick up and move his library—first to New York in 1869 as he fled Spanish colonial authorities, and again back to Cuba after the Spanish withdrew from the island in 1898, where he would ultimately become director of Cuba's Biblioteca Nacional (National Library).

It was not only books that Cubans and Puerto Ricans transported in their quest for independence. As we have already seen, printers, editors, and publishers traveled to pursue their publishing activities. At times, they also transported their publications, and even their own printing presses. For example, when he arrived in New York City from San Juan, Puerto Rico, in 1889, Figueroa brought his printing press, which he used to continue the publication that he was prohibited from producing in San Juan. Soon afterward, he founded his Imprenta América print shop at 284 and 286 Pearl Street in Lower Manhattan. From that base of operations, he collaborated as a political organizer with Martí, most famously as the printer and as an editor of the Cuban Revolutionary Party's *Patria* newspaper after its founding in 1892 to pursue their vision of an Antillean federation that would also include an independent Puerto Rico. Following a similar path, in 1891, Francisco Gonzalo "Pachín" Marín "brought his revolutionary newspaper *El Postillón* to New York from Puerto Rico, where it had been suppressed by the Spanish authorities."[92] Marín would go on to become another key participant in organizing and fighting Cuba's third independence war with Spain. Driven by their principles and their dreams, these media innovators-in-exile knew firsthand that Spanish authorities feared the power of print. They chose to upend their lives to maintain the ability to publish in pursuit of their dreams. Together, they envisioned a form of collective action through print that made the magazine itself a representation of movement and transformation. In retrospect, their ideas make visible different formations and patterns than the more familiar ones from late nineteenth-century print culture.

In *La Habana Elegante*, the idea of telephonic literature, which facilitated the exchange of ideas between writer and reader, also makes it possible to see *modernismo* from a vantage point that has been difficult to access, in retrospect, as a result of the notions of literary value, the forms of mass media, and the formations of Latin American and Latinx identity that solidified after the heydays of these publications. Certainly, the emerging notions of literature as a privileged, autonomous sphere of literary writing, as well as the ideas of Latin American identity and resistance to US imperialism that scholars associated with *modernismo* by the turn of the twentieth century are in evidence in *La Habana Elegante*.[93] At the same time, in light of the magazine's explorations of telephonic simultaneity, one might think of *modernismo* as containing multiple scenes that come into view if one looks back on the period through something like the lens of a kaleidoscope. Rotate the cylinder, and the key terms in the previous scene (*Latin America, literature*) end up reconfigured into a new pattern. There, a competing thread of telephonic *modernismo* that did not become canonical appears. Its defining features are a hemispheric form of *latinidad* and an idea of the literary that, rather than elevating the cultural producer to a separate sphere, put writers and readers in two-way communication with each other—or even, at times, engaged everyone as creators.

As we gaze on that new scene, the term *modernismo*, often dated back to Rubén Darío's 1888 book of prose poems, *Azul* (Blue), brilliantly foreshadows what was to come as literature became an elite, specialized category in the context of twentieth-century mass media. By defining *modernismo* through an idea of literature as a privileged class of writing, Darío helped to secure the movement's value in the eyes of those who interpreted it later from the perspective of the twentieth-century literary field in Latin America. (In this way, he made a move similar to those of Howells and James in repositioning their writing within an exclusive literary sphere, as we saw in the previous chapter.) But such a notion of what one might call canonical *modernismo* also foreclosed some of the possibilities of the movement's most visionary texts. A far less familiar (and also less fully formed) telephonic *modernismo* evident in *La Habana Elegante* might have led to different notions of the literary—and to corresponding ideas of modern media and of *latinidad*. Those ideas centered on leveling hierarchies and on increasing the exchange of ideas across the divides created by writer and reader, producer and consumer, and perhaps also Hispanophone and Anglophone America.

Through the lens of this alternate, telephonic *modernismo*, we might also consider the Nueva York and La Habana that these publications constructed as different kinds of capitals of the nineteenth century—which contrast with Paris, where Walter Benjamin, with Baudelaire's painter of modern life in mind, located a mode of expression characterized by disengaged wanderings and a disinterested gaze in the figure of the flaneur.[94] If the Parisian flaneur's mode of experiencing the city is that of consumption, telephonic *modernismo*'s mode is production—not solely for the purpose of profit (although that is necessary to keep a publication afloat) but also for the purpose of advancing Latin American culture and democracy. Nueva York and La Habana are also not alone in serving as such sites, but rather they are nodes in a network of cities with active print cultures at the time—also including Buenos Aires, Lima, Managua, and Mexico City, to name a few—from which we might also gain a unique vantage point on the diversity and complexity of ideas and innovations of the period's hemispheric print culture. These capitals of the nineteenth century differ from—and at times, resist—the cities (in some cases, the same ones) that Hispanophone innovators cast as sites of materialistic excess. In contrast, the city of telephonic *modernismo* is, like the magazine, a site of collective action. One might also consider, from this perspective, Martí's publication of "Nuestra América" in *El Partido Liberal* in Mexico City soon after it appeared in *La Revista Ilustrada* as an attempt to participate in different nodes of this telephonic *modernista* network simultaneously.

In *La Revista Ilustrada*, Figueroa provides a powerful demonstration of what greater participation throughout this print cultural network might accomplish. Throughout his contributions to the magazine in the early 1890s, Figueroa challenges the predominantly White, elite Hispanophone publishing community in which he participated in New York City to make racial equality a central goal of the future Cuban and Puerto Rican republics that they were working to make possible. Figueroa, who joined *La Revista Ilustrada*'s editorial team with its June 1890 issue, offers perhaps the fullest articulation of what an inclusive future of Cuba and Puerto Rico might look like. At this early stage in his career in New York City, his articles and poetry for the magazine show Figueroa critiquing and revising an editorial strategy that, for all of its ambition and vision to increase access to the changing world of print, remained almost exclusively the product of and for White liberal elites. Through Figueroa's writing, then, *La Revista Ilustrada* becomes a site for gaining insight into the negotiations that would enable Martí, Figueroa, Serra, and others to bridge economic and racial divides as they built support in the early 1890s for a third attempt at Cuban independence.

Even when he does not do so explicitly in his writing for *La Revista Ilustrada*, Figueroa lays the groundwork for future arguments for equal inclusion of Black Cubans and Puerto Ricans in the Cuban and Puerto Rican independence movement. In his inaugural article of the series "Reparos literarios" (Literary criticisms)—in which he debates about literary writing in Latin America with another editor, Nicaraguan Gustavo Guzmán—Figueroa takes issue with a question that Guzmán posed in a previous letter: "¿Cual será la mejor zona, el mejor clima, el mejor terreno, el país más apropiado para producir buen escritores?" (What will be the best area, the best climate, the best terrain, the most appropriate country to produce good writers?)[95] While Gúzman suggests that some locations must be better than others for cultivating the choicest literary fruits (reflecting the very Eurocentrism that Martí would condemn six months later in "Nuestra América"), Figueroa challenges his colleague's underlying assumptions, as well as his choice of words. As Figueroa explains, "Haré caso omiso de la nomenclatura que usted presenta, de sandías, peras, melocotones, fresas, manzanas, guindas y uvas de Málaga, pretendiendo hallar semejanza entre estas frutas y las producciones de la inteligencia, porque no la encuentro apropiada." (I will disregard the nomenclature that you introduce, of watermelons, pears, peaches, strawberries, apples, cherries and grapes of Málaga, pretending to find a similarity between these fruits and the products of intelligence, because I do not find it appropriate.)[96] Great literary writing, Figueroa argues, does not spring from the earth, but rather results from the right kind of social conditions: "No tanto las causas físicas como los hábitos de sociabilidad y cultura son los que nutren el cerebro, haciendo que produzcan abundantes y sazonados frutos." (Not so much the physical causes as the habits of sociability and culture are the ones that nourish the brain, making them produce abundant and seasoned fruits.)[97] While Guzmán imagines literary products as fruits that are not native to the Caribbean and instead thrive in the soil of the Spanish colonizers in Málaga, Spain, Figueroa argues that literature is the result of social and intellectual nourishment that can take place anywhere.

Figueroa redirects Guzmán's line of inquiry away from the very thinking that he and other leaders of color in the Cuban and Puerto Rican independence movement confronted as they revealed "racial division and inequality to be a product of social prejudice, not nature."[98] Just as he did in confronting racial discrimination throughout the 1890s, Figueroa's rebuttal here rejects Guzmán's suggestion of an inevitable hierarchy among literary cultures. He does so by upholding the magazine's commitment to universal education—what Figueroa describes as "una educación liberal, generalizada, racional, que tanto se aparte de dogmatismos exagerados é incongruentes, como de prácticas rutinarias que sacrifican el espíritu á la ietra" (a liberal, widespread, rational education, which departs both from exaggerated and incongruous dogmatism, and from routine practices that sacrifice the spirit to the letter).[99] Figueroa's words take his argument beyond literature. Education provides the key to escaping the rigidity and absolutism of Spanish colonial rule. He provides a glimpse of what he must have hopefully imagined when he envisioned a future democracy in Cuba and Puerto Rico: a freedom of spirit takes the place of dogmatism and rigid routine. Figueroa had himself experienced the latter as a printer and editor who was not able to publish what he wished. Only by fostering "el desarrollo de la inteligencia" (the development of intelligence), regardless of the natural environment, "puede el pensamiento tender su vuelo á las esferas de las grandes concepciones" (can thoughts take their flight into the sphere of great ideas)—and ultimately circulate on paper.[100]

The potential that Figueroa sees in education extends beyond the Spencerian social Darwinism that he references throughout his "Reparos literarios." While he clearly understands the possibilities of education in terms of individual and social progress, he also articulates an ideal that anticipates the community of creators that Martí would mediate six months later in "Nuestra América." For Figueroa, as for Martí, ideas constitute the true currency of a healthy society that is "siempre sujetándose á los objetos que hieren la imaginación" (always conquering the objects that wound the imagination) and that favors "las ideas bulliciosas ó entusiastas que son susceptibles de despertar las ciudades" (the boisterous or enthusiastic ideas that are capable of waking up cities).[101]

Figueroa's intervention introduces another aspect of the story of the media innovation led by Nueva York in the late nineteenth century. For, in this city with a complicated color line, during the very period that historian Rayford Logan in 1954 famously called the nadir of American race relations, New York's Spanish-language press of the 1880s and 1890s envisioned a future Cuban democracy that focused increasingly on ending racial discrimination and achieving social justice. For Figueroa, as for his co-collaborators in *La Revista Ilustrada*—and many of those who worked with him to organize for Cuban and Puerto Rican independence—a more participatory future of print provided the vehicle for democracy's pursuit. The magazine sometimes seems animated by the possibility that such a future was within grasp.

The lost connections and unrealized dreams of *La Habana Elegante* and *La Revista Ilustrada* demonstrate how the experimentation and negotiations of late nineteenth-century media change unsettled and reimagined fundamental categories of human experience, including identity, community, and the possibilities for social and political transformation. Perhaps Figueroa had the diversity and complexity of this changing world of print in mind when he wrote his homage to Johannes

Gutenberg, dedicated to Martí and included in *La Revista Ilustrada*'s January 1891 issue: "Y con la IMPRENTA surge ese Proteo múltiple, inquieto, diligente, vario." (And with PRINT arises that multiple, restless, diligent, various Proteus.)[102] Figueroa's words remind us that new media technologies do not determine their own futures. Those futures result instead from the myriad and often competing possibilities that visionary cultural producers, like those who created *La Revista Ilustrada* and *La Habana Elegante*, discover within them.

4

Revolutionary Workshops

THE US-BASED CUBAN SEPARATIST PRESS
IN THE AGE OF YELLOW JOURNALISM

Near the end of the Spanish-Cuban-American War, the Tampa-based *La Revista de Cuba Libre* (Free Cuba Magazine) took aim at the US yellow press: "Esa prensa vocinglera y *jingoista* . . . ha dicho en estos dias todo lo malo que se puede decir de los cubanos que han demostrado ser tan valientes como los más, tan dignos como los mejores." (That babbling and jingoistic press . . . has said in these days everything bad that can be said about the Cubans who have demonstrated themselves to be as brave as the bravest, as worthy as the best.)[1] As *La Revista de Cuba Libre*'s article urgently defends Cubans, it dismisses the sensational approach most closely associated with the *New York World* and the *New York Journal* in the latter half of the 1890s: "No se detiene á estudiar las cosas ántes de formar un juicio cuando es condición indispensable oir ambas partes ántes de sentenciar." (It never stops to study things before forming a judgment when it is an indispensable condition to hear both parties before sentencing.)[2] The editorial team's immediate purpose is to refute false claims about "los cubanos voluntarios que no cobran sueldo y sufren toda clase de privaciones" (the Cuban volunteers who do not get paid and suffer all classes of privations). But *La Revista de Cuba Libre*'s lead editor, María de la Torriente, may also have had another example of rushed and uninformed judgment in mind—which involved the magazine's own contributor and distribution agent in New York City, Clemencia Arango.

Just under a year before *La Revista de Cuba Libre* first appeared in print, Arango came to fame in the US Anglophone press as the result of a *Journal* article by Richard Harding Davis called "Does Our Flag Protect Women?" The headline invited readers to consider Arango's alleged ordeal with Spanish soldiers as an affront to the United States as well.

Printed with an illustration of Arango surrounded by menacing male soldiers, the article made the sensational and unfounded suggestion that Arango had been sexually harassed by Spanish authorities in Havana when she was taken into custody while boarding a US-bound steamship called the *Olivette*. The episode exemplified a key problem that critics identified with the yellow press: the stories were crafted to inspire the passions of readers and the sale of newspapers with little regard for understanding what happened from those involved. Arango's victimization in Davis's article relied on precisely the kind of hasty judgment called out by *La Revista de Cuba Libre*; she does not appear in Davis's story as a source, but rather as a voiceless victim. By contrast, *La Revista de Cuba Libre* empowered Arango as a woman, a creator, and a leader in the publication's organizational structure. This chapter considers *La Revista de Cuba Libre*, along with the New York-based *Doctrina de Martí*, as periodicals from the Cuban separatist press of the late 1890s that built on their predecessors' foundations to provide some of the clearest examples of how the publications of Nueva York that participated in the democratic literary imagination prioritized collective engagement and collaboration through print for the purpose of achieving racial, gender, and economic justice for Cuba, Puerto Rico, and beyond. While the *Journal* and the *World* leveraged their capital advantage to more fully demarcate the divide between those who actively produced the news (reporters, editors, publishers) and readers who passively consumed news products, *La Revista de Cuba Libre* made their publications into virtual workshops for revolutionary participation.

La Revista de Cuba Libre sought to define a role for women at a time when dominant narratives of women's roles in the Cuban cause, including those circulated by José Martí and his allies, cast them merely as auxiliary supporters. Through its women-led editorial team, *La Revista de Cuba Libre* displayed women's capacity for leadership. This revolutionary publication cited *Patria* and other revolutionary newspapers as its most direct interlocutors, while exhibiting the influence of earlier illustrated magazines. Although this publication, run by a club whose members most likely identified as White, does not address race directly, its contributor list, which included leading male figures of the Cuban Revolutionary Party, offers a hint of the publication's relationship to the increasingly starkly drawn color line in the Jim Crow South, as the

1896 *Plessy v. Ferguson* decision impacted Tampa's historically interracial Cuban community.[3] Like many publications at the time, *La Revista de Cuba Libre* appears to have struck a careful balance in its relationship building with various factions of the Cuban Revolutionary Party; those relationships included contributions from Enrique Varona, the editor of *Patria* who oversaw the publication's shift away from its antiracist agenda after Tomás Estrada Palma assumed the leadership of the party, and from Martín Morúa Delgado, the Afro-Cuban editor of *Revista Popular* in Key West in the late nineteenth century; he is better known for his later role as the first Black Senate president of Cuba in the early years of its independence, who introduced the infamous Morúa Amendment, which banned Black political parties as discriminatory against White Cubans and has been cited as the source of Cuba's Race War of 1912.[4]

For its part, *Doctrina de Martí* devoted consistent attention to "dirigir nuestros esfuerzos para el triunfo de la Independencia de la patria, y para que sean reales y no vaga ficción los derechos del pueblo" (direct our efforts to the triumph of Independence in the homeland, and to ensuring that the rights of the people are real and not vague fiction).[5] A team of Afro-Cuban and Afro-Puerto Rican leaders in the Cuban Revolutionary Party, led by Rafael Serra in collaboration with Sotero Figueroa, Juan Bonilla, and Francisco Gonzalo "Pachín" Marín, among others, established *Doctrina de Martí* in 1896—after Estrada Palma had replaced Figueroa, who had served as *Patria*'s principal editor and printer from the beginning, with Varona.[6] Recognizing that *Patria* no longer provided a platform for promoting the racially egalitarian future they envisioned, they created their own publication, built on "la escuela de Martí" (the school of Martí), who "nos enseñó á ser indóciles contra toda forma de tiranía, contra toda soberbia" (taught us to be indocile against all forms of tyranny, against all forms of arrogance).[7] Boldly declaring indocility against Cuban racism, the periodical focused on ensuring equality for the laborers who made up a key part of the PRC's coalition, which included many Cubans and Puerto Ricans of African descent. As they faced racism within Cuba's independence movement and in the United States during a period of violent suppression of the rights of Black Americans, *Doctrina de Martí* made the print shop both a material means for restoring the collaboration necessary for revolution and a conceptual space in which they could envision how citizens of a nation could work collaboratively to achieve economic and racial justice.

Throughout both publications, editorial notes, articles, and advertisements show the continued expansion of print culture centered on the small print shops of Nueva York's vast network, which included Tampa's Spanish-language publishing community. Their editors and writers worked passionately to increase participation in the Cuban revolutionary movement by appealing to a racially diverse group of working-class readers, on the one hand, and to women on the other. Within their pages, literature represents a fluid category animated by the democratic literary imagination in its pursuit of a more just world.

The advocacy for independence and for economic and social equality in a future Cuban republic in the Cuban separatist press contrasts with what William Randolph Hearst dubbed within the yellow press "the journalism that acts."[8] While the Cuban separatist press built on the idea of newspapers as workshops—as well as a notion of newspapers as soldiers from the Cuban independence movement of the earlier nineteenth century—the yellow press expanded notions of reform-oriented journalism first modeled in *Frank Leslie's Illustrated Newspaper* in the 1860s and 1870s and continued in Pulitzer's efforts to forge a new journalism in the *World* during the 1880s and early 1890s. Even in the reporting from those newspapers that scholars have since seen as ambivalent about the news narration practices of the yellow press, such as Stephen Crane's war correspondence for the *World*, yellow journalism isolated and elevated the reporter. But the choice of a war as the theater in which the *World* and its new competitor, the *Journal*, staged performances in which Cubans—especially Cuban women—appeared as innocent victims saved by heroic reporters also put the idea of acting through journalism to the test. While the *Journal* and the *World* brought together telegraphic technology with scandalous storytelling meant to reach a wide audience, Spanish-language revolutionary newspapers became vehicles for editorial teams and their contributors and readers to exchange ideas and act together to plan future independent nations in Cuba and Puerto Rico. Consisting largely of newspapers printed in the off-hours in small- to mid-size print shops and circulated to small readerships within the Cuban revolutionary movement's network, these periodicals demonstrate what media history misses when it restricts its perspective to that of the largest, commercial publications. These under-studied experiments represent some of the most hopeful examples from nineteenth-century Nueva York's network of how a newspaper might serve the purpose of building democracy.

Newspapers, Revolution, and Late 1890s Media Change

Though divergent, the Cuban separatist press and the yellow press shared an interest in reimagining the newspaper and what it could accomplish. Both communities of print sought to harness the potential of print against the backdrop of media change that had accelerated since the 1870s.

By the 1890s, the capital required to engage in daily news production had widened the divide between the small-scale operations typical of the city's Spanish-language press and English-language dailies like the *World* and the *Journal*, which pushed the boundaries of what was possible at the time in terms of circulation size. *New York Sun* editor Charles Dana, widely respected in the Spanish-language press due in part to his well-known friendship with Martí, noted around that time that "$10,000 was adequate capital to start a solid urban daily in 1830 in New York City; by 1890, one would have needed $500,000 to $1 million."[9] Dana's estimate included staff and material costs that far exceeded what the smaller papers of the Cuban revolutionary press, which tended to be biweekly or monthly publications, would have required: one appeal to readers for financial support, published in the September 30, 1897, issue of *Doctrina de Martí*, estimated *Patria*'s costs at $4,800 per year and those of *Doctrina de Martí* at $900 per year.[10]

The revolutionary Cuban separatist publications of the 1890s operated on a shoestring; few hoped to do more than break even. Many leading writers and editors in the community, including Martí and Figueroa, had gotten their start in New York City in the illustrated publications of the prior decade, whose missions of advancing democracy and Latin American culture always also accompanied (and sometimes competed with) commercial goals. In publications such as *La América* and *La Revista Ilustrada de Nueva York*, Martí, Figueroa, and others were able to earn incomes and develop their ideas, while learning valuable skills in printing, editing, and writing. They became accomplished printers and editors who determined, as the organizing for the 1895 war gained momentum, to direct their talents and networks to promote the Cuban cause and the future democracy that they hoped would follow. Their publications dedicated wholly to the struggle for Cuban and Puerto Rican independence often faced great difficulty in securing the resources to stay in print. By the end of its run in 1897, Serra openly acknowledged in *Doctrina de Martí* a dire need for donations to help subsidize the cost of printing the newspaper, naming "nuestra difícil condición económica para continuar la obra revolucionaria, la obra de amor" (our difficult economic condition for continuing the revolutionary labor, the labor of love).[11] Serra's description of *Doctrina de Martí* as "la obra de amor" indicates the urgency he felt around the vital cause of "modelar en sentido democrático el carácter de la república cubana" (modeling in a democratic sense the character of the Cuban republic).[12] Serra and his colleagues in the Cuban separatist press considered newspapers essential and powerful resources in realizing that goal.

The Cuban separatist press's view of print as a means of revolutionary action built on a long-standing tradition of publishing in exile. Martí's editorial note in the inaugural issue of *Patria*, published on March 14, 1892, for example, repeats a widespread trope in the Spanish-language press: "Eso es PATRIA en la prensa. Es un soldado." (This is PATRIA in the press. It is a soldier.)[13] Martí personifies the paper as an individual soldier with a singular purpose, to mobilize and engage "los cubanos y puertorriqueños de New York, para contribuir, sin premura y sin descanso, á la organización de los hombres libres, en acuerdo con las condiciones y necesidades actuales de las Islas, y su constitución republican venidera" (the Cubans and Puerto Ricans of New York, to contribute, without haste and without rest, to the organization of free men, in accordance with the conditions and current needs of the Islands, and their future republican constitution).[14] This was a vision of action based on enabling collaboration and participation in the process of building the future Cuban and Puerto Rican republics and an Antillean federation.

Other publications within the Cuban separatist press offered variations on that idea. In his editorial note in the first issue of *Cacara Jícara* in 1897, Hernández Miyares (the former editor of *La Habana Elegante* when he was based in Havana) called his new publication "una batalla que daremos semanalmente contra España" (a battle that we will wage weekly against Spain).[15] As a battle rather than a soldier, the newspaper more clearly represents a collective project. It also introduces a temporal dimension to the newspaper's work: an event repeated weekly with the release of each new issue. *Doctrina de Martí* extends that idea in a reflection on *Patria*: "Sin el periódico, no habría podido Martí acortar las distancias para ponerse al habla con los elementos progresistas, organizar el gran Partido, y hacer fondos de guerra." (Without the newspaper [*Patria*], Martí would not have been able to shorten the distances to talk to the progressive elements, organize the great Party, and raise funds for the war.)[16] As a soldier or a battle within the larger fight for Cuban independence, the newspaper makes it possible to coordinate effort across physical distance. The possibility of simultaneous experience, which inspired so many writers, editors, and other media innovators of the late nineteenth century, is reimagined here to mobilize revolutionary action.

Doctrina de Martí's vision of the newspaper in action differed drastically from the one that became a primary innovation of the yellow press during the same period. In 1895, the year that marked the start of the insurrection against the Spanish in Cuba, William Randolph Hearst purchased the *New York Journal*. Cuba's war with Spain subsequently became a major news item precisely during the period when Hearst was developing his brand of journalism with mass appeal, rooted in scandal, fearmongering, and sensationalism. While the *Journal*'s critics saw lurid depictions of crime and catastrophe as the epitome of yellow journalism's approach, Hearst had a different idea of what should drive his newspaper's reputation. For him, the keyword was *action*: "Action—that is the distinguishing mark of the new journalism," he declared in the paper's October 13, 1897, issue. "It represents the final state in the evolution of the modern newspaper."[17] By action, he meant not simply reporting the news, but also making the news: "The newspapers of a century ago printed essays; those of thirty years ago—the 'New journals' of their day—told the news and some of them made great efforts to get it first. The new journal of to-day prints the news, too, but it does more. It does not wait for things to turn up. It turns them up."[18] As Hearst suggests, his approach built on foundations established by the illustrated press of the 1870s led by *Frank Leslie's Illustrated Magazine* and later by the *World*, as Pulitzer followed in Leslie's footsteps to develop his new journalism of the 1880s and early 1890s. Hearst's experiment with putting action into journalism constituted a resource-intensive update to those earlier ideas. Bringing together telegraphic and print technology, he developed his own supersized brand of the heroic reporter who specialized in "acting when public service requires; acting in the way to accomplish beneficent results."[19] Recognizing in the *Journal* a fierce competitor, Pulitzer also poured resources into updating his own paper around this idea.

Initially, Hearst and Pulitzer were not alone in considering action journalism a promising path forward for the future of news. According to Joseph Campbell, "The activist paradigm won admirers, even among Hearst's rivals and foes, and was seen as a promising agent in confronting official corruption and monopolistic excess."[20] One commentator remarked in *The Journalist*, "It is the freshest news brightly presented, the sham sharply punctured and, above all, the feeling . . . that behind and through the paper there beats a warm, generous, human heart alive to the troubles and miseries of humanity and anxious to alleviate them."[21] In this characterization, the writer replaces the blood and gore of the *Journal*'s most infamous stories with the idea of a human heart filled with kindness and understanding (belonging presumably to some intrepid reporter) as the power behind the news. Amid the scandals and corruption of Gilded Age America, the idea of newspapers becoming advocates on a new scale for those impoverished or disenfranchised by the wealthy and powerful must have appealed to some readers and members of the press. But it was the war in Cuba in which Hearst saw the most potential.

Hearst promoted the rescue of Cuban Evangelina Cosío y Cisneros from a Spanish prison by reporter Karl Decker as one of his greatest demonstrations of the journalism that acts. The story was designed as an update of the heroism of the new journalistic reporters of the 1880s. Karen Roggenkamp has shown that "the *Journal* and other national newspapers spared no verbiage in linking the rescue with the most romantic of models. 'The Days of Knight Errantry are still with us,' one headline proclaimed."[22] In Decker's 1897 coffee-table book *The Story of Evangelina Cisneros*, Nathaniel Hawthorne's son Julian Hawthorne, who wrote the book's introduction, lauded this new and improved heroism in similar terms: "No adventure of modern times has so appealed to the imagination of the world; had the knight of La Mancha not been a Spaniard, and had the achievement been less splendidly practical, we might call it Quixotic."[23] The *Journal* essentially remediated the romance to create a spectacle that harnessed the cutting-edge technology available at the time. Hearst poured resources into the endeavor—which involved breaking Cosío y Cisneros out of a women's prison in Havana and smuggling her onto a steamboat to New York, where her journey ended in a public welcome reception. As a laudatory article on the feat published in *Cacara Jícara* emphasized, "Lo que nadie ha podido hacer lo ha hecho por su entusiasmo por Cuba, por su propia cuenta y riesgo, y con su dinero, el verdadero heraldo del periodismo moderno, el *Journal* de W. R. Hearst." (What no one has been able to do has been done as a result of its enthusiasm for Cuba, at its own peril, and with its money, by the true herald of modern journalism, the *Journal* of W. R. Hearst.)[24] In this instance, the journalism that acts appeared to support and extend the efforts of Cubans fighting for independence. At the same time, the emphasis on cost in Hernández Miyares's commentary offers a hint of the very different method that the *Journal* employed. The story's investment in "saving" Cisneros renders her a pawn and a silent victim, rather than a participant in the war effort.

This passive role for readers may have been an unintended consequence of the journalism that acts. Elizabeth Lowry has argued that nineteenth-century newspapers in general "were designed to provoke community action" and the Cosío y Cisneros episode "encouraged women to participate in efforts to free Cuban women from the Spanish."[25] At the same time, as Lowry admits, "Hearst succeeded in swaying mass opinion by turning his readers into uncritical consumers of the Evangelina saga."[26] The story modeled a new kind of mass spectatorship powered, in part, by the telegraph wires that enabled rapid communication between Hearst and his reporters on the ground. Although the telegraph had enabled reporters to send updates to newsrooms in prior wars, Hearst also reversed the flow of information—essentially sending stage directions to his reporters on the ground, who in turn engaged in actions that made them the heroes of their own stories. According to Craig Carey, the *Journal* figured among "a handful of papers [that] were able to exploit unprecedented amounts of cash and other resources to actively create, coordinate, and manipulate war news through the telegraph's short circuit."[27] Telegraphy, in particular, "created the conditions necessary to coordinate 'action' at a distance through the manipulation of discrete signals: the serial data through which news was discretized and delivered across the wire and repurposed in print as the periodical spectacle of sensational journalism."[28] Since photographs could not yet be sent quickly, illustrators in Cuba and in the drafting room back in New York City provided the visual material for these performances.[29]

At their core, the difference between the approaches adopted during this period by the yellow press and the Cuban separatist press came down to making media a means of producing stories for mass consumption rather than as a means of mass participation in shaping and realizing a shared vision of the future. Within the Spanish-language Cuban separatist press, *La Revista de Cuba Libre* set out to ensure roles for women in the latter experiment. The publication's women-led editorial team reimagined the illustrated magazine, a form more typically associated with female readership, to make the work of producing a publication a demonstration of women's leadership in revolutionary activity.

Women, Revolution, and *La Revista de Cuba Libre*

Published biweekly in Tampa, Florida, from December 1897 to August 1898, *La Revista de Cuba Libre* was the official publication of the Club de Justo Carrillo, a women's organization dedicated to fundraising to support Cuba's third war for independence, which had finally started in 1895, after years of tireless coalition building.[30] The magazine appeared as part of a wave of publications in New York City, Tampa, and Key West that surged throughout the war.[31] This rare example of a women-led publication from nineteenth-century Nueva York's network demonstrates how a group that did not have direct access to the production of print created opportunities for themselves to participate and take leadership roles.

The Club de Justo Carrillo launched *La Revista de Cuba Libre* with the clear intention of becoming a recognized part of the Cuban separatist press. The magazine's first issue salutes the "Gobierno y Ejército revolucionario" (Government and Revolutionary Army) while adding, "A la prensa separatista igualmente extendemos nuestro saludo sincero á la vez que le pedimos su apoyo en nuestra tarea." (To the separatist press we also extend our sincere greeting at the same time that we ask for its support in our task.)[32] *La Revista de Cuba Libre*'s women-led team seeks to ensure that they will be noticed by a publishing community dominated almost exclusively by men. The concern was a valid one, given how few opportunities existed for women to participate in the printing and editing professions at the time. María de la Torriente and her editorial team belonged to the privileged elite of Tampa's Cuban exile community, but they were also outsiders to the print shop. As one editorial note reflected, "No se nos oculta que la tarea en que emprendemos con la publicación de nuestro periódico es mayor de lo que nosotras, débiles é inexpertas en el arte podemos resistir." (It is not lost on us that the task we undertake with the publication of a newspaper is greater than we, weak and inexperienced in the art, can withstand.)[33] Employing the all-female *nosotras* (we), the editorial voice appears to speak to potential critics from within the Cuban separatist press. By adopting a gendered humility, the editors invite generosity from those readers who possess the expertise that *La Revista de Cuba Libre*'s leadership lacked. That carefully crafted acknowledgment of the magazine's supposed limitations offers a glimpse of how these women employed their skills and resources to produce a singular publication. Throughout its run of seventeen issues, published biweekly from December 1897 to August 1898, *La Revista de Cuba Libre* shows its women editors making savvy use of networks and fundraising capacity, in addition to developing an editorial strategy that brought together articles and editorial notes that gave women prominent and unconventional roles in the revolutionary effort.

The editorial team's repeated, self-deprecating references to their "periodiquito" (little newspaper) belie the accomplishments of a publication that brought together an impressive contributor list and mix of content.[34] The masthead of each issue boasted a leadership team made up almost entirely of women except with a role as "Presidente de honor" (honorary president) assigned to the club's namesake, Justo Carrillo.[35] An adjacent column on the front page also exhibited a contributor list that featured men and women writers. The women included Arango and one of her companions on the *Olivette* steamer, Rosario Sigarroa, as well as a Havana-based correspondent writing under the pen name Aurora and New York-based Puerto Rican poet Lola Rodríguez de Tió. Among the men were Martín Morúa Delgado, Gonzalo de Quesada, and Enrique Varona. These and other contributors enabled Torriente and her team to publish letters from Havana and Cuba, poetry, articles, news on Tampa's Cuban community, and games, among other types of content. In that context, the editorial team's tendency to suggest their inexperience with frequent references to "nuestro humilde periódico" (our humble newspaper) might be considered strategic. Such claims served as reminders that women were highly capable of participating in the production of print to "servir á la Patria" (serve the Homeland).[36]

The choice made by Torriente and her editorial team to include in their publication's title the word *Revista*, or magazine—a word increasingly employed at the time to distinguish illustrated publications that placed more emphasis on literary or other cultural content from daily *periódicos*, or newspapers—signaled another part of the publication's editorial strategy: The editors rewrote the practices of earlier Spanish-language illustrated magazines, including those of the preceding decades in Nueva York in which many of those who became leaders of the Cuban separatist press got their start, to show how women could contribute in print. The Havana-based correspondent Aurora provides an example of how *La Revista de Cuba Libre* repurposed the genres and conventions of the illustrated press. Aurora's regularly published "Carta de la Habana" (Havana letter) follows the form of the *crónica* dedicated to cultural and society news, while shifting its focus to the war effort. In Aurora's contribution to *La Revista de Cuba Libre*'s inaugural issue, she draws this distinction explicitly: "Quieres que te hable de política y siempre de política; que deje á un lado las modas y sociedades." (You want me to write about politics and always about politics; that I leave aside fashion and society.)[37] Departing from the topics that female correspondents more typically addressed in illustrated magazines, Aurora asserts that her role is to cover the war effort. While writing about politics in Havana is a monumental task—"¡Por donde empezaré!" (Where will I begin!)—she also accepts the role readily "por hacer algo desde aquí por mi patria" (in order to do something from here for my homeland).[38] Moreover, her *crónica*'s title, "De nuestra corresponsal" (From our correspondent), as well as its first line addressed to "querida directora" (dear director), make clear through the use of feminine pronouns that writing and editing are roles occupied in this publication by women. Thus, Aurora's language updates a common practice in the *crónicas* of earlier illustrated magazines to address their readers as the feminine *vosotras*.[39] When Aurora writes in the same genre, she reframes the *crónica* to include female leadership in addition to female readership.

The magazine also included poetry from its network of contributors, including Lola Rodríguez de Tió, who was then based in New York. Her poem "¡Nevando!" (It's snowing!), published in the January 22, 1898, issue, converses with Martí's 1888 "Nueva York bajo la nieve" (New York under snow) considered in chapter 2. Snow, in this poem, represents the speaker's anguish: "En la tierra mucho frío / Y en el alma mucho duelo!" (In the land it is very cold / And in the soul there is much mourning).[40] This pain is the result of the speaker's exile, which in the context of *La Revista de Cuba Libre* might be read as Cuba or Rodríguez de Tió's homeland of Puerto Rico: "Al mirar tanta blancura / —Por contraste singular— / Mas lejos se ve el hogar / Y la ausencia más oscura." (Upon looking at so much whiteness / —by singular contrast— / The farther away one sees home / And the more obscure the absence.) One might also read in this overwhelming whiteness a critique of a racial White dominance in the United States as the speaker experienced the city and displacement from her island. For most of the poem, the speaker conveys a sense of personal anguish as a result of this distance from home, which makes her feel "como huérfana extrangera" (like an orphan abroad). In the final stanza, however, her perspective shifts to something more like that of Martí's in "Nueva York bajo la nieve," as he described New York City during the Great Blizzard that took place a decade earlier. Echoing his account of the suffering of New York City's poorest residents, the poem's speaker reflects, "Sigue nevando, nevando / Y yo con tristeza digo: / ¡Cuantos pobres sin abrigo! / ¡Cuántos ausentes llorando!" (It keeps snowing, snowing / And I say sadly: / How many poor people without shelter! / How many absent people crying!) The snow provides a source of personal sadness as well as reflection on the plight of those with limited resources in the city. Rodríguez de Tió's dedication at the outset of the poem, "A mi hija patria" (To my homeland daughter), takes on particular significance in the context of *La Revista de Cuba Libre*. While it was typical to personify Cuba and Puerto Rico as female, Rodríguez de Tió positions herself as a mother of her homeland, perhaps indicating her own leadership role in advocating for Puerto Rican independence. This mother, in other words, is not the traditionally represented self-sacrificing woman who plays an auxiliary role in the revolution. Rather, she appears in *La Revista de Cuba Libre* as a poet who was by then widely recognized by readers throughout Latin

America, lending her voice to the magazine's effort to show women's leadership in the Cuban and Puerto Rican cause.

While New York-based illustrated magazines of the 1880s such as *La América* and *La Revista Ilustrada de Nueva York* had provided the professional training ground for Martí, Figueroa, and other leaders of the 1890s Cuban separatist press, *La Revista de Cuba Libre* was one of few illustrated magazines explicitly founded to support Cuba's 1895 independence war. The associations with female readership that made the illustrated magazine an appealing form for the editorial team of *La Revista de Cuba Libre* may also have led the editors of publications like *Patria* and *Doctrina de Martí* to choose to take forms that fell into the broader category of *periódicos*. As Jesse Hoffnung-Garskof has noted, even the most progressive visions of racial or class unity pursued by members of the PRC were "heavily invested in a shared experience of manhood."[41] Typically, movement leaders confined women to the roles of selfless and supportive wives and mothers of those on the battlefield and to raising funds through women's clubs like the Club de Justo Carrillo.

Another likely reason for the dearth of illustrated magazines in the Cuban separatist press of the 1890s is that publishing illustrations was costly. From this perspective, too, *La Revista de Cuba Libre* appears to have been exceptional. Following the formula made familiar by New York-based Hispanophone magazines of the 1870s and 1880s, editorial notes in *La Revista de Cuba Libre* frequently reminded readers of the quality of its printing, committed to making improvements over time, and acknowledged printing delays and other challenges. Printed at the print shop of Tampa's *Cuba* newspaper, the "órgano oficial del Partido Revolucionario Cubano en Tampa" (official mouthpiece of the Partido Revolucionario Cubano in Tampa), *La Revista de Cuba Libre* celebrated "el inmenso y variado surtido de tipos" (the immense and varied assortment of types) at this "magnifica imprenta" (magnificent print shop).[42] Later editorial notes call attention to improvements in the magazine's illustrations. As an announcement in the March 19, 1898, issue explained, "Correspondiendo al favor que el público nos ha dispensado y que atribuímos á la noble causa que representamos . . . desde el présente número empezamos á publicar foto-grabados de interés para los cubanos." (Corresponding to the favor that the public has dispensed to us and that we attribute to the noble cause that we represent . . . from the present issue we begin to publish photo-engravings of interest to Cubans.)[43] As did its predecessors in the 1870s and 1880s, *La Revista de Cuba Libre* makes a direct link between its pursuit of the "noble causa" and its increasing capacity for reproducing illustrations. In its late 1890s context, the announcement also suggests that *La Revista de Cuba Libre* had achieved surprising financial success compared to its peer publications.

"40 pesos," an announcement published in the August 27, 1898, issue, shared that the club had raised this amount for the Partido Revolucionario Cubano and hoped to soon deliver more. One of the major functions of women's clubs like the Club de Justo Carrillo was to raise money for the war, and so it is unsurprising that the editors cite a recent dinner organized by the club as a source of the funds. In this case, however, there were additional sources of revenue: "cotizaciones y venta de la *Revista*" (contributions and sale of the Magazine).[44] That the magazine had surplus funds to donate to the cause is surprising in light of the deficits suffered by its colleagues in the Cuban separatist press (including *Doctrina de Martí*). While these women may have lacked publishing experience, they appear fully competent in managing their magazine. One tagline that appeared in an advertisement for the publication describes it as a "periódico fundado para arbitrar recursos a la causa de Cuba" (newspaper founded to raise resources for Cuba's cause), suggesting that fundraising had shaped its purpose from the start.[45] From that perspective, *La Revista de Cuba Libre* might be considered a rare success story among publications that often simply disappeared without formal explanation in print—in many cases, following increasingly ardent appeals for payments of overdue accounts and new subscriptions to help overcome financial hardships.

La Revista de Cuba Libre appears as an intervention in both the Cuban separatist press and the US Anglophone yellow press. The leadership of the Club de Justo Carrillo brought together a team of women, most of whom were not print professionals, who became media innovators in the debate about Cuba's future. They also identified their own heroes, among them Arango, who appears in a very different light than that of the *Journal* article that described her escape from Cuba. In *La Revista de Cuba Libre* she is not a victim, but rather a journalist and sales agent credited on the front page of every issue. One of Arango's companions on the *Olivette*, Rosario Sigarroa, appears in a similar light—as an editor addressed in letters to the magazine, a contributor of *crónicas* from Tampa, and the first to be featured in the "galeria de honor" launched by the publication to recognize heroes of the war effort. She is identified as a hero for her battlefield contributions as an aide and messenger for the PRC and for serving as a Red Cross volunteer, but also for her contributions to the magazine. The article lists among her achievements "sus trabajos, sus crónicas [que] le dieron siempre á nuestro periódico verdadero impulso" (her work, her chronicles [that] always gave to our newspaper real momentum).[46] As I have argued elsewhere, "her work aiding the wounded on the battlefield appears here as a continuation of her heroism in the editorial office."[47] In this way, *La Revista de Cuba Libre* repeatedly repositions the auxiliary roles women were expected to play into leadership roles in the editorial office. But this does not mean that they turned women into stunt reporters like Nellie Bly. Rather, *La Revista de Cuba Libre* showed women leading in the work of revolution, which included the publishing of periodicals.

Rewiring Yellow Journalism

Within a print culture that was engaged in a wide-ranging debate about what the newspaper should become, yellow journalism's bold experiments—and the varying critiques they inspired—raised the question of what, really, a newspaper is for. As the yellow press participated in a growing newspaper industry and journalistic profession, and the Cuban separatist press pushed the limits of print as a means of mobilizing participation in creating a new, more just nation, these communities of print offered increasingly divergent answers to that question.

The *World*'s and the *Journal*'s methods of making the newspaper a vehicle for stories that would attract the widest possible audience increasingly relied on the power of celebrity. Looking to popular fiction as a model, Hearst hired bestselling authors and promoted them in his headlines. Among them was Stephen Crane, who served as a war correspondent for the *Journal* in Greece (during the Greco-Turkish War in 1897) and afterward wrote for the *World* from Cuba. In a dispatch from Greece for the *Journal* that appeared in that newspaper on June 13, 1897, the headline touted Crane's literary credentials by referencing his 1895 bestselling novel—which had inspired critical acclaim, as well as controversy, for its portrayal of a soldier's personal experience of war, with which Crane, at the time, had no firsthand experience: "That Was Romance, 'The Red Badge of Courage'—A Story. This is Reality, The Battle To-day in Greece—A Fact."[48] While Nellie Bly's race around the *World* at the turn of the 1890s sought to make Bly into a star who could outshine Jules Verne's success as a fiction writer, Hearst simplified the process by hiring literary stars who would bring their spotlight to the *Journal*.

Scholarship on Crane's war correspondence has tended to credit his writing with a self-reflexivity and element of critique that was uncharacteristic of the yellow press.[49] Even as a self-doubting reporter, however, Crane contributed to yellow journalism's effort to isolate and elevate the reporter on a stage provided by Cuba's war with Spain. In one article from Cuba featuring Theodore Roosevelt's Rough Riders, Crane confesses, "I know nothing about war, of course, and pretend nothing, but I have been enabled from time to time to see brush fighting, and I want to say here plainly that the behavior of these Rough Riders shook me with terror as I have never before been shaken."[50] His claim not to "pretend" anything about war appears to depart from the sensationalism of yellow journalism, and perhaps also the literary impressionism for which his novel received widespread acclaim, by offering a "plainly" narrated account. Yet Crane's value to the *World* was precisely to bring his own literary sensibilities to his reports for the yellow press, as he employed his signature impressionistic style to highlight the heroism of the US soldiers and war correspondents on the scene. Indeed, Crane casts himself in a role that sounds very much like that of *Red Badge of Courage* protagonist Henry Fleming as he decides to flee from the returning troops after his first experience in battle: "For my part, I was frightened almost into convulsions."[51] From that personal perspective, Crane unveils the "spectacle of heroism" on which the rest of the dispatch centers.[52]

The spectacle that Crane constructs consists of the personal dramas of the soldiers: "There was nothing to be seen but men straggling through the underbrush and firing at some part of the landscape. This was the scenic effect."[53] When the soldiers arrive in an open space that could provide a more panoramic view, their bodies fill the scene: "The Rough Riders advanced steadily and confidently under the Mauser bullets. They spread across some open ground . . . and there they began to fall, smothering and threshing down in the grass, marking man-shaped places among those luxuriant blades."[54] Crane's method of narrating news of the war imprints the Cuban battlefield with the bodies of heroic US soldiers. As the article continues, the figure of the war correspondent appears on the soldiers' heels as another important element of the action. Following the "heroic rumor [that] arose, soared, screamed above the bush," he encounters a fellow correspondent who "lay, shot through the body."[55] Surrounded by soldiers and having suffered a similar fate to those who "began to crawl, walk and be carried back to where, in the middle of the path, the soldiers had established a little field hospital," the correspondent takes position here as another type of soldier.[56] Empowered by this new role, Crane explains to a group of passing US soldiers who ask what he is doing, "I am a correspondent, and we are merely carrying back another correspondent who we think is mortally wounded."[57] The word "merely" belies the powerful transformation that takes place. Crane brings himself into the story as a war correspondent who not only observes the romantically charged trials and triumphs of war but acts in them as well.

The image of the war-correspondent-turned-soldier provides a stark contrast to the use of the figure of the soldier-turned-newspaper in the Spanish-language press. As a writer with his own investment in celebrity in his literary and journalistic writing, Crane ultimately contributes to the separation between writer and reader that yellow journalism accelerated. The war correspondent operating as a soldier must take actions and make judgments and then tells readers about them after the fact. By contrast, treating the newspaper as a soldier requires the active cooperation of the varying elements of the newspaper.

A departure from yellow journalism also took place in the Anglophone mass press of the late 1890s. In his 1897 book *Facts and Fakes about Cuba*, *New York Herald* reporter George Bronson Rea mocked the "'intrepid war correspondent' of a leading New York daily, who never leaves the safe environments of the city, and who sees the most marvelous battles, and celebrates astonishing interviews with unknown Cuban chiefs, and mixes names and geography in such a manner as to cause the insurgents to jump one hundred and fifty miles in an hour."[58] Rea had lived in Cuba before the war, and his knowledge of the island helped him to become one of the few correspondents who managed to circumvent

Spanish regulations and travel with the revolutionaries. The invective he directs at those reporters who did not share the same access transforms the "marvelous battles" of the yellow press—and even the less triumphant, impressionistic moments captured by Crane—as baseless, potentially dangerous, forms of fiction. Reliability of information is how Rea distinguishes his own reporting from yellow journalism.

A key distinction Rea draws between his reporting and that of the yellow press is his consideration of multiple sides of the same story. His analysis culminates in an account of an argument that he claims to have had with Cuban General Máximo Gómez. According to Rea, Gómez objected to a story by Rea about the capture by Cuban revolutionaries of the small town of Paredes. The story alleged that the Cubans had left their wounded behind, and Gómez feared that such a report would "hurt the Cuban cause."[59] When Gómez insists on his version of the story, in which the battle "was a great victory," Rea refuses to accept the general's report over the testimony of the several participants in the battle whom he met in his travels: "I am convinced that the people told me the truth, and I will believe them in preference to a one-sided report."[60] While Rea participates in the dismissive attitude toward military leaders in the war effort that was ubiquitous in the yellow press, he also does something new. His description introduces a concept that was still in its infancy at the time—of telling a news story from both or multiple sides. The example that Rea uses to promote such an approach calls into question the role of advocacy for a cause in journalism. His critique also anticipates what would ultimately become a goal of journalistic objectivity by suggesting that the viewpoints of multiple participants can prevent the inaccuracies of a "one-sided report."[61] Moreover, it is important to note that "both-sides" journalism, which became widely idealized by the twentieth century, did not often include a perspective that was critical of US capitalism and foreign policy. In her analysis of *Times* foreign correspondent Dorothy Stanhope's reporting from Cuba in the years following the withdrawal of the Spanish, Nancy Mirabal notes that Stanhope's reports repeated the patronizing and racist depictions of Cubans that appeared in the yellow press: "[Stanhope] justifies the land rush and speculation by making those from the United States worthy of economic opportunities, and Cubans, despite their years of struggle and sacrifice, unworthy" and "she envisioned a Cuba, not for Cubans, but for US residents."[62] These were precisely the concerns that *La Revista de Cuba Libre* voiced in its editorial team's own critique of the yellow press—but now embedded in a new paradigm of journalism focused on objectivity.

Before that shift to journalistic objectivity in the early twentieth century, yellow journalism represented one possible direction for the future of news in a print culture characterized by diversity and complexity. Drawing on notions of heterogeneity developed in studies of nineteenth-century Latin American print culture, John Patrick Leary has asked, "What if we consider the generic heterogeneity of 1890s newspaper writing less as an interregnum, anticipating and preparing what came after, and more as a reflection of a decade of crisis in both the country and its intellectual professions?"[63] For Leary, such a line of inquiry enables a comparison between the newspaper writing of leading reporters for the yellow press, including Crane and Davis, and the *crónicas* of Hispanophone writers, including the Havana-based Julián del Casal and the New York-based José Martí: "Crane, Davis, Casal, and Martí perform this professional anxiety in quite different ways, and they may locate modernity in different places, but they shared a common investment in stylization as a mark of literariness and intellectual autonomy in a modernizing profession that endangered both."[64] The premature deaths of both Casal (of tuberculosis in 1893) and Martí meant that neither writer engaged with the yellow press of the late 1890s, but the leaders of the Spanish-language press who outlived them, including Serra, Figueroa, and Torriente, continued to innovate during this time of political crisis and media transition. They shared with the writers and editors of the yellow press an interest in using print to improve the world. But the Cuban separatist press's commitment to motivating action throughout the entire print community ultimately offered another path forward, if briefly. This path illuminated by the democratic literary imagination diverged not only from the capitalistic model represented by the yellow press, but also from the emergent notions of literary distinction that Leary identifies as common ground connecting Crane, Davis, Casal, and Martí. Instead, the Cuban separatist press modeled making newspapers virtual workshops for collaboration and democratic participation.

Here, we might return to the August 6, 1898, issue of *La Revista de Cuba Libre*, which devoted its front page to a critique of the yellow press. The article demonstrates the emptiness of the yellow press's form of action, especially in comparison to *La Revista de Cuba Libre*. In the yellow press, the editors note "el poco conocimiento con que se tratan muchos particulares" (the little understanding with which many details are treated).[65] It is a press whose "afan de alborotar y de hablar hasta de lo que ignoran, solo consiguen su propio desprestigio" (eagerness to fuss and talk even about what they ignore, only achieves their own discredit).[66] The choice of words—*ávida* with its sense of eagerness and greed, and *afán*, evoking again eagerness associated with desire and haste—associates the yellow press with a kind of unthinking impulse. In contrast, the *Revista* posits the careful consideration of "ambas partes" (both sides) as a prerequisite of determining just outcomes. *La Revista de Cuba Libre* holds the newspaper accountable to the democratic ideal that the United States so vitally represented for Hispanophone writers even as it also fell far short of that ideal at home and abroad.

The title of *La Revista de Cuba Libre*'s article, "El cuarto poder . . . americano" (The . . . American fourth estate), evokes journalism's role in achieving and upholding democracy. The article thus suggests that the greatest flaw of the yellow press is its failure to fulfill its promise of being a protector of democracy—at home or abroad. Instead, in the case of Cuba's struggle for independence, the newspapers "ofender á mansalva á los que su gobierno favorece" (greatly offend those whom its government favors).[67] If journalism as it is conceptualized in the United States serves to defend democracy, then yellow journalism departs from that course in a dangerous and destructive way. The eager pursuit of increased sales and circulation comes at the cost of democracy itself.

Within the Cuban separatist press, *Doctrina de Martí* most clearly articulated an idea of the newspaper as a site for embarking on the work of nation building while the war was still being waged and afterward. To that end, Serra and Figueroa set out to make *Doctrina de Martí* a means of enabling democratic participation as an ongoing work in progress.

Doctrina de Martí's Revolution in Print

In *Doctrina de Martí*, Serra brings together his astute observations about the history on which the newspaper built with a savvy approach to updating the newspaper for his fast-changing media context. Serra knew well the small-print community rooted in the print shops of Nueva York that were responsible for the expansion of the Hispanophone illustrated press there since the 1870s. As in earlier magazines, advertisements in *Doctrina de Martí* limn the outlines of the New York-based Hispanophone network in which the publication participated. A. W. Howe, which printed *Doctrina de Martí*, was located at 115 Park Row, and so occupied the same building that housed the editorial office of Hernández Miyares's *Cacara Jícara*, founded in 1895. Regular advertisements for Figueroa's print shop, Imprenta América, also appeared in the paper, declaring, "Teniendo ya algunos años de establecida está en relación con las mejores casas de grabados de la ciudad." (Having already been established for some years, it [Imprenta América] has connections to the best engraving houses in the city.)[68] Nueva York, as we can see, maintained its web of connections.

At the same time, some of the material aspects of New York City print culture and the hemispheric network in which it participated are less visible in the pages of *Doctrina de Martí* than they were in earlier publications. Serra rarely addressed print quality or print capacity in editorial notes in *Doctrina de Martí*. And while the illustrated magazines in which Figueroa participated—and continued to print in the 1890s—touted their network of writers and readers as one of their primary strengths, *Doctrina de Martí* was produced by a smaller, New York City-based team.[69] Within its pages, *Doctrina de Martí* presents an evolving vision of how the print shop and the newspaper constitute means to achieving Cuban and Puerto Rican democracy. In this vision, the key actors were not reporters, but rather those who considered economic and racial equality the essential foundation of a future independent Cuba and Puerto Rico. In this way, the newspaper extended and revised the idea of the newspaper as a soldier that circulated widely in the publications of nineteenth-century Nueva York.

Understanding *Doctrina de Martí*'s ideas about revolution and the role of the newspaper in achieving it requires understanding *Patria*'s successes and failures. Founded by Martí in 1892, *Patria* inspired a new wave of US-based Spanish-language newspapers dedicated to Cuban and Puerto Rican independence. As with the earlier generation of nineteenth-century Spanish-language periodicals, these publications were varied in their political and social commitments, and it is easy to overstate the role of egalitarian ideals within them. White elites seeking to maintain their social and economic privilege remained a powerful force. Yet, to a much greater degree than during the earlier wars for Cuban independence, the wave of newspapers that surged during the late 1890s made room for discussions about democracy and how to achieve it. The always precarious coalition that made the war possible was made even more uncertain given the degree to which it included working-class Cubans, many of whom were of African descent. But, for a time, *Patria* attempted—imperfectly, incompletely, but also ambitiously—to provide a platform for debate and collaboration for all those brought together by the PRC.[70] After Estrada Palma took over the leadership of the party in the fall of 1895, however, *Patria* lost its previous "careful balance . . . between profiles of wealthy, white patriots and profiles of exemplary black soldiers, poets, and teachers."[71] Serra and a team of collaborators, including Figueroa and Bonilla, created *Doctrina de Martí* to pick up where *Patria* left off. Informed by their deep experience in the print shops and editorial offices of Nueva York, they pursued "la práctica de la verdadera democracia, que es de donde tiene que surgir el bien de la República" (the practice of true democracy, which is where the good of the Republic must arise).[72]

Throughout *Doctrina de Martí's* three-year existence, Serra and his collaborators, especially Figueroa, promoted the revolution as a collaborative project that did not end with the removal of the Spanish from the island. In an editorial note published in the first issue, they described the challenge they faced:

Echar al déspota fuera de nuestra patria; y también combatir y vencer contra sus enfermizas tradiciones; purificar las costumbres; darle derechos y completa garantía á la mujer; abolir los privilegios, no tan solo en la ley escrita sino también en la ley moral; consagrarse á toda obra de provecho común; aplicar los progresos de la inteligencia á las necesidades de la vida; establecer la igualdad; difundir la instrucción, y preservar con toda su grandeza la justicia. Revolucionemos.

(To take the despot out of our homeland; and also to fight and defeat his sick traditions; to purify customs; to give rights and full security to women; to abolish privileges, not only in written law but also in moral law; to devote oneself to all works of common good; to apply the advances of intelligence to the needs of life; to establish equality; to spread education; and to preserve justice in all its greatness. Let us revolutionize.)[73]

The process of revolutionizing encompasses a set of goals that starts, rather than ends, with freeing Cuba from Spain. The real revolution lay in dismantling the hierarchies that the Spanish put in place and working together for public goods, including education, and ultimately, equality and justice. In *Doctrina de Martí*, this process is always facilitated by the newspaper through its editors, writers, printers, and readers.

In the same inaugural issue of *Doctrina de Martí*, Figueroa offers further insight into the revolutionary views that informed the periodical's editorial strategy: "La palabra *revolución* tiene más trascendencia de la que generalmente se le dá." (The word *revolution* has more significance than it is usually given.)[74] Echoing the sentiment of "Nuestra labor," Figueroa explains that the term extends beyond the war for independence to the future work of nation building and beyond: "Tendremos patria, y continuaremos revolucionando no ya contra los españoles, sino para arrojar lejos de nosotros los vicios que pueda habernos inoculado el coloniaje desapoderado y rampante." (We will have a homeland, and we will continue to revolutionize no longer against the Spanish, but in order to cast off the vices that may have inoculated us against dispossessed and rampant colonization.)[75] Revolutionizing constitutes a process of decolonization of Cuba's own population after the departure of the Spanish. Such a process brings together action with ideas: "Nuestra labor revolucionaria no es pasajera, sino permanente, y hemos de sembrar ideas que quedan y fructifique." (Our revolutionary work is not temporary but permanent, and we must sow ideas that remain and bear fruit.)[76]

Figueroa defines a key role within such ongoing revolution for "el periodista honrado" (the honest journalist), a category in which he includes himself. He commits to upholding for *Doctrina de Martí* "la misión de la prensa digna, que corrige y enseña, á la vez que es válvula de seguridad por donde se escapan las quejas populares" (the mission of the dignified press, which corrects and teaches, while at the same time being a safety valve through which popular complaints escape).[77] The newspaper's work takes place in two directions—following from the journalist's insights and teachings and from the public's frustrations and criticisms.

Figueroa's characterization of the journalist updates earlier notions from Spanish- and English-language magazines of their civilizing mission. In Figueroa's view, journalists must be attentive to their readership, "si no quieren caer envueltos en el general anatema que alcanzan los que no saben ó no quieren dar satisfacción a la opinión pública" (if they do not want to fall into the general anathema that those who do not know or do not want to satisfy public opinion achieve).[78] Journalism is a means of serving the public, which includes enabling continued communication and collaboration between a publication and its readers.

The reconceptualization of the newspaper in *Doctrina de Martí* centers on the image of the *taller*, or workshop, which carries dual meanings in Spanish as both an artist's studio and a space for skilled production. Both Serra and his lead collaborator, Figueroa, were intimately familiar with the *taller*, having made their livings in the trades of cigar rolling and printing, respectively. Throughout *Doctrina de Martí*, and in Serra's writings more broadly, the *taller* illustrates the need for a majority to come together to overpower the tyrannical minority of the Spanish in Cuba. The article "Sin justicia no hay union" (Without justice there is no union), published in the June 15, 1897, issue, argues that workers are uniquely qualified to understand the type of union that leads to liberation: "Los obreros de LA DOCTRINA podemos hablar de unión, porque para ello hemos trabajado y trabajaremos siempre." (The workers of LA DOCTRINA can speak of union, because for this we have worked and will always work.)[79] Workers have the history and experience to create the kind of coalition that Cuba needs.

An essay included in Serra's 1896 *Ensayos políticos* dedicated to "los artesanos" (the artisans) elaborates that idea. The essay assigns metaphorical significance to the *taller* as a space in which the unity of a nation might be envisioned:

En un taller, por ejemplo, se ve lo que [es] en una nación. Cien hombres empleados en una casa sufren las caprichosas exigencias injustas de un solo hombre, ayudado por dos ó tres dependientes, porque realmente entre estos hombres que son la mayoría, no hay dos verdaderamente unidos.

(In a workshop, for example, one sees what is in a nation. A hundred men employed in a house suffer the capricious unjust demands of a single man, aided by two or three dependents, because actually among these men who are the majority, there are not two truly united.)[80]

It is not that the *taller* is necessarily an ideal place. Indeed, as it is described here, it can also be a site of oppression. But it is also a space where workers can find the tools, as well as the community, to fight that oppression. Such tools include the knowledge obtained through reading: "Los pueblos que menos leen son los pueblos más esclavos, porque todo lo ignoran; no saben más que lo que les conviene á sus tiranos." (The people who read the least are the most enslaved people, because they are ignorant of everything; they know nothing more than what suits their tyrants.)[81] The description recalls the central role of *lectores*, or readers, in many of the tobacco workshops, whose workers became a key constituency in the Partido Revolucionario Cubano. Like the tobacco factories, the workshop envisioned here is not only a space of production; it is also a site of learning and of organizing to cast off oppression: "Deshabilitemos á nuestros tiranos con nuestra unión, con nuestra actividad y nuestra cordura" (Let us disable our tyrants with our union, with our activity and our sanity.)[82] In the workshop, workers have previously modeled the kind of union that recognizes the rights of all those who participate in it.

A notable difference appears between this characterization of the *taller* and the one provided in the illustration of the *taller* of *La América Ilustrada*'s "El taller del obrero" (The worker's workshop) considered in chapter 1. There, an individual described as the "modern worker" exemplifies the kind of activity and contemplation that leads to productive participation in democracy. In Serra's characterization, the *taller* is not a place for solitary character building, but rather a place for collective organizing. It is an idea that captures well what Serra sought to achieve with his newspaper.

Serra identified a similar purpose for *Doctrina de Martí*. In editorial notes, he described it as a space for achieving unity across the many groups and individuals involved in the wide-ranging coalition that sought Cuban independence. One note published in *Doctrina de Martí*'s inaugural issue echoes Martí's introduction to *Patria* considered earlier in this chapter: "Nuestra misión es de unir. Pero unir de veras. No con la unión desventajosa y desigual de ginete y el corcel." (Our mission is to unite. But to unite for real. Not with the disadvantageous and unequal union of the rider and the steed.)[83] The metaphor suggests that the major threat to unity is inequality, and anything that claims unity without addressing that inequality is not authentic. Clearly, in the context of *Patria*'s power shift, which reinstituted White liberal elites to leadership positions and actively pushed leaders of African descent like Serra and Figueroa to the margins, the problem of racial equality very much motivated *Doctrina de Martí*'s editorial strategy, not to mention the life's work of its editor and key contributors. But the periodical relied less on direct discussions of race than on references to the working class in its discussions of how to achieve equality.

This emphasis on the central role of the working class in *Doctrina de Martí* builds on and extends the imagery and ideas about how to create a new kind of government for Cuba that Martí advocated most famously in "Nuestra América." There, Martí assigned creativity a central role in the task of developing uniquely Latin American approaches to governing. Serra offers his own take on the importance of creativity in another article in *Doctrina de Martí*: "Nos enseñó el ilustre Martí, que un pueblo compuesto de distintos elementos vivos y maniatados por un mismo yugo, deben estar sinceramente unidos, y representados por igual en todas las capacidades contributivas á la creación del País." (The illustrious Martí taught us that a people composed of different living elements and bound by the same yoke must be sincerely united, and represented equally in all contributing capacities to the creation of the Country.)[84] The word *creación* signals that the work of building an independent Cuban nation constitutes a creative act. While Martí characterized such creativity as manual labor that did not necessarily take place in the print shop, Serra returns to the print shop—or the *taller* more broadly—to envision the collaborative work necessary to build a truly democratic Cuba.

What kind of *taller* could facilitate creative production across distances? How does one achieve the collaboration that such work requires when the physical workshop is not close enough (or large enough) to accommodate all who need to be involved? How does one traverse the vast distances that separate a community scattered in exile across Europe and the Americas? In *Doctrina de Martí*'s unique formulation, it is a workshop in which Cubans can help create a Cuban nation. As in the *taller* magazines of the 1870s, this idea of the newspaper as *taller* also differs from Julio Ramos's characterization of the Latin American *crónica modernista*, noted in the introduction, as "a kind of experimental workshop" where "literature began to insistently announce the project of autonomy."[85] If, as Ramos has argued, the workshop of the *crónica* emerged, in part, to invent "a new individuality that presupposes the progressive dissolution of the public, communitarian spaces of the modern city," then the Cuban separatist press might be considered an attempt to keep the dream of collective action alive and to reinvent it through modern media.[86]

The workshop of the newspaper that *Doctrina de Martí* constructed thus provides a powerful illustration of the democratic literary imagination centered on participation and collaboration, in contrast to notions of the literary associated with individuality and distinction that appear in one, much better-known strain of *modernismo*, and that would solidify in the twentieth century. In the pages of the Cuban separatist press, editorial notes, brief articles, and updates, often printed anonymously and representing a collective editorial voice, provide the genres through which the periodicals' writers and editors envision new possibilities and negotiate the terms on which they will create new worlds. Such texts are not literary from the perspective of familiar notions of genre or authorship; rather, they push boundaries through language. And they constitute fiercely hopeful and creative efforts to write new possibilities into existence.

The thing about this kind of work in progress is that it doesn't make a very good commodity. It will never be fully formed. It also doesn't make a very polished object of study. But the less polished objects of study may well be the most revealing ones.[87] When we look beyond the familiar genres, and signs of what was to come—which is to say, what we already know—powerful alternatives come into view. Within the Cuban separatist press of the late 1890s, one such alternative was *Doctrina de Martí*, which achieved one of nineteenth-century Nueva York's clearest visions of achieving unity through a participatory print culture motivated by achieving true democracy.

Small Press Alternatives to Emerging Mass Media

La Revista de Cuba Libre's editors, as well as Figueroa and Serra, followed their purpose when the US intervention ended the war. They went to Cuba—Figueroa with his printing press in tow—to participate in the work of nation building.[88] Under the direction of Sigarroa, a new publication called *Cuba Libre* appeared in Havana in 1899 as the replacement promised by *La Revista de Cuba Libre*. Figueroa and Serra, too, founded new publications there.[89] Their departure makes it all too easy to overlook the smaller publications that remained in the shadows of the English-language press. Yet Cuban separatist publications published in the United States, like *La Revista de Cuba Libre* and *Doctrina de Martí*, provide a reminder that there is more to the story of the emergence of modern media than the largest-circulating newspapers—or the discourses of literature and journalism that they helped to shape.

Writers and editors of that community took advantage of the relative accessibility of printing presses, cheaper paper, and, in some cases, improved processes for reproducing images to make newspapers a primary vehicle for supporting the war effort and planning the independent Cuba that would come afterward. Some—as Martí famously did during his tenure as president of the Partido Revolucionario Cubano and editor of *Patria*—frequented the telegraph offices in Lower Manhattan to gather information that informed their newspapers' content. All saw a new world of print that made it possible to reach people more quickly and more frequently, if not always simultaneously, through newspapers and magazines. Those small, original, determined, and often idealistic publications offer just one example of the communities of print that took shape alongside the mass-circulation Anglophone press, often as alternatives to it.

The story of these publications calls for further exploration of smaller presses in late nineteenth-century print culture. For example, during the period when the Spanish-language press thrived in Lower Manhattan, the area was also home to T. Thomas Fortune's *New York Age*, which at the time was a leading Black newspaper in the United States. The *New York Age* not only occupied the same buildings (its offices were at 4 Cedar Street, in the same building where *El Espejo* operated from 1874 to 1893), its goals also intersected with those of the Spanish-language publishing community. The *New York Age* reported on the activities of Afro-Cubans and Afro-Puerto Ricans who participated in Masonic lodges in the city; Hoffnung-Garskof notes, "It is also clear that the Cubans became readers of the *New York Age*, and depended on it as a source for the news that they transmitted to Spanish-speaking readers in Cuba and the migrant communities."[90] Following the US intervention in Cuba in 1898, the Anglophone Black press in New York City and beyond also became increasingly critical of US imperialism. Some identified the hypocrisy of US claims to promote freedom and democracy. Referencing the devastating prevalence of lynching in the United States at the time, the *Weekly Blade* (based in Parsons, Kansas) opined in its June 11, 1898, issue, "Now, while Uncle Sam can find time to shoot Spaniards for their cruelty to Cubans, he ought to take a little of the time and make a thorough search among the persecuted part of the Americans about his own door mat."[91] Other papers warned of the racism that the United States would spread to Cuba. In the August 20, 1898, issue of the Richmond *Planet*, an editorial observes,

> The Cubans are reported to be dissatisfied with the terms of the protocol as signed by representatives of the United States and Spain. . . . It is the same old story. . . . The dark-skinned inhabitants of the island will be the victims of race prejudice, and this combined with Spanish contempt will make their wretched lives miserable. It is indeed a gloomy outlook with not a ray of light visible upon the horizon of their future.[92]

This bleak observation contrasts sharply with the hopeful ambitions focused on racial justice and gender equality (although not always together) visible in the Cuban separatist press. In the Anglophone Black press and in the Spanish-language press that participated in the democratic literary imagination during this period, the struggle for democracy during the very years when systemic racism in the United States became so deeply and violently entrenched was always part of the story. That story, infamously, never found a place in the yellow press— even when it appeared to support the Cuban cause through stories that made heroes of their own White male US journalists.

To recover the history of communities that grappled the most with the challenges and opportunities of media and democracy, we must recognize that important developments of late nineteenth-century media change might not have taken place in the well-resourced newsrooms and legendary moments that have dominated US media history. As publications like *Doctrina de Martí* and *La Revista de Cuba Libre* took advantage of the ability of smaller presses to mediate new audiences without the prohibitive investment required for the largest presses, they raised the possibility of making newspapers into vehicles for mobilizing creativity on a massive scale. At a crossroads in media and journalistic history, the Cuban revolutionary newspapers of the US-based Spanish-language press engaged in an extraordinary experiment. As Anglophone mass-circulation newspapers were shaping a future of print based on increasing circulation, this small-press vision of participation in the production of knowledge, ideas, and a shared future would persevere in the twentieth century in other types of democratic institutions and countercultural publications.

5

Work in Progress

EDITORSHIP FROM THE MARGINS OF PRINT AND
AT THE LIMITS OF LITERATURE IN NUEVA YORK

The October 20, 1894, issue of the New York-based Spanish-language anarchist newspaper *El Despertar* (The Awakening) reflects on a dream it does not intend to realize. Referencing the advertising that supports the English-language mass-circulation press in New York City, the anonymous article notes that with similar funds, "pudiera publicarse nuestro periódico EL DESPERTAR, diario, imprimiendo 50,000 ejemplares por espacio de ocho meses ó un año, sin cobra suscripción" (our newspaper *EL DESPERTAR* could be published, daily, printing 50,000 copies for eight months or a year, without a subscription charge).[1] In this paper that dreams big in pursuit of justice and economic equality, this possibility of becoming a daily newspaper with a robust readership constitutes a path that its founding editors, Spaniard Luis Barcia and Cuban José Cayetano Campos, refuse to take. To be sure, a bit of longing lingers as the unsigned article imagines a solid (if modest, by the standards of the mass press) daily run of 50,000 copies supported with nearly a year's worth of funding. The idea that the paper might be distributed for free must have been tempting for a publication whose readers suffered low wages and gaps in income due to strikes and unemployment—along with resulting hunger, health issues, and, at times, displacement. But the dream of financial sustainability entertained fleetingly here primarily sets up a stark contrast to the precarity with which Barcia and Cayetano Campos—and many of their colleagues in the anarchist press, as well as the Cuban separatist press—would have been familiar. For those intersecting (and sometimes conflicting) communities of print, pursuing the revolutionary possibilities of print or the growing business of journalism had become forking paths.

The article in *El Despertar* expressed little doubt that the big-business approach chosen by the Anglophone mass-circulation newspaper that

Barcia and Cayetano Campos observed most closely, Joseph Pulitzer's *New York World*, would continue to be traveled by many more publications: "No pasará mucho tiempo sin que en la plaza del *City Hall* de New York, centro del mercado periodístico de los Estados Unidos, sino del mundo, se levante otro edificio tan alto como el del periódico *The World.*" (It will not be long before, in the City Hall Plaza of New York, the center of the journalistic market of the United States, and indeed the world, another building as tall as that of the newspaper *The World* is built.)[2] The description references the gold-domed skyscraper that the *World* had opened in 1890 on Newspaper Row, a gleaming testament to that newspaper's commercial success. As discussed in chapter 2, *El Despertar* printed frequent commentary on the *World*—often to point out what Cayetano Campos and his team saw as the hypocrisy of that paper, which promised to combat political and business corruption for the masses. For the editors of *El Despertar*, the *World's* skyscraper in its prime location in Lower Manhattan just across the street from City Hall must have also signaled the extent of the challenge that he and others faced as they worked to "introducir ideas nuevas tan en contraposición con el llamado *orden* actual" (introduce new ideas so oppositional to the so-called current *order*).[3] How could he harness print's potential to enable social revolution at a time when, as contemporary anarchist Lucy Parsons put it in a speech reprinted in *El Despertar*, newspapers representated "una venenosa institución de las clases directoras" (a venomous institution of the ruling classes)?[4] Parsons's view, shared by many in the anarchist press, helps to elucidate the unique challenges and roles played by editors who operated at the margins of late nineteenth-century print culture. Many such editors struggled to maintain a presence in print, on which they relied to build their movement, to create and cultivate contributions, and ultimately to circulate the stories that would keep their dreams alive.

This chapter brings into focus the role of editorship, including some of its transformations, within the publishing community of late nineteenth-century Nueva York. Since the Spanish-language illustrated magazines of the 1870s, editors had played a key role in pursuing the possibilities of the changing world of print—especially to mediate a hemispheric audience that could mobilize support for Cuban and Puerto Rican independence from Spain and increase the visibility and status of Latin American culture on the hemispheric (and world) stage. Martí advanced the political potential of the Spanish-language illustrated magazine starting with his transformation of *La América* from an advertising circular into a vehicle for articulating earlier versions of the unified hemispheric community before he arrived at the term "Nuestra América."[5] In magazines such as *La América* and later *La Revista Ilustrada de Nueva York*—which owner-editor Eliás de Losada similarly transformed from an advertising circular to a means of circulating revolutionary ideas (including Martí's "Nuestra América, discussed in chapter 3)—editorship combined the pursuit of a hopeful vision for the future of Cuba, Puerto Rico, and Latin America with running a modest business funded through a combination of advertising, subscriptions, and, in some cases, job printing. By the 1890s, this model had begun to change. The Cuban separatist press ran largely on volunteer labor, as did the Spanish-language anarchist press that, at times, exhibited shared goals. Less able or less willing to rely on advertising, these 1890s publications scraped together the funds they needed to operate from subscriptions and donations. Understanding editorship within such publications sheds light on the possibilities and the limits of print at the end of the nineteenth century. During a period characterized by oppression of workers and immigrants, as well as violent treatment of racialized BIPOC communities, editorship even at the margins was itself a kind of privilege. It must be understood in relation to other forms of activism, such as public lectures, protests, and building archives and edited collections of suppressed histories. Such editorship also generated fleeting and fragmented forms of literary innovation—for which creating a market for recognized literary genres was never the goal.

This chapter's analysis pursues such understanding by situating the editorial team of *El Despertar*—which Barcia and Cayetano Campos led until around 1895, when both men moved on to other publications and Pedro Esteve became the primary editor—alongside the women editors of the Havana-based *Minerva*, which is known to have circulated in New York City during its first run in the late 1880s; its team of editors included E. T. Elvina (the pen name for Etelvina Zayas), Cecilia (the journalistic pseudonym for Úrsula Coimbra de Valverde), América Font, Cristina Ayala (née María Cristina Fragas), Natividad González, and K. Latina (the pen name used by Catalina Medina). In *El Despertar*, Cayetano

Campos worked to make the future of anarchism seem possible during a period of violent suppression of anarchist organizing and publishing. Along the way, the periodical updated notions of the potentiality of the newspaper and the magazine from the earlier nineteenth-century Nueva York. No longer associated with the workshop as a metaphor for collaboration, newspapers and magazines become a space for creating hope and envisioning revolutionary change as a long game. *Minerva* provides a reminder of the limits of print culture, especially for those whose access to publishing was systematically and violently suppressed. That publication's female editors received credit only as contributors, and many of them chose pen names to protect their identity in this paper centered on advocating for the rights of Black women. Both publications help to explain a turn toward making history within the publishing community of Nueva York, exemplified in Teófilo Domínguez's collection of biographical sketches on Afro-Cuban contributors to the Cuban independence movement, called *Figuras y figuritas: Ensayos biográficos* (Big and small figures: Biographical essays), and in Arturo Schomburg's writing and curation of texts from the African diaspora that would ultimately lead to the establishment of the New York Public Library's Schomburg Center for Research in Black Culture. Together, these examples demonstrate the unique forms and possibilities of editorship as "a practical way for marginalized groups to develop collective and collaborative forms of expression" during a period when Nueva York's writers and editors grappled with the limits of magazines and newspapers for mobilizing collaboration and collective action.[6] Editors and editorial teams cultivate dreams. They envision worlds that they seek to realize through print. They make publishing into a means of movement making. At times, they also push literature into new possible formations—many of which look quite different from the forms made familiar by the twentieth-century literary field. In such a context, as Jim Casey and Sarah Salter have noted, "editorship, like community, is always a work in progress."[7]

The examples provided by *El Despertar, Minerva*, and Domínguez's and Schomburg's efforts to rewrite history suggest that editors and the teams they bring together employed the democratic literary imagination in varying ways to make media a means of mobilizing participation in making a more just world. Continuing a pattern identified in the publications of Nueva York reaching back to the 1870s, editorial notes, articles, updates, lists of distribution agents, and sometimes advertising served as significant sites for articulating new ideas and possibilities. In addition, the examples brought together here also point to the need to look outside print. Indeed, Lucy Parsons's critique (quoted at the outset of this chapter) of newspapers as protecting elites provides a reminder that the work of mediating change—starting with circulating the stories that the best-resourced newspapers of Newspaper Row refused to tell— extended into the lecture hall, to protests in the street, into myriad private conversations that never made it to print, as well as to Domínguez's and Schomburg's prescient impulses to address absences and omissions in the archival record.

The Newspaper and the Book in *El Despertar*'s Democratic Literary Imagination

In contrast to the newspapers of the Cuban separatist press of the 1890s, which tended to depict Cuba's triumph over Spain as imminent, those in the anarchist press knew well that they were playing a long game for their own social revolution. References to the Haymarket Affair of 1886 continued to appear, as new acts to suppress the anarchist movement proliferated. In that context, the metaphors that the editorial team of *El Despertar* employed to depict the power of print changed. Eventually, the idea of the workshop that animated the most visionary papers of the Cuban separatist press, especially *Doctrina de Martí*, became a site of oppression without the possibility for change. As *El Despertar* recognized revolutionary change as a distant hope, the book, rather than the newspaper or magazine, began to appear as the preferred metaphor in the efforts of Cayetano Campos and his editorial team to inspire and mobilize a transitional community of anarchists. In *El Despertar*, editorship constitutes a role that reaches far beyond the editorial office; it is about fueling hope, building community, and finding opportunities to keep the movement alive. Barcia, Cayetano Campos, and Esteve played these roles successfully enough to make that newspaper "the longest-running Spanish-language anarchist periodical in nineteenth-century United States."[8]

In many ways, anarchist newspapers of the late nineteenth century, in Spanish and in English, offer some of the best examples of Nueva York's democratic literary imagination—even as the anarchists considered democracy a corrupted institution. As Kathy Ferguson has noted in her study of Anglophone anarchist print culture in the United States and Britain, "Most political movements have their publications, but . . . the anarchist movement gave birth to a remarkable number of publications, each a center of a radical community, usually with a small print run (a few thousand, commonly) but inviting an intense engagement."[9] Esteve described such engagement through the newspaper in a pamphlet on the 1893 Anarchist Conference published by the printing house of *El Despertar*: "One of the best and most economic tools for propaganda and agitation is the newspaper, whose columns can be used for education campaigns, and at the same time, so that those who work for our cause can communicate with each other."[10] Here, the revolutionary work performed by the newspapers echoes the image of the *taller* signaled in Cuban separatist newspapers like *Doctrina de Martí*. Both the physical print shop, which was a space of collaboration and a site for selling books and newspapers, and the newspaper are sites for conducting their collaborative work in progress.

The editing role in this type of publication included serving as a teacher and a source of inspiration. As Christopher J. Castañeda has noted, "Transnational anarchist print networks were built around people like Campos, who were artisans of print culture, writers, and thinkers, and committed individuals who shared ideas, reprinted famous anarchist essays, and reported news about labor, economics, and society as well as promoted subscriptions and collected funds."[11] In such roles, editors like Cayetano Campos needed to spark hope and creativity even in the face of daunting odds. A glimpse of this important work appears in a letter addressed to another contributor to the editorial collective of *El Despertar*, Gerardo Quintana, by Juan Bonilla, an organizer with Martí, Serra, and Figueroa of the Cuban separatist movement. Published in the April 15, 1893, issue of *El Despertar*, the letter advocates for independence for Cuba and also enters into the debate about anarchist methods by asserting that education, not violence, will propel social revolution. According to Bonilla, "Para implantar nuevos sistemas, hay que crear nuevos espíritus, á nuevas formas moldes nuevos." (In order to introduce new systems, new attitudes must be created, new forms and new molds.)[12] His words elucidate an important point of intersection between Nueva York's anarchist and Cuban separatist communities, even as they disagreed on the importance of nationalism in the struggle for equality: both believed in the importance of creativity, in the need to empower individuals to participate in creating new forms. Bonilla's letter also references an article published in the July 1892 issue of *La Revista Ilustrada de Nueva York*, further demonstrating the overlap between these two communities of print.

Yet, as *El Despertar*'s editors assumed the wide-ranging responsibilities of editors pursing revolutionary change, the metaphor of the workshop appeared to reach the end of its usefulness as they grappled with the rise of what one article called the "industria periodística" (journalistic industry).[13] A series of articles published by Cayetano Campos in 1894, called "El literato por fuerza" (The man of letters by force), shows him grappling with the challenge of realizing the transformative potential of print, in contrast to increasingly prevalent profit-driven models in the writing of literature in particular. For those writing under such conditions, "la literatura es un arte mecánico sujeto á la fría imitación de un modelo y en el que para nada entra la inspiración y el pensamiento" (literature is a mechanical art subject to the cold imitation of a model, and in which inspiration and thought do not enter at all).[14] Cayetano Campos's language demonstrates his priorities centered on the democratic literary imagination as a means of imagining and mobilizing for a more just world in contrast to what he depicts here as the loss of originality, inspiration and thought in an approach to literature that has become cold and mechanical. The references to alienated work recast the workshop as a site of oppression rather than of creativity and collaboration: "Creo firmamente que el taller es un presidio y que el trabajador no es otra cosa sino un humilde y abyecto esclavo." (I firmly believe that the workshop is a prison and that the worker is nothing more than a humble and abject slave.)[15] Cayetano Campos's concern is not only about the experience of individual workers, in which he includes writers whose work has been reduced to writing for profit. As he indicates in another article in his series on literature, this literary mechanization has also threatened the very potentiality of print, which he continues to acknowledge as an "arma potente" (powerful weapon) even though it has fallen "en manos de esos desalmados" (into the hands of those heartless ones) of the industrial press.[16]

Additional reflections in *El Despertar* extend Cayetano Campos's ideas about literary writing into print culture more broadly. An article signed Palmiro de Lidia (the pen name for Cuban Adrián del Valle) offers a telling articulation of the problem of capitalist consolidation in the world of print: "Cada periódico se convierte en almacén ambulante de la opinion que más convenga á sus mercantiles intereses." (Each newspaper becomes a mobile shop for the opinion that best suits its mercantile interests.)[17] The image of the mobile shop contrasts sharply with the earlier hopeful views of the potential of print—from the mobile libraries of *La Revista Ilustrada de Nueva York* to the collaborative workshops of *Doctrina de Martí*.

In the face of this looming loss of print as a lever of change, *El Despertar* responds with characteristic creativity and determination, providing a means of conceptualizing its unfinished social revolution as a book still being written. In a 1901 article, prominent anarchist theorist Ricardo Mella appeals to his community of "propagadores de ideales nuevos" (propagators of new ideas) with another metaphor, centered on the book: "Hay un libro inmenso, más eloquente que ninguno: el libro de todos, de la experiencia de todos." (There is an immense book, more eloquent than any: the book of all, of the experience of all.)[18] As he emphasizes the need to combine theory and practice, knowledge and action, Mella initially appears to imply that this is a book already written, waiting to be read: "Que vayan unos cuantos á buscar y rebuscar entre las páginas del pobre saber humano la esencia misma de todas las razones." (Let a few go to search and search again through the pages of poor human knowledge for the very essence of all reasons.)[19] But as the description continues, it becomes clear that this book is not yet completed; many of the reasons for human suffering are not yet recognized and addressed: "Siempre la incontable muchedumbre quedaráse á obscuras si esas razones no se las escribe en el libro universal de la realidad ambiente, de la práctica cotidiana." (Always the innumerable crowd will remain in the dark if these reasons are not written in the universal book of environmental reality, of everyday practice.)[20] The invitation offered by Mella's description is not simply to read this book, but also to contemplate its vast dimensions and power, and ultimately to help create it: "Larga, muy larga, será quizá esta obra. Tan larga como se quiera, demanda toda nuestra paciencia y toda nuestra perseverancia.

Es así como se afirma un método y es así como quisiéramos ver á cada momento traducido el ideal." (Long, very long, perhaps this work will be. As long as you want, it demands all our patience all our perseverance. This is how a method is affirmed and that is how we would like to see the ideal translated at every moment.)²¹ Mella emphasizes the role of print as a means, not an end in itself. Editorship, in this context, is a vast and shifting role—as much about organizing and educating as it is about overseeing the contents of the printed page. To this list of tasks, Mella's choice of words also adds translation, implying an ethical imperative to recognize and negotiate cultural difference. These ongoing practices capture the idea of the work in progress that we have seen throughout the publications of nineteenth-century Nueva York.

Another example of editing as work in progress appears in the Havana-based periodical *Minerva*, an extraordinary publication from the late 1880s published by and for Afro-Cuban women, which circulated throughout the network of Nueva York.

Minerva's Letters of Hope

Founded in Havana in 1888, the first issue of *Minerva* offers another model of editorship from the margins of print culture—in the context of censorship, violent repression, and limited access to print.²² Nominally, *Minerva*'s editors were men: Miguel Guala and Enrique Cos. However, *Minerva* likely advertised these men as the magazine's editors because women could not legally hold public positions in Cuba at the time. According to María del Carmen Barcia Zequeira, in practice, "the magazine was edited by a group of women who, although they only appeared listed as collaborators, were actually in charge of preparing the different sections."²³ Although the biographical details of many of these women have yet to be uncovered, what we know about Cristina Ayala and Cecilia provides an indication of *Minerva*'s connections to Nueva York and its publications' interlocutors, especially in Cuba's Black press.²⁴ Ayala was born enslaved in 1856. Following emancipation in Cuba in 1886, she became a leader among "a small but dynamic group of aspirational Black women" who set out to "break with the social stigma of enslavement in order to gain recognition as racial equals."²⁵ A teacher, poet, and political organizer, Ayala contributed to several publications, including

El Pueblo Libera and *El Sufragista*, as well as *Minerva*. Similarly, Cecilia, who was a musician as well as a writer and educator, contributed to a variety of publications within Cuba's late nineteenth-century Black press, including *La Fraternidad*. The child of a Black mother and White father, she grew up in a community of free people of color in Cienfuegos, and she devoted her career to advancing Black women's rights in Cuban society. Along with these and other Black women leaders and political organizers based in Cuba, the magazine also brought together a network of contributors, readers, and distribution agents that extended *Minerva*'s reach outside Cuba, especially to New York City, Key West, and Tampa.[26] Its most famous contributors from those cities were Rafael Serra and Martín Morúa Delgado. Among this women-led editorial team's contributions to the magazine—as well as those contributed by their interlocuters and readers within and outside Havana—*crónicas* and letters to the editor played key roles in creating a collective transnational voice through this "revista quincenal dedicada a la mujer de color" (biweekly magazine dedicated to women of color).

To pursue its mission to promote the education of Black women in Cuba and beyond, *Minerva* follows the format of many illustrated magazines of the period—such as *La Habana Elegante* and *La Revista Ilustrada de Nueva York*—including sections dedicated to politics, cultural criticism, society news, and poetry. An article in the November 30, 1888, issue, "Mis opiniones" (My opinions), by contributing editor América Font, explains, "La mujer debe aspirar, repito, á salir de la esclavitud de la ignorancia; y para poder ser libre, en este concepto, debe ser instruida; pues donde no hay instrucción no hay libertad." (Woman must aspire, I repeat, to leave the slavery of ignorance; and in order to be free, in this sense, she must be taught; for where there is no education there is no freedom.)[27] The metaphor that connects ignorance to slavery takes on particular weight in this publication whose editors and contributors included women who had themselves been enslaved. *Minerva*'s first issue, in October 1888, appeared only two years after the Spanish royal decree that abolished slavery on October 7, 1886. As Natividad González notes in her article "La ignorancia" in the December 15, 1888, issue, "La mujer de color . . . hace poco tiempo yacía sumida bajo el yugo vil de esclavitud, que hace poco tiempo era tratada con sumo despotismo, con . . . miles crueldades." (The woman of color . . . until recently lay subsumed

under the vile yoke of slavery, who until recently was treated with ut-
most despotism, with . . . thousands of cruelties.)[28] Here and throughout
Minerva, the magazine provides a space for acknowledging the painful
and very recent past of slavery along with its legacies of inequality that
the women of *Minerva* continue to confront.

Minerva intertwined its advocacy for women's education with discussions of marriage and family. An article titled "La familia" (The family)
that appeared in the December 30, 1888, issue reflected, "La esclavitud
jamás ha producido esposas, sino concubinas; mas ya que pasó la servidumbre, pase también la degradación." (Slavery has never produced
wives, but concubines; but now that servitude is over, so is the degrada-
tion.)[29] In that context of recent and hard-won liberty, the magazine
embraces "la alta misión de constituir la familia" (the high mission of
establishing the family), including the role as "la que debe inculcar en el
tierno corazón de sus hijos las ideas de orden, de moralidad y de amor
al prójimo" (the one who must inculcate in the tender hearts of her
children the ideas of order, morality, and love of one's neighbor).[30] A
combination of what Font calls "la virtud y la instrucción" (virtue and
education) are the means of empowerment for Black women in Cuba
and beyond.[31]

It is clear throughout the pages of *Minerva* that the publication plays
a vital role for its writers and readers. A letter from a reader in the April
15, 1889, issue, signed La Güinera, expresses her joy and relief at finding a
copy of *Minerva*. She describes the "entusiasmo que se había apoderado
de mi corazón al leer esos buenos artículos que tanto honor hacen á
nuestra raza, y esas bellísimas poesías donde he admirado el talento y la
cultura" (enthusiasm that had taken hold of my heart to read those great
articles that do so much to honor our race, and those beautiful poems
in which I have admired talent and culture).[32] The publication's display
of Afro-Cuban women's talent and intellect is a welcome source of joy.
The reader goes on to explain that she was so moved by an article in the
preceding issue that "me ha impulsado á escribir hoy" (it has prompted
me to write today).[33] Quoting an article from the previous issue, she
applauds its assertion "que la prensa ilustrada sabe que la clase de color
viene con sus propios esfuerzos trabajando por la emancipación de la
ignorancia" (that the illustrated press know that the class of color comes
with its own efforts working for the emancipation from ignorance).[34]

This letter from a reader shows a writer-reader exchange that celebrates *Minerva*'s contributions to the illustrated press in service of uplifting Afro-Cuban women. She closes by addressing the magazine's contributors: "Proseguid, distinguidas damas, pensad que vuestros buenos trabajos se esperan con anhelo, se leen con sumo gusto y se aprecian en lo que valen." (Proceed, distinguished ladies, know that your good works are eagerly awaited, read with great pleasure, and appreciated for all they are worth.)[35] Creating and inspiring their community appear here as key functions of this editorial collective's work.

The magazine's *crónicas* play a key role in building and celebrating a much-needed community by and for Black women within the magazine. *Minerva*'s editor in charge of contributing the society news associated with the *crónica* was Elvina. Although Elvina echoes many *cronistas* in claiming that her section of the magazine is "la más insignificante, como insignificante es quien la escribe" (the most insignificant because the one who writes it is insignificant), it is actually the heart of the magazine.[36] In Elvina's columns, updates on community marriages, club meetings, cultural events, and new publications provide the magazine's most constant window on its community. In addition, she provides regular reflections on the progress and challenges of the magazine—as front-page editorial notes often did in the publications of Nueva York.

In her installment in *Minerva*'s December 30, 1888, issue, Elvina recognizes the team of women who run the publication, extending "mi felicitación al Director de este quincenal, y á sue [sic] redactores masculinos; pero muy especialmente á mis hermanas en colaboración, *Cecilia, Onatina*, America Font, Lucrecia González, y Cristina Ayala, Natividad González . . . y á la *debutante* en el presente, que oculta su nombre bajo el anagrama de *K. Latina*" (my congratulations to the Director of this biweekly magazine, and to its male editors; but especially to my sisters in collaboration, Cecilia, Onatina, America Font, Lucrecia González, and Cristina Ayala, Natividad González . . . and to the debutante in the present issue, who conceals her name under the anagram K. Latina).[37] Distinguishing between the men named as the publication's editors and its women contributors, Elvina promotes her "hermanas en colaboración" as the real power behind the magazine: "Todo lo que es MINERVA . . . se lo debe á ese grupo, á esa pléyade de damas, ilustres dos veces por sus virtudes é inteligencias, y una vez más ilustres porque desechando pueriles temores no negaror su valiosa ayuda . . . para esta modesta publicación." (All that is MINERVA . . . is owed to that group, to that Pleiades of ladies, illustrious twice for their virtues and intelligences, and again more illustrious because, discarding childish fears, they did not withhold their valuable support . . . for this modest publication.)[38] Her description of these women depicts them as models of the twin pillars of virtue and intelligence on which *Minerva* builds its case for advancing Black women's education. In addition, she recognizes the courage of these women in putting their voices in print.

The prevalent use of pen names in *Minerva* indicates something of the risks these women faced. As Nancy Mirabal has noted, "There was a reason why Afro-Cuban women did not sign their names. It was dangerous to express their views openly in such a public medium. The women who wrote for *Minerva* were harassed, intimidated and threatened with jail and exile."[39] For example, Elvina indicates in one of her articles that she has told Cos that concealing her identity behind the pen name E. T. Elvina "es condición *sine qua non*, para escribirle esta seción [*sic*] del periódico" (is a condition *sine qua non* for writing this section of the newspaper for him).[40] Despite Elvina's insistence here, she does reference her real first name at the outset of her "Notas quincenales" in the December 15, 1888, issue. (In that same issue, a front-page portrait of Cecilia on the cover identifies her as Úrsula Coimbra de Valverde.[41]) We do not know why Elvina changed her position, but it is not likely that she did so out of a sense of reduced danger. As Elvina herself noted in a reflection published just two weeks earlier, "Difícil es la misión de la prensa en nuestra raza." (The mission of the press is difficult in our race.)[42] Although she does not elaborate on the reasons, for her readers the risks as well as the possibilities of this groundbreaking publication that circulated the ideas, concerns, and hopes of its hemispheric network of Black women editors, writers, and readers would have been clear.

Elvina's weekly *crónica* serves as a primary site in the magazine for building a kind of transnational community and support network. We see displayed within her columns the friendship of the magazine's women editors. When one of these women, Cecilia, loses her baby in childbirth and nearly dies herself, Elvina expresses her heartfelt condolences and concern: "Comienzo á estas notas bajo la impresión de dolor, que me causa el estado de mi distinguida amiga é ilustrada colaboradora de MINERVA, *Cecilia*." (I begin these notes with a feeling of sorrow, caused by the state of my distinguished friend and enlightened contributor to MINERVA, Cecilia.)[43] Her column is also a site from which she connects *Minerva* to other publications in Cuba and abroad. In the December 30, 1888, issue, for example, she includes an enthusiastic review of a new publication in Key West, *Revista Popular*, directed by Martín Morúa Delgado. She explains the significance of this publication that "no vendrá á ser . . . un periódico más, no; vendrá á ser una publicación que acreditará el movimiento intelectual que en nuestra raza viénese operando de manera ventajosa en el actual momento" (will not become one more newspaper, no; it will become a publication that will accredit the intellectual movement that in our race is operating in an advantageous way at the present time).[44] As she sends *Revista Popular* "en nombre de MINERVA . . . mi saludo á la *Revista*, deseándolo todo género de prosperidades" (on behalf of MINERVA . . . my greetings to the Magazine, wishing you every prosperity), Elvina situates the new publication alongside her own as part of a vital, growing press by and for Afro-Cubans.[45]

Throughout *Minerva*, letters from readers also help to create a sense of a tight-knit, if also widespread, community. The November 30, 1888, issue devotes three pages to a letter from María Storini, who says that she was born enslaved in Cuba and since "he tenido la suerte de residir algún tiempo en algunas de las principales capitales extranjeras" (I have been fortunate enough to reside for some time in some of the major foreign capitals).[46] She shares her idea of creating a new organization dedicated to advancing Black women's education: "Debo decirle que, lectora asidua de su periódico, concebí la idea, desde que ví su primer número, de dar á luz un pensamiento que hace tiempo acarició con carácter de irrealizable." (I must tell you that, as an assiduous reader of your paper, I conceived the idea, from the moment I saw your first issue, of giving birth to a thought that I have long cherished as unrealizable.)[47] Storini's letter exemplifies the ideal of writer-reader collaboration that runs throughout the publications of Nueva York. The magazine inspires the reader to share an idea that she had previously deemed impossible, which the magazine, in turn, circulates in its pages. As Storini goes on to explain, "todas contribuiríamos con nuestro óbolo á la obra" (we would all provide our small contributions to the work).[48] *Minerva* becomes the means of making connections and spreading ideas for an end—in this case achieving Black women's rights and education—outside the magazine.

This role of the magazine in creating community, circulating possibilities, and strengthening actions to support the magazine's mission runs throughout the issues of *Minerva*. The magazine is a vehicle for affirming support for Black women's education, commiserating over individual challenges and loss, and at times providing mutual aid. Elvina uses her column for something like the latter purpose, for example, when she begins her December 15, 1888, column with an appeal for donations to help "una jóven de nuestra raza la cual es víctima de una terrible enfermedad: un *tumor canceroso* en el pecho izquierdo" (a young woman of our race who is the victim of a terrible illness: a cancerous tumor on her left breast).[49] She asks her readers to turn her words into action: "Yo espero, queridas hermanas . . . que no seréis sordas, y que contribuiréis con vuestro óbolo, por pequeño que sea, á aliviar á una hermana en desdicha." (I hope, dear sisters . . . that you will not be deaf, and that you will contribute with your resources, however small, to relieve a sister in distress.)[50] *Minerva* mobilizes help for those who need it, as part of its mission to support and advocate for Black women.

Returned from her sick leave, Cecilia offers a reflection called "Gratitud" (Gratitude) in the February 15, 1889, issue that characterizes the unique power of this publication. Thanking her colleagues for their support as she recovered from childbirth complications, she writes, "Me siento orgullosa de pertenecer á una raza que por sí sola y á costa de sacrificios, procura elevarse á la altura de las demás y lucha, trabaja y estudia para vencer." (I am proud to belong to a race that on its own and through sacrifice, seeks to rise to the level of others and struggles, works and studies to be victorious.)[51] Cecilia's words summarize the work of this magazine, which gives voice to the injustices of the past and empowers its contributors and readers to pursue "el camino de nuestra regeneración y de la gloria" (the path of our regeneration and glory).[52] Cecilia also recognizes the historic significance of the publication: "Gracias, incomparables hermanas, MINERVA ocupará un puesto predilecto en las páginas de la Historia." (Thank you, incomparable sisters, MINERVA will occupy a favorite place in the pages of history.)[53]

Like many of the publications of Nueva York, *Minerva* struggled to make ends meet, and ultimately only managed to stay in print for about a year. Adding to *Minerva*'s challenges was the fact that "the colonial Spanish government did not take kindly to the public critiques of slavery, racism, and the demands for Cuban independence, especially from Afro-Cuban women."[54] In the January 26, 1889, installment of her "Notas quincenales," Elvina notes that "nuestro modesto quincenal, nuestra pobre MINERVA, ha estado amenazada de muerte" (our modest biweekly magazine, our poor MINERVA, has been threatened with death).[55] While the magazine survived apparent economic and political difficulties at that time, it ceased publication about six months later, publishing its final issue on July 19, 1889. Its short-lived run makes it no less significant as a publication that modeled an approach to collective editorship by and for women. It also provides an indication of the limits of print. For, as the women of *Minerva* acknowledged, the ability to circulate their ideas in print was a rare privilege that involved risks and sacrifices. It could not be the only means of advocating for equality.

Within the publishing community of Nueva York, in the decade after *Minerva*'s first edition reached the end of its run, some editors, like Teófilo Domínguez, began to look toward history as a lever of change.

Making History in Teófilo Domínguez's *Figuras y figuritas*

Domínguez's *Figuras y figuritas* demonstrates an urgent awareness of the need to rewrite the archival record as part of the effort to build a more just future in Cuba and beyond. In her analysis of this text, Mirabal offers a helpful overview of this collection of short biographies of Afro-Cubans who contributed to the Cuban and Puerto Rican independence movement: "Of the seven profiled, four—Rafael Serra, Juan Bonilla, Margarito Gutiérrez, and Manuel de Jesús González—migrated, lived, and worked in New York. The other three, Joaquín Granados, Emilio Planas, and Julian González settled in Tampa."[56] Published in 1899, the book, whose essays included some that circulated in Cuban separatist newspapers while the war was still underway, stands at the threshold between the conclusion of the war effort and the beginning of the work of building a new Cuban nation.

The preface to the book by Pedro Duarte, called "Carta abierta" (Open letter), reflects on the transitional moment in which it appeared in print. In the book's biographical sketches, Duarte notes, "No veo solamente un núcleo de hombres que han logrado adquirir y desarrollar conocimientos que han de serles muy útiles, sino que . . . sospecho que esos dignísimos ciudadanos serán futuros mentores de la generación que viene." (I see not only a nucleus of men who have managed to acquire and develop knowledge that has been very useful to them, . . . I suspect that these very worthy citizens will be future mentors of the coming generation.)[57] The history narrated by the book is well positioned to inform and inspire future generations, especially given Domínguez's selection of figures to profile: "Nadie con más razón, ni con más aptitudes que éllos podrán enseñar á vencer obstáculos, porque de seguro que serán ejemplos vivos y palpitantes para nuestra pobre y modesta juventud." (No one with more reason, or with more aptitude than they have, will be able to teach how to overcome obstacles, for they will surely be living and pulsating examples for our poor and modest youth.)[58] Domínguez's biographical essays reanimate a history with direct bearing on Cuba's unfolding future.

Domínguez was an active writer and editor in one of the major nodes of Nueva York's publishing network, Tampa, Florida. There, he directed the weekly political and literary magazine *El Sport* from 1897 to 1899. Domínguez's choice of figures to profile in his book reflects his perspective informed by his earlier editorial roles and his engagement with Nueva York's network. This is not a book that discusses contributions on the battlefields of Cuba. Rather, it catalogues the intellectual and political organizing contributions made by key Afro-Cuban writers and editors of the Spanish-language press dedicated to the independence movement.

Domínguez's first biographical essay, on Rafael Serra, strategically frames the historical narrative provided by the book. The text describes Serra's geographical trajectory, from his birth in Havana, Cuba, to his voluntary relocation in 1888 to Key West because of his support for Cuban independence, which ultimately led him to New York City, "donde Serra ha adquirido los más notables triunfos, tanto en la tribuna, como en el periodismo" (where Serra has acquired his most notable triumphs both on the public stage and in journalism).[59] As if to legitimate those successes, Domínguez highlights Serra's close associations with "los elementos más ilustres de Cuba que trabajaron por sacudir la dominación española en nuestra tierra" (the most illustrious elements of Cuba who worked to shake off Spanish domination in our land), including Máximo Gómez, Antonio Maceo, and José Martí (*FF*, xvi). He was "uno de los que formó parte de aquel heróico contingente de abnegados patriotas" (one of those who formed that heroic contingent of self-sacrificing patriots), when Gómez and Maceo launched an ultimately unsuccessful effort to invade Cuba in 1885 and 1886 (*FF*, xvi). And he "tomó parte activa" (took an active part) in the founding of the Partido Revolucionario Cubano and its newspaper *Patria*, while also working "en unión de Martí y otros patriotas" (in union with Martí and other patriots) to found the educational organization for Afro-Cuban and Afro-Puerto Rican workers, La Liga (*FF*, xvii). After establishing this close collaboration with the greatest figures of the Cuban independence movement, the essay introduces *Doctrina de Martí* as Serra's greatest contribution "de todas las empresas políticas con que Serra ha buzcado el triunfo de la buena causa" (of all the political enterprises with which Serra has pursued the triumph of the good cause) (*FF*, xix).

The choice to highlight *Doctrina de Martí* as Serra's most important endeavor, especially over *Patria*, is significant. As discussed in chapter 4, Serra founded *Doctrina de Martí* expressly for the purpose of including the Afro-Cuban and Afro-Puerto Rican perspectives on Cuba's future that *Patria*'s new leadership pushed out after Martí's death. As Jesse Hoffnung-Garskof has argued, after Tomás Estrada Palma took over the leadership of the Partido Revolucionario Cubano and gave Enrique José Varona the job of editing *Patria*, "the writers who surrounded Estrada Palma told the history of the movement in ways that emphasized the sacrifices of the heroic white professionals while reducing blacks and artisans to passive roles."[60] Moreover, Domínguez's account reverses the ongoing erasure of Afro-Cuban and Afro-Puerto Rican contributions to Cuban independence, making *Doctrina de Martí* supersede *Patria* as the publication that "vino á sostener enhiesta la bandera del *Partido Revolucionario Cubano* propagando entre el pueblo, ó sean los distintos elementos de Cuba, las salvadoras doctrinas del apóstol caído: *La Republica Cordial, con todos, y para todos*" (came to hold the flag of the Cuban Revolutionary Party, propagating among the people, or the different elements of Cuba, the saving doctrines of the fallen apostle: The amiable republic, with all and for all) (*FF*, xix–xx). Domínguez does not miss the opportunity to describe this role for *Doctrina de Martí* in terms of its historical significance. Through *Doctrina de Martí*, Serra "añadió á la larga historia de su vida política páginas brillantes" (added brilliant pages to the long history of his political life) (*FF*, xx). *Doctrina de Martí* appears in this account as the true voice of the values centered on the idea of racial and economic justice that Serra helped to construct with Martí, Figueroa, Bonilla, and others.

The remaining six biographical sketches continue to elaborate the contributions of the publications of the Cuban separatist press that were most committed to racial and economic equality. They include Key West's *El Pueblo* and *Revista Popular* (cited in *Minerva* as an important new vehicle for Afro-Cuban thought and political organizing). Domínguez's essay on Joaquín Granados, who contributed to both publications, among others in Key West and Tampa—in addition to serving as the director of two important Cuban publications, the Havana-based newspaper *La Fraternidad* and the Matanzas-based weekly *El Progreso*—emphasizes the enormous obstacles that Granados "surgió, construyéndose á sí mismo por entre la ruína moral de nuestro pueblo en época tenebrosa y de triste recordación" (emerged, pulling himself up out of the moral ruin of our people in a dark and sadly remembered time) (*FF*, xxvi). Born to enslaved parents and raised by a family with minimal resources that was unable or unwilling to pay for his education, Granados "empezó á instruirse de propios esfuerzos; adquiriendo un libro hoy y otro después, con la abnegación propia de quien desea vencer todos los obstáculos" (began to instruct himself by his own efforts; acquiring a book today and another later, with the self-sacrifice of one who wishes to overcome all obstacles) (*FF*, xxvii). This self-determination and refusal to accept limits led Granados to demonstrate "desde muy jóven . . . sus facultades de periodista en numerosos trabajos de colaboración" (from a very young age . . . his faculties as a journalist in numerous collaborations) and ultimately to become "escritor de nota [que] á menudo era solicitado para empresas en que necesitábase su concurso valioso" (a writer of note [who] was often called upon for undertakings in which his valuable assistance was needed) (*FF*, xxvii). As his support for Cuban independence led him from Cuba to Key West and ultimately to Tampa, he became an "incansable defensor de la clase proletaria" (tireless defender of the working class) and an accomplished writer of prose and poetry "que son fiel expresión de la exquisita sensibilidad de su alma pura" (that are faithful expressions of the refined sensibility of his pure soul) (*FF*, xxix). Against all odds, Granados makes himself into an accomplished intellectual, organizer, and poet.

The essay on Juan Bonilla, who was born in Key West and moved to New York City in 1881, highlights his contributions to a range of publications in Havana, including *La Fraternidad, La Igualdad,* and *Minerva*; Key West, including *Revista Popular*; and New York City, where he wrote for *Doctrina de Martí* and the *New York Age*, in addition to serving as the secretary of La Liga. Domínguez positions Bonilla's wide-ranging contributions as the direct result of his close collaboration with Martí: "Todo el que haya tenido la dicha de poder apreciar de cerca, los buenos ejemplos que el único apóstol cubano de nuestros dias José Martí, supo inculcarles á los que tuvo á su lado . . . encontrará tres figuras salientes entre sus discípulos: Gonzalo de Quesada, Rafael Serra y Juan Bonilla." (Everyone who has had the joy of being able to appreciate closely, the good examples that the only Cuban apostle of our days José Martí knew how to instill in those he kept at his side . . . will find three outstanding figures among his disciples: Gonzalo de Quesada, Rafael Serra and Juan Bonilla) (*FF*, xxxviii). In that context, "Bonilla pertenece á esa clase de hombres que viven para el pueblo, no del pueblo" (Bonilla belongs to that class of men who live for the people, not by the people) (*FF*, xxxviii). As in the previous essays, Bonilla and the publications that promoted racial and economic equality to which he contributed appear as the most important contributors to the independence movement.

The final essay of the book, on Manuel de J. González, another leader of La Liga in New York City who also contributed to *Patria* and *Doctrina de Martí* in New York and *La Fraternidad* in Havana, situates González's contributions within a larger set of themes. This essay consists primarily of a reflection provided by Serra, who notes that "lo mismo que en el campo de la guerra material, pasa en el campo de las ideas donde siempe [*sic*] con entereza de corazón luchan los ménos por obtener el mayor grado de felicidad posible para todos los hombres" (as in the field of material warfare, it happens in the field of ideas where always with fortitude of heart a small minority fight to obtain the greatest possible degree of happiness for all men) (*FF*, lxv–lxvi). The comparison emphasizes the significance of intellectual rather than battlefield contributions to the separatist movement. It also amplifies the book's careful framing of its Afro-Cuban subjects as the most important architects of the ideals and values that underpin both the war against Spain and the nation-building work that was then underway. These are the figures, the book suggests, who are best positioned to realize the potential of the revolution as envisioned by Martí:

En esta lucha que desde los primeros años de nuestra vida hemos venido librando tanto contra el egoismo y la vanidad que son el gérmen de la tiranía del hombre contra hombre, como contra la ignorancia y la apatía . . . en esta lucha empeñada contra los vicios que corroen á opresores y oprimidos, hemos tenido ocasión de conocer la entereza y flaqueza de cada uno de los hombres con quienes hemos tenido necesidad de unirnos.

(In this struggle that from the first years of our life we have been waging both against selfishness and vanity, which are the seed of man's tyranny against man, and against ignorance and apathy, which are the origin of abjection, of misery, from the indifference and apathy . . . in this hard-won struggle against the vices that corrode the oppressors and the oppressed, we have had the opportunity to know the integrity and weakness of each of the men with whom we have had need to unite.) (*FF*, lxvi)

Serra claims he writes these words to demonstrate his ability to recognize in González "la gracia del talento y una existencia enriquecida de virtudes" (the grace of talent and an existence enriched by virtues); in addition, they reveal a pattern demonstrated throughout *Figuras y figuritas* (*FF*, lxvi). The struggle that so many of these figures encountered "desde los primeros años de nuestra vida" (from the first years of our life) is rooted in the racism and oppression—which Serra links here to egoism, vanity, ignorance, and apathy—that they all faced. With the wisdom of someone who knows from deep experience what it takes to cast off such deeply rooted injustices, Serra also references the vices that "corroen á opresores y oprimidos" (corrode oppressors and oppressed), which test the strengths and weakness of each individual. Only those who are true leaders like González and the others featured in the book, Serra suggests, have the strength and courage to come together to fight enormous obstacles and prevalent distractions.

The conclusion to *Figuras and figuritas* makes explicit the book's approach to making history:

> La historia íntima de un pueblo, ó de una clase social, no es posible llegar á su íntegro conocimiento si quedan ignorados ciertos detalles, los que pareciendo insignificantes á primera vista, á poco que se medite, sobre la importancia relativa que interesa al gran todo, viene la comprensibilidad natural, indicando que, la omisión de los mismos más bien obstaculizan el análisis que se intentare.

> (The intimate history of a people, or of a social class, cannot possibly reach full knowledge if certain details are ignored, those that seeming insignificant at first sight, when one meditates a little, on the relative importance that concerns the great whole, bring natural comprehensibility, indicating that, the omission of those very details rather hinders the analysis being attempted.) (*FF*, lxxiii)

The statement offers a prescient assessment of the consequences of suppressed histories. Domínguez makes a case for uncovering the details that have been relegated to the shadows, deemed insignificant, suggesting instead that they hold the key to true understanding. He is also quite clear that the overlooked history that he addresses here is Afro-Cuban history: "Pocas veces hemos visto que se hayan tenido en cuenta las grandes dificultades que halló en su camino la raza de color para mejorar sus condiciones morales y materiales." (Seldom have we seen any consideration of the great difficulties encountered by the race of color in improving its moral and material conditions) (*FF*, lxxiii). Domínguez's book boldly identifies the work that remains to be done in the new Cuban republic after "tres largos siglos de servidumbre" (three long centuries of servitude) and names the men of *Figuras y figuritas* as both heroes of Cuban history and leaders of the path forward for Cuba (*FF*, lxxv).

Much like the publications of Nueva York and its network, history from this perspective is a means to a democratic end. The book concludes with a call to action: "Preparémonos para recibir la herencia de nuestros padres, porque á esta generación corresponde distribuirla entre hermanos con equidad." (Let us prepare ourselves to receive the inheritance of our fathers, for it belongs to this generation to distribute it among brothers and sisters with equity) (*FF*, lxxxiv). Rafael Serra, Juan Bonilla, Margarito Gutiérrez, Manuel de Jesús González, Joaquín Granados, Emilio Planas, and Julian González appear in this book as the founding fathers of a Cuban nation that was still a work in progress. It was also work that could not be accomplished by Domínguez's editorship of newspapers alone. According to Mirabal, *Figuras y figuritas* reflects "a conscious decision to build [an] archive and insure Afro-Cuban male historical relevance and visibility within an exile and immigrant community that perpetually sought to dimmish their intellectual and political contributions."[61] By the turn of the twentieth century, writing history constituted an increasingly urgent part of the work to advance Nueva York's commitment to equality, which Schomburg also took up.

Activating the Archive in Schomburg's Letters to the Editor and *Crónicas*

Schomburg never served as an editor, but his writing and notion of the archive as a site for public engagement align with and extend Nueva York's approach to editorship as a means of community building for powering efforts to achieve racial equality. His distinguished career, which led to the establishment of the New York Public Library collection that is now called the Schomburg Center for Research in Black Culture, began in the clubs and publications of the Cuban and Puerto Rican independence movement of New York City. Born in Puerto Rico in 1874, Schomburg moved to New York City in 1891, where he befriended Serra, met Martí, joined the Revolutionary Committee of Puerto Rico, and in 1892 co-founded the Club Las Dos Antillas (Two Islands Club) to advocate for Cuban and Puerto Rican independence. He served as its secretary for most of the 1890s and also reported the club's activities to *Patria*.[62] As scholars have discussed, the archiving and publishing practices that Schomburg learned in his teenage years through political organizing and publishing in late nineteenth-century Nueva York played a role in his later innovations in making history.[63] According to Laura Helton and Rafia Zafar, "The documentary zeal of the revolutionaries likely fed young Schomburg's penchant for archiving, and indeed some of the books in his collection date from this period, including Teófilo

Domínguez's *Figuras y figuritas*."[64] His participation in late nineteenth-century Nueva York also informed his later writings for the *New York Times*, the *New Century*, and *The Crisis*. Kevin Meehan has argued that Schomburg built on and updated "the nineteenth-century liberal romantic and nascent revolutionary nationalism of Martí" by bringing together African and Caribbean perspectives on decolonialism and activism.[65] Schomburg's method involved not only assembling his famous archive, but also organizing and writing to make it publicly available—both as a record of "historical agency in the black working masses" and a source of inspiration for ongoing cultural and political activism.[66]

The sixteen letters to the editor that Schomburg published in the *New York Times* between 1901 and 1905 provide a revealing window on the transformation that took place both for Schomburg and for Nueva York after the end of the Spanish-Cuban-American War. Since so many of the organizers of the Cuban and Puerto Rican independence movement moved back to Cuba or had died in the war, Nueva York underwent a major transformation almost overnight. As Helton and Zafar have noted, "After 1898 . . . Schomburg lost his political community, and like many other Afro-Cubans and Afro-Puerto Ricans frustrated by a stalled revolutionary project, he had to reinvent himself" while "watching racial injustices unfold simultaneously in Puerto Rico, Cuba, and the United States."[67] It was during that period that Schomburg offered his perspective to the *New York Times* on a range of topics related to his antiracist agenda, including US imperialism in Puerto Rico, lynching, and disenfranchisement of Black voters in the United States. In these letters, Schomburg extends Nueva York's project of pursuing social justice to new outlets and audiences.

In the pages of the *New York Times*, Schomburg positions himself as a voice of reason and a moral compass, calling on the United States to live up to its democratic ideals. At times, he states his position from the perspective of a Puerto Rican observing the aftermath of 1898 on the island.[68] In a letter entitled "Questions by a Porto Rican," published on August 9, 1902, Schomburg addresses the US Immigration Bureau policy of "prohibiting the coming to the United States of residents and natives of Porto Rico and the Philippines, except after passing the same examination as is enforced against other alien immigrants" who are not from territories of the United States.[69] His letter points out the unspoken prejudice behind such policies: "Does the citizen naturalized in Porto Rico and the citizen naturalized in Ohio differ in any degree of excellence? They are American citizens, and as such entitled to the privileges and immunities enjoyed by all citizens of the United States."[70] In this period preceding the 1917 Jones-Shafroth Act, which granted statutory US citizenship to Puerto Ricans, Schomburg calls attention to the second-class status afforded to "the Territories."[71] It was also a period when the *New York Times* and many other leading Anglophone dailies "promoted themes of underdevelopment, inferiority, and spectacle" in coverage of the new US territories even as so-called journalistic objectivity became the guiding principle of the news industry.[72] Schomburg repeatedly calls out such moments of racism and hypocrisy in his letters to the *New York Times*, as he addresses a range of contemporary issues, in measured and direct prose.

Several of his letters address lynching, as in his June 28, 1903, letter, "Lynching a Savage Relic," in which he observes, "The letter on 'The Law's Delay,' published by you on June 24, seems to have been written while the mind was under some heavy emotional impulses."[73] Schomburg takes issue with "the statement that the mob who lynched and burned a negro murderer at Wilmington, Del., was 'composed of average American citizens, of men very much like us.'"[74] Positioning himself on rational and moral higher ground, Schomburg argues,

> There is a feeling among Christian people when an outcast has committed a horrible murder that the majesty of the law ought to be allowed to punish him with the severest penalty. This is preferable to having "men like the rest of us" take the law in their hands, usurp established justice, and create in its place the partial administration of justice and punishment of culprits to the satisfaction of mob rule.[75]

He exposes this effort to disguise the horror and irrationality of mob rule as the will of "average American citizens." He makes visible the hypocrisy and immorality of such a claim: "Those who took part in the Wilmington (Del.) lynching 'constitute a representative American community,' says the letter, but the moral reasoning is weak: for what is the use of fixed principles of right and wrong if they are to be treated as mere abstractions and not as the practical guide of conduct?"[76] As Schomburg's question asks readers to consider the immorality of mob rule, it also invites consideration of the unspoken racial lines drawn by the claim of its link to "a representative American community."

Another powerful intervention appears in Schomburg's December 20, 1903, letter, "Union League Club's Actions," in which he points out the systemic racism experienced by Black communities of the US South: "The Constitutions of various Southern States are not only in open opposition to the United States Constitution, but actually in contravention of the very Declaration of Independence," enabling "notorious practices by which those States are depriving the negroes from the lawful exercise of their political and natural rights."[77] By asserting that these state constitutions defy the founding principles of the United States, Schomburg invites his readers to recognize their deeply cynical practices of voter disenfranchisement: "Who will deny that the various qualifications or clauses were not carefully drawn up by the offending States as traps to positively deprive the majority of negroes from the exercise of their political rights?"[78] As Schomburg's letters identify and ask readers to recognize instances of racism in the United States and its territories, they also reveal something of his view of the possibilities of print at this transitional stage in his career.

In his letter from October 18, 1903, "Tillman Trial and Verdict," Schomburg lauds as "just and fair criticism of how things can be done without impunity and without danger in South Carolina" a *Times* editorial that denounced the acquittal of South Carolina Lieutenant Governor James Tillman in his trial for the murder of newspaper editor Narciso Gener Gonsales.[79] Tillman fatally shot Gonsales for what he saw as irreparable harm to his reputation caused by Gonsales's newspaper, and he argued successfully in court that the murder was an act of self-defense. This trial, which pitted Tillman's sense of Southern honor against Gonsales's right to press freedom, inspires Schomburg to articulate his own view of the press:

> The press is like the safety valve of a boiler—always ready to blow through printed papers the abuses or unlawful acts done against the welfare, peace, and prosperity of the community. It checks the spirit of anarchy and tyranny, and like the bugle call, is ready to reverberate the sound of

danger and bring to the defense of the State the good citizens to remove the oppressor and re-establish the proper conditions of order.[80]

Schomburg's words describe the role that his own editorials play in the *Times*—as well as a view of the newspaper that reaches back to nineteenth-century Nueva York. By releasing and exposing the hot air of unlawful abuse and corruption through the solid material of print on paper, the press diffuses tensions and protects communities. When necessary, it also sounds the alarm, calling the community to action to fight off oppression. It is a vision of the press that Schomburg acknowledges in his letter "seems to be in peril of death in the State of South Carolina."[81]

Schomburg's run of letters to the editor written to *the New York Times* ends around 1905, and his subsequent writing appeared primarily in the Black press—suggesting another change in his approach by the 1910s. His article "General Evaristo Estenoz" for the July 1912 issue of *The Crisis* exhibits such a shift, while demonstrating how Schomburg carried on the legacy of nineteenth-century Nueva York. Vanessa Valdés has categorized Schomburg's essays from this period as *crónicas*, arguing that Schomburg made use of the genre because it "afforded a discursive space for the introduction of Spanish-speaking men of African descent in periodicals written and read by an Anglophone African diasporic audience."[82] Referencing Rotker, Valdés links Schomburg's essays to Martí's use of the genre to explore the idea that "journalism represented the democratization of writing because it was available to a broader audience than the book-buying public" and to include "a more subjective perspective, whereby the writer could reference his/her own personal narratives and emotions."[83] In essays like "General Evaristo Estenoz," we see Schomburg adapting the *crónica* genre to his own style. In contrast to the artistic license and emotional appeal that characterize Martí's *crónicas*, Schomburg does comparatively little editorializing. On the contrary, the same tactics that he uses in his letters to the editor published in the *New York Times*—focusing on facts, appealing to reason—largely drive the narrative in this essay. Yet the essay also shares in something of the vision and ambition that Martí brought to his *crónicas*. Within the pages of *The Crisis*, Schomburg opens up a new vista in the struggle for racial justice—inviting his Anglophone US readers, especially African

Americans—to see the struggle in Cuba as part of, or at least parallel to, their own.

Like many of Martí's *crónicas* from Nueva York, Schomburg's "General Evaristo Estenoz" starts with a news item: "The cable has flashed over the world the news that in Cuba General Evaristo Estenoz has taken up the gage of battle for the rights of his dark fellowmen, and that a crisis in Cuba is the result."[84] In addition, like Martí, who wrote many of his *crónicas* about the United States for an audience in Latin America, Schomburg needed to explain this news item to an audience—in this case Anglophone African American readers—that was likely unfamiliar with the news and its context. He references his late friend Serra, explaining that "soon after the close of the Cuban War and the establishment of the republic, he [Evaristo Estenoz] associated himself with Rafael Serra, the lamented Negro philosopher" (GEE, 143). Serra and Estenoz, Schomburg explains, became the architects of a new Independent Colored Party in Cuba, "its object being to promote the interests of the colored race, to urge the government to recognize their rights as citizens and taxpayers, and to accord them a fair proportion of the elective and appointive offices" (GEE, 143). As in his letters to the *New York Times*, Schomburg makes a rationally and morally grounded case for equality and justice, noting Serra's book *For Whites and Blacks*, which argues that "since both races had fought to make the republic possible, they should enjoy in common the burdens and the benefits of the country," is a founding text of the Independent Colored Party (GEE, 143). The essay also references the ICP's newspaper, *Previsión* (Foresight), edited by Estenoz, as an indication of the party's widespread popularity—and also perhaps a demonstration of the ideal role of the newspaper that Schomburg shared in the *New York Times*: "So great was the demand for this publication that the press could not turn out enough copies to supply the thousands of readers" (GEE, 143). The healthy demand for the party's newspaper serves as evidence of its democratic success.

The essay explains that the recent turmoil in Cuba is a result of the suppression of this party and its movement. As discussed in chapter 4, the source of this suppression is a contributor to nineteenth-century Nueva York's network, Martín Morúa Delgado: "When the government found that it could not deal with the situation, it . . . persuaded him to introduce in that body his notorious 'Amendment No. 17' of the electoral law, which, in effect, forbade the formation of any political party along racial lines" (GEE, 143). Schomburg is reserved in his criticism of Morúa Delgado: "For this perfidy Delgado was rewarded with the appointment to the portfolio of secretary of war, but he was ever afterward looked upon by the Negroes of Cuba as a Judas to his race. Although he did not, like Judas, go out and hang himself, he died, it is said, of a broken heart" (GEE, 143). While the essay depicts Morúa Delgado as a traitor to his race, it does so succinctly and unemotionally, suggesting that Morúa Delgado was a pawn in the travesty and offering him at least partial redemption through reference to his "broken heart."

The remainder of the essay describes the organized and violent repression of the ICP: "The Negroes began to realize, when their leaders were thrown into prison on the eve of election, that the white Cubans had determined that they should not have any representation save what was bestowed on them as a charity" (GEE, 143). We see here the themes of injustice and hypocrisy that also appeared in the *New York Times* letters:

> Many Cuban Negroes curse the dawn of the Republic. Negroes were welcomed in the time of oppression, in the time of hardship, during the days of the revolution, but in the days of peace and of white immigration they are deprived of positions, ostracized and made political outcasts. The Negro has done much for Cuba; Cuba has done nothing for the Negro. (GEE, 144)

This is a heart-wrenching observation coming from someone who experienced the hope and energy of nineteenth-century Nueva York firsthand. Far from realizing the dream of racial equality in a democratic republic, Afro-Cubans and Afro-Puerto Ricans view the new nation as a curse and an oppressive and extractive force: "The black men of Cuba have taken to the woods because conditions are intolerable, because, as my friend, the late Jose Martí the apostle of Cuban freedom, said: 'So long as there remains one injustice to repair in Cuba the revolutionary redemption has not finished its work'" (GEE, 144). Only in his concluding lines, in calling Martí a friend, does he choose to divulge something of his proximity to the situation in Cuba. He does so in the context of acknowledging that the work of Nueva York—namely, the dream of a democratic Cuban republic—is an unfinished project. This reference to work in progress might be the essay's tightest link to the *crónica* genre, even as it also diverges from the model of the genre forged in Nueva York. In this sense, "General Evaristo Estenoz" participates in the *crónica* genre for its optimistic attempt to write a better world into existence, no matter how terrible the odds might seem. Schomburg himself suggests something of this optimism in another *New York Times* letter, in which he reflects on the racism faced by Black Americans: "I believe that if we were to try to better things, try to be a little more optimistic in our views, these matters can be remedied: we may succeed in time in partly overcoming the existing conditions without sacrificing genuine affections for doubtful ones."[85] This radical hope might be considered one of the legacies of nineteenth-century Nueva York that Schomburg carried into both his writing and his work as a researcher and collector of archival materials relevant to Black history and culture. Like Domínguez through *Figuras y figuritas*, Schomburg seeks to put the past in conversation with the present. He does so by taking on a much broader swath of the archival record. As César Salgado has argued, Schomburg's collecting was ambitious both for its geographic and historical reach, as he set out to create "an archive that could redefine the Renaissance as the Afro-Latin cultural outcome of Southern European and North-and-Central African socioeconomic and migratory exchange and integration at the very moment of transatlantic expansion."[86] For Schomburg, recovering this history is necessary not simply to set the record straight, but also to blaze a path forward for achieving a more just world.[87]

From that perspective, we might reconsider one of Schomburg's most widely read texts, "The Negro Digs Up His Past," published in the March 1925 issue of *Survey Graphic* and reprinted that same year in *The New Negro*, edited by Alain Locke. The text, which might also be associated with the *crónica* genre, is a call to action, a manifesto, a declaration of a new possibility unfolding:

> History must restore what slavery took away, for it is the social damage of slavery that the present generations must repair and offset. So among the rising democratic millions we find the Negro thinking more collectively, more retrospectively than the rest, and apt out of the very pressure of the present to become the most enthusiastic antiquarian of them all.[88]

Schomburg's words recall Martí's tendency to write about possibilities unfolding: "Democratic millions" are rising and "thinking more collectively" as they look toward the past to address the challenges of the present. Schomburg also emphasizes the significance of the collective in his archival findings: "But weightier surely than any evidence of individual talent and scholarship could ever be, is the evidence of important collaboration and significant pioneer initiative in social service and reform, in the efforts toward race emancipation, colonization and race betterment" (NDHP, 671). His words emphasize the significance of collaboration to advance racial justice that has happened in the past, and he points out that this is an ongoing project that must be undertaken so that "the full story of human collaboration and interdependence may be told and realized" (NDHP, 672). He suggests that he is not looking for individual heroes of history, but rather the webs of organizing— networks, we might say, like that of nineteenth-century Nueva York. Given his experience in that very community, Schomburg would have known what to look for, and he also knew how to model such collaboration in his own work.

In this way, Schomburg's approach to researching Black history and curating an archive brings the democratic literary imagination of nineteenth-century Nueva York to the production of knowledge. Reflecting on his method, Helton and Zafar have argued,

> Schomburg's assemblage, vital to our understanding of the Black archive today, was not a solo endeavor but one forged over decades of collaborations: with his comrades in the Negro Society for Historical Research, with librarians at Fisk University and the 135th Street Branch, and with Afro-Cuban artists in the final years of his life. Schomburg models archive-building as a multisensory, collective, open-ended enterprise.[89]

Just as his predecessors (and, in some cases, friends and colleagues) in nineteenth-century Nueva York repurposed the magazine and newspaper forms to enable greater participation in the spread of ideas and in organizing to realize racial equality in Cuba and Puerto Rico, Schomburg remediates the archive to advance the antiracist project that was his life's work beyond the anticolonial struggle against Spain and into the twentieth century. As Valdés has observed of what Schomburg achieved as he brought his collection to the New York Public Library, "Whereas archives are generally conceived to be vaults, mausoleums that withhold knowledge from the general populace under the guise of protecting those items deemed highly valued, often by the state or a private corporate entity, Schomburg's collections reveal a democratic impulse."[90] The periodicals of Nueva York starting in the 1870s envisioned, in a newly networked world, creating a virtual space where editors, writers, printers, and readers could work together to realize a democratic vison in Cuba and beyond. Schomburg created another such space for facilitating new forms of collaboration to create a more just world—this time a physical one for the purpose of putting history in conversation with ongoing efforts to achieve racial equality—when he opened what was then called the Division of Negro Literature, History and Prints as a special collection of the 135th Street Branch Library in Harlem.

Schomburg's life's work anticipates and informs recent efforts to engage understudied texts and absences in the archival record, to which this book contributes. Some of the best articulations of the potentiality of such work come from scholars working within the digital humanities to interrogate colonial knowledge structures and rewrite the archival record to recover marginalized and suppressed histories and call attention to archival fragmentation, absences, and omissions that have contributed to the suppression of those histories. In their 2023 "US Latinx Digital Humanities Manifesto," Gabriela Baeza Ventura, María Eugenia Cotera, Linda García Merchant, Lorena Gauthereau, and Carolina Villarroel "incite/invite the DH community (scholars, programs, projects, libraries, organizations, and foundations) to seriously reflect on how all DH practitioners can reimagine relations of knowledge production in the digital age."[91] As a demonstration of collaborative idea sharing itself, the manifesto critiques the "underfunded, underrecognized, nontenured, at-risk" status of such work within the broader field of digital humanities and at the predominantly White institutions (PWIs) of higher learning that "often do not acknowledge the experience and cultural knowledge of Latinx scholars." It also articulates a hopeful path forward, drawing on the authors' deep collective experience in the recovery of archival materials relevant to the enduring history of Latinxs in the United States and in the use of Latinx digital humanities methods to engage researchers, students, and the public in archive creation and knowledge production.

Their list of eleven guiding principles of such work emphasizes that, in their approach, Latinx digital humanities "foregrounds relationships and community building over the development or implementation of digital tools" and "rejects extractive models of research and digital production. It engages communities not just as sources of 'data' but as partners in the production of knowledge." This is a vision of "knowledge made by and for communities in struggle [that] has the power to raise consciousness and transform practices of knowledge" and extends across various sites, including universities, K-12 schools, community organizations, libraries and more. The authors acknowledge that through this work

> we walk in the footsteps of intellectuals like Martha Cotera, founder of the Chicana Research and Learning Center, a major resource for information on Chicanas and women of color in the 1970s; Nicolás Kanellos, founder and director of Arte Público Press and Recovering the U.S. Hispanic Literary Heritage Program, who spearheaded the unified methods to locate, preserve, and make available the written legacy of Latinxa/os/x in the United States; and Arturo A. Schomburg, who established a massive repository on Black culture for the New York Public Library.

Following from this genealogy, we might consider Schomburg a proto-digital humanist—one who saw that as "certain chapters of American history will have to be reopened" (NDHP, 671), doing so will require not only new sources, but also new methods of increasing participation in the production of knowledge.

The forms of editorship in evidence in the publications of nineteenth-century Nueva York participate in this tradition of community collaboration and empowerment. It is a role most typically undertaken by teams to produce a publication in service of a broader vision. As such, editorship in nineteenth-century Nueva York joins the genealogy shared in "A US Latinx Digital Humanities Manifesto." Across the editorial, authorial, archival, and digital humanities projects described in this chapter, the final product—whether it's a magazine, an archival collection, or a digital tool or product—is always a means to an end. In that context, the literary itself transforms in ways that have flickered into view throughout this book. Sometimes the literary still takes the form of a familiar genre, such as a poem, or a novel, or a manifesto. But the literary also resides in that spark of imagination that fuels collective efforts to write the world that could be into existence—through forms and platforms that, like communities themselves, never stop changing. As scholars today, we can find such works of the democratic literary imagination in myriad forms within and outside the archival record, and they call on us, too, to become participants making democracy.

Afterword

In her 2023 book *Democracy Awakening*, US historian Heather Cox Richardson writes, "America is at a crossroads. A country that once stood as the global symbol of democracy has been teetering on the brink of authoritarianism."[1] Richardson roots this crisis in the nineteenth century, specifically in "the thinking behind the Confederacy—that people are inherently unequal and some should rule the rest."[2] Following his election to his first term in 2016, President Donald Trump "and his followers embraced the false past of the Confederates and insisted they were simply trying to follow the nation's traditional principles. Eventually, they tried to overturn the results of the 2020 presidential election to stay in power."[3] Their ideology and their actions stand in direct opposition to another thread of US history, whose origins Richardson locates in the beginnings of the nation itself:

> People in the U.S. had never lost sight of the promise of democracy because marginalized people had kept it in the forefront of the national experience. From the very first days of the new nation, minorities and women had consistently, persistently, and bravely insisted on their right to equality before the law and to a say in their government.[4]

Although always a work in progress, US democracy has served as a symbol of hope, a standard against which to demonstrate injustices, a means of making the case for social change.

As I familiarized myself with the publications of nineteenth-century Nueva York in writing this book, it struck me how much the United States played such roles for that community of writers and editors. I have returned many times to the passionate statement from an 1887 article in

La Revista Ilustrada de Nueva York that I included in the introduction: "Escribimos para nuestra raza, para nuestra patria inmensa, que es toda la grande América que fué hispana, que padeció bajo el poder colonial y que sigue padeciendo bajo sistemas que proclamamos como redentores." (We write for our people, for our immense homeland, which is all of the great America that was Spanish, which suffered under colonial power and that continues to suffer under systems that we proclaim as redeemers.)[5] I hear in these words, probably written by Nicanor Bolet Peraza, who fled the authoritarian regime of his home country in Venezuela, the burning determination that fueled that publication's project to create a better future for Cuba and Puerto Rico. Its editors and writers engaged in an ongoing anticolonial struggle against Spain, and advocated for the new nations of Latin America, where writers including Bolet Peraza and Martí were never able to find the press freedom that the United States afforded them—try as they did.

These writers saw hopeful models in US public education, press freedom, agriculture, and, to some degree, industry—even as those same models were also stunted or corrupted by the racism, sexism, and extreme wealth inequality of Gilded Age America. Most of the writers and editors of nineteenth-century Nueva York—most famously Martí—did not overlook these flaws. For many of them, the United States also represented a growing threat of exporting its racist structures and extending its imperialist reach further into Latin America. And yet, for those same writers and editors, the ideal of democracy met an urgent need, as Nueva York imagined and pursued its own democratic vision for the nations of nuestra América. With eyes wide open to its menacing dangers, these writers and editors also needed the United States to be a beacon of hope.

The publications of nineteenth-century Nueva York have led me to see in a different light the symbols of that hope located in Lower Manhattan, which I see regularly on my way to work, and which date back to the late nineteenth century. On the ferry from Hoboken, I pass the Statue of Liberty, whose arrival from France in 1885 both Bolet Peraza and Martí wrote about, as New York correspondents for publications that participated in Nueva York's network. They both represented the statue as a symbol of democratic possibility that reached far beyond the borders of the United States. The enormous statue of Benjamin Franklin referenced in chapter 1 still stands outside the buildings that now house my university. To me now, he reminds me of all the writers and publications from that neighborhood who existed in the shadows of the Anglophone mass press, for whom he served as a sort of figurehead. But I suspect that for the members of nineteenth-century Nueva York who lived and worked in that area and passed him regularly, he might also have been another source of hope—of the promise of democratic institutions that the writers and editors of Nueva York dedicated their lives to building through the work that they conducted on and off the printed page. In a sense, those monuments became more relevant to me—as the publications of nineteenth-century Nueva York began to feel urgently relevant as well.

I wrote this book because nineteenth-century Nueva York represents an important and previously overlooked part of the story of the emergence of literature and mass media in the United States. But I have also come to think that those who are continuing the struggle for just democracies today may need the writers and editors of nineteenth-century Nueva York. We need their hope, their wisdom, the lessons we might learn from their successes as well as their failures—and also the inspiration and energy that we might experience from the idea that democracy's struggle today could pick up where nineteenth-century Nueva York left off.

One of the clues that nineteenth-century Nueva York left behind was the work its participants carried out at the convergence of media, education, and democratic participation. It is telling that many of those who contributed to the publications of nineteenth-century Nueva York were also advocates of public education. They wrote treatises on the importance of education for women and people of color. Many participated in the institution known as La Liga de Instrucción, discussed in chapter 5, which was a night school for Afro-Cubans and Afro-Puerto Ricans founded by Serra in New York in 1890, versions of which also existed in Havana and Tampa. Martí briefly edited a children's magazine for the purpose of education, *La Edad de Oro* (The Golden Age). The democratic literary imagination of the publications and archival interventions of nineteenth-century Nueva York emerged in that context. Incipiently, they explored the possibility of what David M. Berry has called in a digital humanities context "the promise of a collective intellect" generated through "a society or association of actors who can think critically together, mediated through technology."[6] They did so within the limits of their own media moment, when access to print remained for the most part a privilege, even as they worked against that current. But those limits might also help us to recognize the limits and possibilities of our own media moment.

I will conclude with a few examples in which I see the legacy of nineteenth-century Nueva York in our digital age—and at a political moment when democracy in the United States and around the world is under attack. It is tempting to say that social media might realize the participatory aims of that community, but I would argue that the business models that enable the largest social media platforms to profit on division and on spreading misinformation make them more like a personalized, twenty-first-century version of the yellow press. To find the legacies of the publications of nineteenth-century Nueva York that made media a means of pursuing a democratic ideal, we need to look for the projects and platforms that sit at the intersection of media, education, and democratic participation in our digitally dominated media system.

Consider, for example, the Spanish-language podcast *Radio Ambulante* (Mobile Radio), hosted by Peruvian American novelist Daniel Alarcón, which "uses long-form audio journalism to tell important but neglected and under-reported Latin American and Latino stories."[7] In 2016, when *Radio Ambulante* joined National Public Radio (NPR) with a base in New York City, Alarcón stated in the press release,

> There are more than 50 million Spanish speakers living in the US, and we too are part of the "public" in "public radio." . . . It's exciting to be part of NPR, helping it sound a little bit more like America. NPR shares our journalistic values, our commitment to good storytelling, and our desire to innovate.[8]

Like so many of the innovators of nineteenth-century Nueva York who preceded him, Alarcón envisions a media community that centers the lives, communities, and innovations of Spanish speakers—asserting the hemispheric meaning of *America* in the process. One might say that *Radio Ambulante* realizes nineteenth-century Nueva York's vision of a hemispheric, Hispanophone print culture—in a digital context. As he put it in a 2013 interview, "One of the premises of *Radio Ambulante* is the idea that . . . political borders may be real, but cultural borders are much more fluid. And . . . with 55 million Latinos in the country, the United States is a Latin American country as well."[9] This podcast envisioned as a walking radio follows in the footsteps of the mobile library first articulated in *La Revista Ilustrada de Nueva York.*

A range of digital humanities projects aimed at increasing participation in the production of knowledge about marginalized and suppressed histories might also be considered efforts to extend the collaborative *taller* model into the digital age. They include the Colored Conventions Project, co-directed by P. Gabrielle Foreman and Jim Casey, and the Chicano por Mi Raza Digital Memory Project and Archive, founded by Maria Cotera and Linda García Merchant, both of which are designed to engage students and the public in continuing to expand the project. They also include new digital repositories, such as the University of Houston's Recovering the US Hispanic Literary Heritage Project's new "Periodicals in the US-Mexico Border Region" database, which provides free access to more than two hundred digitized publications from this region, and the Puerto Rican Literature Project, which provides access to poetic texts of Puerto Rico and the diaspora that "are currently located in various physical archives or have never been archived before."[10] Another example is Marissa López's Picturing Mexican America, a series of public humanities initiatives centered on a mobile app that "displays images of 19th century, Mexican Los Angeles to users based on their location."[11] The project website announces, "We're looking back at history to help us understand our present!"[12]

In New York City, a number of digital and public humanities initiatives—of which I can only provide a sampling here—might be said to have taken up Schomburg's vision of activating the archival record for scholars, artists, and the public. They include the work of Khalil Gibran Mohammed to increase the role of public research during his tenure at the New York Public Library's Schomburg Center for Research in Black Culture. CUNY's Centro de Estudios Puertorriqueños (CENTRO) under the leadership of Yomaira Figueroa-Vásquez is also a model of an archive and research center that prioritizes community engagement, through initiatives that include public workshops on family and community archiving, an interdisciplinary digital research and data hub, and a media team that partners with filmmakers and writers to produce educational media like *Puerto Rican Voices*, which recently won two Emmy Awards. At the Museum of the City of New York, Puffin Curator of Social Activism Sarah Seidman and Curator of Community Histories Angel "Monxo" Lopez are modeling community-centered publicly engaged approaches to New York City history, through exhibitions like *Changing the Face of Democracy: Shirley Chisholm at 100* and *Byzantine Bembé: New York by Manny Vega*. Teatro Pregones/Puerto Rican Travelling Theater preserves and disseminates narrative, history, and culture in non-academic and community-based settings. The Loisaida Center's exhibitions and annual festival provide public venues for activating and celebrating Nuyorican history. The Nuyorican Poets Café, undergoing at the time of this writing a major renovation of its historic space at 236 East Third Street, continues to engage established and aspiring poets through virtual and in-person readings and poetry slams. Historian and artist Kamau Ware's Black Gotham Experience offers walking tours and creates digital projects—such as *Buffalo Sonnet*, a digital comic book that reflects on the experience of Black veterans of the Spanish-Cuban-American War in the former San Juan Hill neighborhood of Manhattan—to "revisit untold and suppressed stories through a practice that invites people to walk, talk, and reimagine the past to expand public consciousness" and build "intentional experiences at the intersection of aesthetics and scholarship to learn, heal, and *remember together*."[13] Through their digital map, the Latino Catskills, Cristina Pérez Jiménez and J. Bret Maney are "resituating the rural Catskills region, located 100 miles northwest of New York City, as a generative space of Latino culture and identities."[14] In my own work, building on my New York City's Nineteenth-Century Spanish-Language Press digital mapping project, a team of colleagues and I have launched at Pace a new digital mapping platform for scholars and students, called The Ground Beneath Our Feet, dedicated to facilitating student participation and community collaboration in geospatial data curation and digital mapping projects that recognize our campus's location on unceded Lenape land near the African Burial Ground at the convergence of Chinatown, the Civic Center, the Financial District, and the Seaport, and uplift Lower Manhattan's previously obscured people, places, and events.

A few patterns emerge from these examples: they explore new ways of telling underrepresented stories, often through digital media, and with an interest, like that of their predecessors in nineteenth-century Nueva York, in mobilizing new communities. Most also do so by engaging students and/or the public in contributing these stories or participating in the production of knowledge through engagement with archival materials. Most are nonprofit or public endeavors that rely on federal and foundation funding, individual donations, and the support of an educational institution or library. It will not be easy to shape a different future for digital media that prioritizes democratic participation from these starting points, especially as many of them (universities, libraries, public media) are under attack from the very authoritarian threat identified by Richardson. Indeed, that reality is clearer than ever as I revise this afterword in April 2025, still reeling from the barrage of executive orders and cuts to federal funding designed to reign in these very institutions. To give one personal example, my own National Endowment for the Humanities (NEH) grant that funded, in part, the Ground Beneath Our Feet initiative at Pace was canceled along with many others as the Trump administration reoriented the agency's priorities to a "National Garden of Heroes" sculpture garden with its heroes to be drawn from an approved list. (None of the writers and editors considered in this book are on it, with the exception of Ben Franklin.)

As the fight to save democracy becomes more urgent daily, nineteenth-century Nueva York provides a reminder of the long history of the ongoing struggle to achieve antiracist, democratic ideals. Nueva York's participants provided significant steps along the way to the forms of democracy that our hemisphere—and our world—has yet to experience.

ACKNOWLEDGMENTS

This book, like the nineteenth-century Nueva York that it explores, would be nothing without the communities that have supported it and helped shape its ideas over its long development.

First, I thank my PhD advisor at Brown University, Stephanie Merrim, for always prioritizing creativity and courage in her own and her students' research. Special thanks also to Esther Whitfield and Kevin McLaughlin, and to colleagues Catalina Ocampo, Amy Vegari, Teresa Villa-Ignacio, Katie Chenoweth, John Funchion, Katerina Gonzalez Seligmann, and Genie Brinkema for invaluable conversations. Brown's Cogut Institute for the Humanities provided essential support, as did the Centro de Estudios Martianos in Havana, particularly Carmen Suárez León and Salvador Arías.

My engagement with media studies was enriched by my time as a postdoctoral Visiting Scholar in Comparative Media Studies at MIT. I am especially grateful to William Uricchio and David Thorburn for welcoming me into their intellectual community and encouraging this project—and to Julia Panko for our brainstorming sessions.

Two seminars at C19: Society for Nineteenth-Century Americanists biannual conferences also played important roles in the development of this project: "Latina/o Lives in the Hemispheric Century," led by Jesse Alemán and Maria A. Windell, and "The Hemispheric South and the (Un) Common Ground of Comparability," organized by Anna Brickhouse and Kirsten Silva Gruesz. These seminars not only provided essential feedback and research leads, but also brought me into the C19 community, which has influenced and encouraged my work, including John Alba Cutler, Carmen Lamas, Rodrigo Lazo, and Marissa López, who has been ever since an inspiring and generous mentor and collaborator. More recently, I am grateful to have been in conversation with Marissa, John, and Laura Lomas as a contributor to Cambridge University Press's *Latinx Literature in Transition* series, volume 2. Two collaborators in that volume, Renee

Hudson and María del Pilar Blanco, also informed my approach, and my chapter in the collection, "Modernism's Workshops: Printing Latinx Literary Modernities in New York City," helped me to develop my ideas about *Doctrina de Martí* from the perspective of its legacy in New York City's early twentieth-century Spanish-language press.

A National Endowment for the Humanities (NEH) Summer Scholar fellowship to attend the "City of Print: New York and the Periodical Press" Summer Institute led by Mark Noonan at CUNY's New York City College of Technology also greatly influenced this book, especially through conversations with Mark, Ayendy Bonifacio, Jim Casey, Joey Kim, Jean Lee Cole, Adam McKible, Sarah Salter, Jesse Schwarz, and Daniel Worden. Sarah and Jim subsequently organized an illuminating American Antiquarian Society symposium on "Editorship as Collaboration: Patterns of Practice in Multi-Ethnic Periodicals." A chapter that I contributed to an edited collection that resulted from that meeting, "Revolutionizing Women's Roles in the Late Nineteenth-Century Spanish-Language Press," in *Immigration and Exile Foreign-Language Press in the UK and in the US*, edited by Stéphanie Prévost and Bénédicte Deschamps, helped me to develop my ideas about *Revista Ilustrada de Cuba Libre*.

Another NEH Summer Institute at the University of Tampa, "The Immigrant Communities of Florida and José Martí in Cuban Independence and the Dawn of the American Century," led by James López and Denis Rey, gave me the opportunity to share and receive helpful feedback on a draft of chapter 4. Kenya Dworkin provided an energizing exchange of ideas at that event and afterward.

I am also grateful to the University of Houston's Recovering the US Hispanic Literary Heritage project for its foundational and ongoing work to index and make available historical Spanish-language texts published in the United States. Thank you also to Nicolás Kanellos, Gabriela Baeza Ventura, and Carolina Villarroel for their encouragement of this project.

I relied on many archives and special collections. Thank you to the staff at the Biblioteca Nacional José Martí in Havana, especially Araceli García Carranza and Orlando Freire Santana, and to Carmen Santillán and Pablo Luzzati at the Museo, Biblioteca y Archivo Histórico Municipal in San Isidro, Argentina. At Washington University in St. Louis, thank you to Micah Zeller and Clara Fehrenbach. Thank you also to the John Hay Library at Brown University; Butler Library at Columbia University; the

Manuscripts, Archives, and Rare Books Division, the Milstein Microform Collection, and the Vartan Gregorian Center for Research in the Humanities at the New York Public Library; the Elmer Holmes Bobst Library at New York University; and the Newberry Library in Chicago.

I am grateful to my incredible colleagues at Pace University who have provided advice and shared ideas, including Sarah Blackwood, Chris Campanioni, Sarah Cunningham, Stephanie Hsu, Maria Iacullo-Bird, Erica Johnson, Iride Lamartina-Lens, Meghana Nayak, Sid Ray, Eugene Richie, and Rebecca Tekula. A sabbatical and a book completion grant helped me through the final writing stages.

I have incorporated portions of two previously published articles into my introduction and chapter 3. Thank you to Oxford University Press and *American Literary History* for permission to reprint my article "American Alternatives: Participatory Futures of Print from New York's Nineteenth-Century Spanish-Language Press," which appeared in issue 30.4 (2018), pp. 677–702. Thank you to Duke University Press and *English Language Notes* for permission to reprint "Telephonic *Modernismo: Latinidad* and Hemispheric Print Culture in the Age of Electricity," which appeared in *English Language Notes*, issue 56.2 (2018), pp. 90–103. I am especially grateful to *American Literary History* editor Gordon Hutner for his attentive editing and to the guest editors of the *English Language Notes*, Jesse Alemán and Maria A. Windell, for the opportunity to explore their theme of "Latinx lives in hemispheric context."

In the final stretch of completing the manuscript, Jean Lee Cole, whom I first met through the "City of Print" NEH Summer Institute, provided invaluable editing. I am also very grateful to the anonymous reviewers of my manuscript, who were generous and engaged readers and provided thought-provoking and helpful comments. Thank you especially to Eric Zinner and Furqan Sayeed at New York University Press for understanding this project and supporting it so attentively.

Finally, I thank my family for their steadfast support: my parents, Ron and Lauren Kreitz, and Amy Kimball, Lisa Smith, and Murray Smith. My sons, Theo and Felix Smith, who love books as much as I do, have cheered me on through the final phases of this project. My husband, best friend, and partner in all things, Weston Smith, has encouraged with great patience, insight, and love every stage and more described here. Thank you for believing in me, always.

NOTES

INTRODUCTION

1 Nicanor Bolet Peraza, "Carta de Nueva York," *La Habana Elegante*, November 6, 1887, 4. The *Paris Herald* later became the *International Herald Tribune* and more recently the *International New York Times*.

2 Ibid.

3 Ibid.

4 On the Atlantic telegraph cable and its cultural significance despite its short-lived period of operation, see Supp-Montgomerie, *When the Medium Was the Mission*.

5 Gitelman, *Always Already New*, 27.

6 My use of the term "media system" draws on media studies. As Briggs and Burke explain, "To think in terms of a media system means emphasizing the division of labour between the different means of communication available in a given place and at a given time without forgetting . . . that old and new media can and do coexist and that different media may compete with or echo one another as well as complement one another." "Printing in Its Contexts," 19.

7 Mexico City, for example, appears as another important center of organizing and exchange of ideas in the Cuban independence movement in Muller, *Cuban Émigrés and Independence*; and Blanco's forthcoming *Modernist Laboratories* shows how the laboratory operated as a powerful metaphor specific to a Mexican context in late nineteenth-century scientific and *modernista* magazines in Mexico City. In addition, Valenzuela's forthcoming *Reading Centroamericanismo* recovers the role of Central American writers, including Nicaraguan Román Mayorga Rivas, in Spanish-language periodicals in Nueva York and beyond. Looking beyond Spanish-language publishing networks, two foundational texts on the multilingual nature of US print culture in the nineteenth century are Conolly-Smith, *Translating America*; and Mizruchi, *The Rise of Multicultural America*. A recent study that considers New York City's Yiddish press during a similar time frame, in which I found helpful parallels to the patterns of Nueva York discussed here, is Brinn, *A Revolution in Type*.

8 In my shifts in terminology in the preceding sentences—from Black, Indigenous, and people of color (BIPOC), to Afro-Cuban, to African American—and throughout this book, I seek to be attentive to geographical and temporal contexts. I also recognize the ongoing debate within Latinx studies about the use of "Black" versus "Afro-Latinx" to describe Latinxs of African descent, and I have

employed both of these terms with attention to the individuals and communities described in each case, as well as the context of my argument. I will discuss my use of the term "Latinx" later in this introduction.

9 Histories of Latin American journalism typically look to the early twentieth century for the beginning of a Latin American mass press, as in Rivera, *El escritor y la industria cultural*. My view of the Spanish-language press in the nineteenth-century United States and Latin America follows studies that have challenged the idea of a uniform march toward the realization of a mass press that arrived belatedly in Latin America. As Silva Gruesz has noted of the earlier nineteenth century, "Of the six cities in the New World with populations greater than 100,000 in 1825, four—Mexico City, Havana, Rio de Janeiro, and Bahia—were in Latin America, so the sheer numbers of readers and potential readers there is impressive." *Ambassadors of Culture*, 22–23. See also Mejías-López's discussion of the hybridity of reading publics in Europe and Latin American in *The Inverted Conquest*, 30.

10 Cutler, "Toward a Reading," 124–25.

11 Lamas, *The Latino Continuum*, 213–14.

12 Brickhouse, "The Black Legend of Texas," 735.

13 Kaestle and Radway, "A Framework," 16.

14 Fox, "Commentary," 643.

15 Ibid.

16 Lazo, "Introduction," 8.

17 Coronado, *A World Not to Come*; and López, *Chicano Nations* are powerful demonstrations of this point.

18 Coronado, *A World Not to Come*, 30.

19 That very neutrality is one of the sources of debate for those who see the term as one that should belong to the LGBTQ+ community. Another important limitation is the word's awkwardness to pronounce in Spanish, making it a term that privileges English speakers. In the context of debates centered on these and other objections to the term, I consider "Latinx" as a kind of imperfect placeholder, as our language continues to evolve.

20 Silva Gruesz, *Ambassadors of Culture*, xi.

21 Irwin, "Almost-Latino Literature," 122.

22 Silva Gruesz credits "Latin American intellectuals since Bello and Bolívar" with the idea that "all are members of the same family with strong affective and genealogical ties." *Ambassadors of Culture*, 189.

23 Aching, *The Politics of Spanish American "Modernismo,"* 115.

24 Nicanor Bolet Peraza, "La influencia americana," *La Habana Elegante*, September 1, 1895, 8. The word *raza* is difficult to translate in this context, as it can mean "race," "people," or "nation." The difficulty is not only one of translation, but also of changing meanings of the word in Spanish and English. As Gilroy notes, "It is significant that prior to the consolidation of scientific racism in the nineteenth century, the term 'race' was used very much in the way that the word 'culture' is today." *The Black Atlantic*, 8.

25 "Importante," *La Revista Ilustrada de Nueva York*, October 1890, 28.

26 On the origins of the term *Latin America*, see Holloway, introduction.

27 An essential study on this topic is Muñoz Martinez, *The Injustice Never Leaves You*.

28 On race and racism in US newspapers, see González and Torres, *News for All the People*.

29 These included Cirilio Villaverde and Félix Varela. On Cubans in nineteenth-century New York, see Pérez, *Sugar, Cigars, and Revolution*; Hoffnung-Garskof, *Racial Migrations*; Mirabal, *Suspect Freedoms*; Lazo, *Writing to Cuba*; and López Mesa, *La comunidad cubana*.

30 My book contributes to recent interventions meant to address this gap, including Hoffnung-Garskof, *Racial Migrations*; and Pérez, *Sugar, Cigars, and Revolution*.

31 Allen, "The Will to Translate," 85–86.

32 On the Spanish-language anarchist press in New York City, I have found especially helpful Castañeda and Feu, *Writing Revolution*; Feu, *Fighting Fascist Spain*; Lomas, "'El Negro Es Tan Capaz'"; Schaffer, *Anarchists of the Caribbean*; and Streeby, *Radical Sensations*.

33 "Honor a nuestro periódico," *La América Ilustrada*, November 30, 1872, 339.

34 "A todos," *Doctrina de Martí*, August 6, 1896, 1.

35 "La anarquia y los anarquistas," *El Despertar*, October 15, 1901, 2.

36 Pease, "José Martí," 52.

37 Valdés, *Diasporic Blackness*, 75.

38 "Constitución para Cuba," *Doctrina de Martí*, January 30, 1897, 3.

39 "Nuestra labor," *Doctrina de Martí*, July 25, 1896, 1.

40 Uricchio, "Historicizing Media," 30–31.

41 Uricchio, "Storage," 128.

42 In a Latin American context, Reynolds, Navitski, and others have situated experimentation within the region's literary movement of *modernismo* in relation to photography and early film. See, for example, Reynolds, "'La Lente Indiscreta'"; and Navitski, "'Ese pequeño arte.'" In a US context, see Gunning, *D. W. Griffith*; and Musser, *The Emergence of Cinema*.

43 See Bolter, *Remediation*.

44 Menke, *Telegraphic Realism*, 10. An inspiring example of this kind of media studies in a Latin American context is Wells, *Media Laboratories*.

45 Silva Gruesz, "Utopia Latina," 58.

46 Coronado, "Historicizing," 51, 52.

47 Gitelman and Pingree, "Introduction," xvi.

48 Murphy has shown that a hemispheric imaginary powered by US imperialism also took shape during the same period. She also notes that "Californio, Tejano, and Latin American writers . . . offered alternatives to dominant formulations of hemispheric interconnection and difference." *Hemispheric Imaginings*, 9. On hemispheric imaginings in the earlier nineteenth-century Spanish-language

press, see also Leary, *A Cultural History of Underdevelopment*. On the role of the hemisphere in the nineteenth-century Black press, see Mirabal, *Suspect Freedoms*, chap. 1. As she points out, "Cubans . . . did not have a monopoly on hemispheric thinking. African Americans in New York continuously wrote about their place within the hemisphere" (58).

49 Kern, *The Culture of Time and Space*, 314.

50 See also Connery, *Journalism and Realism*, which identifies "a paradigm of actuality" that took shape from the 1830s to the 1880s, as writers and editors in the US Anglophone press responded to "more curiosity about the actual and the present" (5, 6).

51 Uricchio, "Storage," 129. The citation in the following sentence is also from this source and page.

52 Kern, *The Culture of Time and Space*, 316.

53 Murray, "Inventing the Medium," 5.

54 Anderson, *Imagined Communities*, 44.

55 Aching, *The Politics of Spanish American "Modernismo,"* 147.

56 Kreitz, "The Metaphors We Use," 5.

57 Fagg et al., "Introduction," 94.

58 Margolis, *Fictions of Mass Democracy*, 21–22.

59 Jenkins, *Textual Poachers*, 24.

60 Jenkins et al., *Participatory Culture*, 2.

61 See, for example, the discussion of the Amateur Press Association in Petrik, "The Youngest Fourth Estate."

62 Fraser's notion of subaltern counterpublics might appear more applicable here, but I would argue that a defining feature of what nineteenth-century publications envisioned for their hemispheric community was the dominant role that they were meant to play. See Fraser, "Rethinking the Public Sphere."

63 Costanza-Chock, *Design Justice*, 89.

64 Ibid., 90.

65 Lazo, *Letters from Filadelfia*, 30–31.

66 Coronado, *A World Not to Come*, 176.

67 When referring to the *crónica*, I have used the Spanish word, in order to avoid the confusion of the wide applicability of the word "chronicle" in English. Foundational texts on the *crónica modernista* include Aníbal González, *La crónica modernista*, Ramos, *Divergent Modernities*; and Rotker, *The American Chronicles of José Martí*.

68 Ramos makes a similar point in his discussion of the way in which *cronistas* positioned their writing in opposition to the telegraph in *Divergent Modernities*, chap. 6.

69 Gitelman, *Always Already New*, 153. Other studies bringing together literary and media history that have influenced my approach include Blackwood, *The Portrait's Subject*; Chenoweth, *The Prosthetic Tongue*; Goble, *Beautiful Circuits*; Lieberman, *Power Lines*; Menke, *Telegraphic Realism*; Panko, *Out of Print*; and Wells, *Media Laboratories*.

70　The subfield of comparative media studies has provided some influential exceptions, including Thorburn and Jenkins, *Rethinking Media Change.*

71　Lazo, *Letters from Filadelfia,* 3.

72　Coronado, *A World Not to Come,* 388, 393.

73　On this topic, see Cutler's consideration of Latinx literary modernities in "Latinx Modernism."

74　Kreitz, "Modernism's Workshops," 245. In "Modernism's Workshops," I explore the legacy of nineteenth-century Nueva York in early twentieth-century New York-based publications.

75　See, for example, Lomas, *Translating Empire;* García Marruz, *Temas martianos;* Ramos, *Divergent Modernities;* and Rotker, *The American Chronicles of José Martí.*

76　Lomas, *Translating Empire,* 85.

77　Suárez León, "La América," 158.

78　Casey and Salter, "Challenges and Opportunities," 103. See also Casey and Salter, "With, Without, Even Still."

79　Woo, "The Colored Citizen," 110.

80　Bonifacio, "'Se Habla Español,'" 120.

81　This phrase comes from the title of Risam's 2019 book, *New Digital Worlds.*

82　Risam, *New Digital Worlds,* 4–5.

83　Hartman, *Wayward Lives,* xiii.

84　Augst, "Archives," 4.

85　Gitelman, *Always Already New,* 26.

86　Ibid.

CHAPTER 1. *TALLER* MAGAZINES

1　The *Times* was the only one of these newspapers located on Park Row at the time, but the *Tribune* and the *Sun* would move there soon afterward. The *New York World* opened its iconic building there in 1890.

2　"La Metropoli Americana," *La América Ilustrada,* May 15, 1872, 138.

3　Valdés, *Diasporic Blackness,* 21.

4　*OED Online,* "network, n., sense 5.b," *OED Online,* accessed January 5, 2025, www.oed.com.

5　*OED Online,* "network, n., sense 4.a," *OED Online,* accessed January 5, 2025, www.oed.com.

6　*OED Online,* "magazine," accessed February 1, 2023, www.oed.com.

7　Lazo, *Writing to Cuba,* 22. As noted in the introduction, more recently, Lazo has argued that an early nineteenth-century "trans-american elite" contributed to and inspired what became a hemispheric print culture—centered, at that time, in Philadelphia—which circulated primarily books and pamphlets that advocated independence for the colonies of Spanish America (*Letters from Filadelfia,* 33). By the 1870s, both the political and media landscapes had changed: most of the region's independence movements—with the exception of those in Cuba and Puerto

Rico—had succeeded, and publishing more frequently with more visual content became easier.

8 On "The Painter of Modern Life" and *The London Illustrated News*, see Gluck, *Popular Bohemia*; and Hiddleston, "Baudelaire and Constantin Guys."

9 On the growth of the English-language illustrated press during this decade, see Brown, *Beyond the Lines*, 8.

10 Published from 1867 to 1868, this magazine centered on promoting public education.

11 On *La Revolución*, see Poyo, "With All, and for the Good of All," 22–28; and Pérez, *Sugar, Cigars, and Revolution*, 202.

12 Velleman, "The Cuban Emigrado," 112.

13 On the history of these and other presses, see Moran, *Printing Presses*.

14 Harris, *Personal Impressions*, 9–10.

15 Qtd. in ibid., 33. Harris suggests that this phrase first appeared in promotional materials for the Lowe Press, citing the description of that press in the catalog of the American Institute, held in New York's Crystal Palace in 1857.

16 "Para impresores, encuadernadores y editores," *El Mundo Nuevo*, June 25, 1872, 368.

17 Rowell, *Rowell's American Newspaper Directory*, 1879, 241.

18 Rowell, *Rowell's American Newspaper Directory*, 1877, 221.

19 Ibid.; Rowell, *Rowell's American Newspaper Directory*, 1879, 235.

20 Rowell, *Rowell's American Newspaper Directory*, 1871, 102; Rowell, *Rowell's American Newspaper Directory*, 1877, 213.

21 Rowell, *Rowell's American Newspaper Directory*, 1871, 102.

22 Ibid., 102, 101. This was before Joseph Pulitzer purchased the *New York World* in 1883 and subsequently pushed that publication's daily circulation beyond 200,000—an amount that had rarely been achieved previously by daily newspapers and that had more typically been achieved over months or longer by the century's bestselling novels.

23 Ibid., 103, 104.

24 Chapter 4 will consider this context.

25 J. C. (José Carlos) Rodrigues, "Office of the Novo Mundo, New York, February 14, 1875," New York, 1875, *Readex: Readex AllSearch*. The notice provides one of the clearest pictures available today of what the business of the Spanish-language illustrated press looked like at the time.

26 Leslie's Publishing House forged this partnership one year after discontinuing a Spanish-language edition of *Frank Leslie's Illustrated Newspaper*, called *La Ilustración Americana*, which ran from 1866 to 1870. According to Ambio, Cirilo Villaverde, author of the foundational Cuban novel *Cecilia Valdés*, contributed to *La Ilustración Americana* in the 1860s. Ambio, "Illustrating Identity," 313. On the role of Miriam Florence Follin (better known as Mrs. Frank Leslie) in pursuing the Spanish-language market, see Silva Gruesz, *Ambassadors of Culture*, 187. A brief mention of the role played by Follin as an assistant for the New York-based *El Noticioso* in 1859 appears in Stern, *Purple Passage*, 30–31.

27 "Dos palabras de introducción," *El Mundo Nuevo*, May 25, 1871, 2.

28 Ibid.; Brown, *Beyond the Lines*, 62.

29 "Dos palabras de introducción."

30 "Estatua de Benjamin Franklin, recientemente erigida en la Plaza de los Impresores, Nueva York," *El Mundo Nuevo*, February 25, 1872, 236.

31 Prettyman, "*Harper's Weekly*," 26.

32 "Dos palabras de introducción."

33 Silva Gruesz, *Ambassadors of Culture*, 187.

34 Lomas, *Translating Empire*, 87, 97.

35 Valdés, *Diasporic Blackness*, 35.

36 "Dos palabras de introducción."

37 "To Advertisers," *El Mundo Nuevo*, May 25, 1871, 16.

38 Ibid.

39 Silva Gruesz, *Ambassadors of Culture*, 193.

40 "Imprenta polyglota," *El Mundo Nuevo*, May 25, 1871, 16.

41 Ibid.

42 Hallet y Breen also appeared to have been used at times as a disguise for pro-independence books that were actually published in Cuba. According to Velleman, while still living in Cuba, Néstor Ponce de León "published the introduction to *Información de Reformas de Cuba y Puerto Rico*, produced in a clandestine edition executed in Guanabacoa, Cuba, despite the appearance of 'New York: Hallet y Breen' on the title page." "The Cuban Emigrado," 103–4.

43 See, for example, Charvat, *Literary Publishing in America*.

44 Lazo locates Philadelphia's appeal to Hispanophone writers in the early nineteenth century in its "association with the drafting of the Declaration of Independence and the US Constitution," as well as the press freedom that the city provided compared to the Spanish colonies. *Letters from Filadelfia*, 25.

45 On the role of the sugar industry in what he calls in his subtitle "the making of Cuban New York" in the nineteenth century, see Pérez, *Sugar, Cigars, and Revolution*.

46 Silva Gruesz, *Ambassadors of Culture*, 176.

47 Ibid., 175–76.

48 "Población," *El Mundo Nuevo*, August 25, 1871, 1.

49 Ibid.

50 "Año nuevo," *El Mundo Nuevo*, January 10, 1872, 178.

51 Antonio Bachiller y Morales, "Primeros periódicos en América," *La América Ilustrada*, May 10, 1873, 147. Emphasis in original.

52 "Notas literarias," *La América Ilustrada*, November 15, 1872, 327.

53 "Ferrocarriles y telégrafos," *La América Ilustrada*, December 15, 1872, 359.

54 Ibid.

55 "Colaboradores," *La América Ilustrada*, January 15, 1872, 14.

56 "La América Ilustrada," *La América Ilustrada*, January 15, 1872, 2.

57 "Libertemos a Cuba," *La América Ilustrada*, July 30, 1872, 211.

58 Ibid.

59 Ibid.

60 Ibid.

61 Ibid.

62 "El decreto de Valmaseda," *La América Ilustrada*, April 15, 1872, 98.

63 Ibid.

64 Ramos has shown how *La Nación* led the region in ushering in a new "distinction between literature and the use of a specifically journalistic language." *Divergent Modernities*, 96. Chapter 2 will discuss two of Martí's contributions to *La Nación*.

65 "Bartolome Mitre," *La América Ilustrada*, January 15, 1872, 2.

66 Ibid.

67 "Atado el mundo," *La América Ilustrada*, January 30, 1872, 19.

68 Ibid.

69 Ibid.

70 Like Ponce de León, the guide's author was a Cuban exile, and he also had arrived in New York in 1869, as the fighting in what would become the Ten Years' War in Cuba entered into its second year. He promptly became involved in the city's Spanish-language illustrated press, contributing to *El Mundo Nuevo*, *La América Ilustrada*, *Museo de las Familias*, and *El Educador Popular*—the latter two of which Ponce de León edited. On *El Educador Popular*, see Velleman, "*El Educador Popular*." Ambio, "Illustrating Identity" considers *El Educador Popular* and *El Ateneo*.

71 On Constantin Guys as the source of Baudelaire's M.G., see Gluck, *Popular Bohemia*, 100–101.

72 Baudelaire, "Le Peintre," 11.

73 Ibid., 10, 12.

74 Ibid., 9.

75 Pearson, "*Frank Leslie's Illustrated Newspaper*," 86.

76 Brown, *Beyond the Lines*, 55.

77 See, for example, Ramos's discussion of the *crónica* as defined in opposition to the reporter and the telegraph in chapter 4 of *Divergent Modernities*. US-based Anglophone literary writers engaged in their own version of this strategic positioning, as chapter 2 will consider.

78 Quoted in Monsiváis, *A ustedes les consta*, 39.

79 In New York City in 1897, Hernández Miyares established his own pro-independence newspaper, *Cacara Jícara*, in which he expressed his frustration with Spanish censorship, which had limited his ability to support the Cuban cause in *La Habana Elegante*. Chapter 3 will discuss *La Habana Elegante*, and chapter 4 will consider *Cacara Jícara* in relation to the late 1890s US yellow press.

80 Enrique Hernández Miyares, "Crónica," *La Habana Elegante*, December 6, 1885, 5.

81 Ibid.

82 Ibid.; Baudelaire, "Le Peintre," 7.

83 Advertisements for the 1872 edition appeared in *El Mundo Nuevo* and *La América Ilustrada.*

84 Pérez, *Sugar, Cigars, and Revolution*, 179.

85 Bachiller y Morales, *Guía*, 170. The article in *El Mundo Nuevo* is "Piedra de fabricar artificial," May 25, 1871, 14.

86 Bachiller y Morales, *Guía*, 103.

87 Ibid., 19–20.

88 Lazo, "La Famosa Filadelfia," 70.

89 See, for example, Ramos, *Divergent Modernities*, chap. 5.

90 "El obrero moderno," *La América Ilustrada*, April 20, 1873, 124. All subsequent citations are from this one-page article.

91 Lomas, *Translating Empire*, ix, 37.

92 Silva Gruesz, *Ambassadors of Culture*, 192.

93 Ramos, *Divergent Modernities*, 189, 188.

94 Ibid., 166.

95 "Una nevada en la Habana," *La Habana Elegante*, May 29, 1887, 6.

96 Baudelaire, "Le Peintre," 9.

97 "Una nevada en la Habana," 6.

98 Ibid., 7.

99 Ibid.

100 Ibid.

101 Ibid.

CHAPTER 2. HEROIC REPORTERS AND NETWORKED AUTHORS

1 "She's Broken Every Record," *New York World*, January 26, 1890, 1.

2 Although Bly sent telegrams from the road, the articles describing her trip were written by anonymous reporters working from the *World*'s office in New York City. Bly's own version of the story appeared in a series of columns after her return, which was also collected in book form as *Nellie Bly's Book*.

3 Roggenkamp, *Narrating the News*, 26.

4 "She's Broken Every Record."

5 "The Coming Newspaper," *The Journalist*, February 13, 1892, 2.

6 The term "new journalism" was used by Matthew Arnold in his 1887 essay "Up to Easter" to describe what he considered a more sensational and less intellectually stimulating form of journalism found in newspapers in Britain and the United States at the end of the nineteenth century.

7 Cordell, "Reprinting," 418.

8 Ibid.

9 They also provided the blueprint for the "journalism that acts," later known as yellow journalism, which defined Hearst's strategy and Pulitzer's competing practices in their coverage of Cuba's 1895 war with Spain and the US intervention (qtd. in Campbell, "1897," 193). Chapter 4 will consider this topic.

10 "She's Broken Every Record."

11 Bly, *Nellie Bly's Book*, 271.

12 "Around the World," *New York World*, November 14, 1889, 1.

13 Baudelaire, "Le Peintre," 8.

14 Bly, *Nellie Bly's Book*, 269.

15 Crinkle, "Howells Out of His Sphere," *New York World*, December 22, 1889. Page numbers on the microfilm were not legible.

16 Ibid.

17 Kaplan, *Social Construction*, 16.

18 Crinkle, "Howells Out of His Sphere."

19 Ibid.

20 "Life in the Metropolis," *New York Sun*, October 4, 1886, 1.

21 "To Coney Island at Last," *New York Sun*, March 15, 1888, 3.

22 Ibid.

23 Ibid.

24 Eytinge, "The Reporter," *The Journalist*, September 12, 1891, 5.

25 Schudson, *Discovering the News*, 71.

26 Shuman, *Steps into Journalism*, 55.

27 Dana, *The Art of Newspaper Making*, 102.

28 Qtd. in Juergens, *Joseph Pulitzer*, 32.

29 After its purchase by Alfred Ochs in 1896, the *Times* published a series of articles that objected to the "freak journalism" of the *World* and the *New York Journal*. The critique followed the *Journal*'s transformation during the previous year under the leadership of William Randolph Hearst. See, for example, "Freak Journalism and the Ball," *New York Times*, February 12, 1897, 6; and "A Question of Freak Ethics," *New York Times*, July 3, 1897, 6.

30 Davis, "A Derelict," 162.

31 Ibid., 167.

32 Lutes offers an insightful reading of the shifting status of Henrietta Stackpole in revisions of James's novels in *Front-Page Girls*.

33 Henry James, *The Princess Casamassima*, 205 (hereafter cited in the text as *PC*).

34 Trilling, *The Liberal Imagination*, 80.

35 See, for example, Tilley, *The Background of The Princess Casamassima*.

36 Seltzer, *Henry James*, 55.

37 Qtd. in Anne Throne Margolis, *Henry James*, 25. James's column shared similarities to what would become the *crónica modernista*. Indeed, scholars have cited the French *chronique* that James references here as a model for the *crónica*. See, for example, Aníbal González, *La crónica modernista*.

38 Reid, letter to Henry James, 217.

39 James, letter to Whitelaw Reid, 219.

40 Ibid.

41 Ibid.

42 In addition to his novels from this period, the publication of "Pandora" and "Georgina's Reasons" in the *New York Sun* in 1884 offers another indication of

James's interest in finding a place for his prose in relation to the expansion of newspapers. On the publication history of these short stories, see Johannings-meier, "Henry James's Dalliance."

43 While James's reading of London newspapers has been noted as an influence on *The Princess Casamassima*, I am arguing that the novel conversed more directly with the innovations taking place within newspapers in New York City, which remained the center of James's publishing activities even after he relocated to London.

44 Baudelaire, "Le Peintre," 12.

45 Henry James, "Preface to Volume 5," n.p.

46 Ibid.

47 Howells, *A Hazard of New Fortunes*, 128 (hereafter cited in the text as *HNF*).

48 Hartsock has made a similar claim that *Hazard* "serves as an insightful cultural critique of mainstream journalistic practice." *A History of American Literary Journalism*, 61. Yet his assertion that the novel objects to "mainstream factual or objective journalism [that] does not personalize or attempt to engage in an exchange of subjectivities" (61) shows how difficult it has been to situate *Hazard* in relation to its own media moment. As the analysis herein demonstrates, it was actually the highly personal writing exemplified by the *World*'s romantic reporting that motivated the novel's critique, along with its search for alternatives.

49 Hochman also notes March's inability to write in her brief reading of *A Hazard of New Fortunes* in *Getting at the Author*, 46.

50 Hochman, *Getting at the Author*, 3.

51 Ibid., 92. Hochman's examples include Miriam Rooth in Henry James's *The Tragic Muse* (1890), Lily Bart in Edith Wharton's *House of Mirth* (1905), "the French woman" in Willa Cather's short story "Peter" (1892), and Caroline Member in Theodore Dreiser's *Sister Carrie* (1900).

52 Kaplan, *Social Construction*, 1.

53 Sundquist, *American Realism*, 9.

54 Ibid., 4.

55 "High realism" is the term Glazener employs to "specify an entity responsible for many of the effects that critics such as Amy Kaplan and Kenneth Warren have attributed to realist texts, especially the effects of producing and enforcing social hierarchies." *Reading for Realism*, 14. Another example of understanding realism as a forum for debate about the literary is Barrish, *American Literary Realism*.

56 Bentley, *Frantic Panoramas*, 9

57 Kaplan's view of realism complements this view. She argues, "Rather than as a monolithic and fully formed theory, realism can be examined as a multifaceted and unfinished debate reenacted in the arena of each novel and essay." *Social Construction*, 15.

58 Howells, *Criticism and Fiction*, 9.

59 Ibid., 17.

60 Prettyman, "Serial Illustrations," 180.

61 Prettyman, "*Harper's Weekly*," 27.
62 Kaplan, *Social Construction*, 47, 48.
63 Ibid., 53.
64 Prettyman, "*Harper's Weekly*," 45.
65 "The Coming Newspaper."
66 Kaplan, *Social Construction*, 53.
67 Forman, "A Successful Magazine and the Men Who Make It," *The Journalist*, April 30, 1892, 2.
68 Ibid.
69 Henry James, *The Art of Fiction*, 70.
70 In support of the Cuban cause, the *New York Sun* became the first site ever to fly the Cuban flag, designed in New York by Narciso López, at its building at the corner of Nassau and Fulton Streets in May 1850.
71 Rotker, *The American Chronicles of José Martí*, 93.
72 Martí, "Nueva York bajo la nieve," 11:417; Martí, "New York Under Snow," 225. Hereafter, both the Spanish-language original and Esther Allen's translation will be cited in the text parenthetically as NY. All translations of this text are Allen's.
73 As Lomas has noted, "Martí's modernism rebels against the dominant literary ideology of realism in the United States of the 1880s. Hermetic rather than transparent, Martí's writing conforms neither to romanticism nor to realism, decades before the official arrival of modernism to the Anglophone literature of the United States." *Translating Empire*, 24.
74 Martí, "Fiesta de la liga de la propiedad literaria," 370.
75 Martí, "Prólogo," 64, 63; Martí, "Prologue," 45. Translations of this text are by Esther Allen.
76 Martí, "Prólogo," 68; Martí, "Prologue," 49.
77 Howells, *Criticism and Fiction*, 25.
78 Rotker, *The American Chronicles of José Martí*, 42.
79 Ibid., 61.
80 Henry James, *The Art of Fiction*, 52.
81 Martí, "Fiesta de la estatua," 11:115.
82 Lomas, *Translating Empire*, 4.
83 Ibid.
84 Martí, "Un drama terrible," 11:334; Martí, "Class War in Chicago," 197 (hereafter cited parenthetically in the text as DT). All translations of this *crónica* are by Esther Allen.
85 On the Haymarket Affair and its role in transforming Martí's understanding of the labor question in the United States, see Conway, "The Limits of Analogy"; and Lomas, "'El Negro Es Tan Capaz.'"
86 Rotker, *The American Chronicles of José Martí*, 93.
87 Conway, "The Limits of Analogy," 46.
88 Ramos, *Divergent Modernities*, 130.
89 Ibid., 112.

90 Ibid., 120.

91 Ibid., 131.

92 Ibid.

93 Ibid.

94 Martí, "A los lectores de 'La America'"; Martí, "From *La América*," 130. The translation is by Esther Allen. On Martí's transformation of *La América* from an advertising circular to a vehicle for his democratic vision for the region, see Lomas, *Translating Empire*; and Suárez León, "La América."

95 Camacho, *El poeta en el mercado*, 29. Camacho has collected and analyzed Martí's contributions from the only extant issue of *El Economista Americana*.

96 Ramos, *Divergent Modernities*, 131.

97 José Martí, "Réplica," *La Habana Elegante*, March 31, 1889, 4.

98 Qtd. in "Joseph Pulitzer—National Monument."

99 "El remedio," *El Despertar*, June 1, 1892, 2.

100 Ibid.

101 Ibid., 3.

102 Ibid.

103 "El divorcio de Vanderbilt," *El Despertar*, March 20, 1895, 1.

104 Ibid.

105 Ibid.

106 Ibid.

107 Ibid.

108 Ibid.

109 "Paso a la verdad," *El Despertar*, December 1, 1891, 2.

110 Ibid.

111 Ibid.

112 "True Stories of the News" was the name of a column in the *World*. See Roggenkamp, "Elizabeth Jordan."

113 "La anarquia y los anarquistas," *El Despertar*, October 15, 1901, 2.

114 Ibid.

CHAPTER 3. MOBILE LIBRARIES AND TELEPHONIC LITERATURE

1 "Nueva era," *La Revista Ilustrada de Nueva York*, January 1891, 2. As noted in the introduction, scholars have widely discussed the difficulty of translating nineteenth-century uses of the term *raza* into English.

2 Ibid.

3 Ibid., 1.

4 Chamberlin and Schulman, *La Revista Ilustrada*, 5.

5 Aching, *The Politics of Spanish American "Modernismo,"* 28.

6 One might argue that the choice of the library at all—as opposed to a study or workshop—marks a step in this same direction. In New York City, the nineteenth century marked the beginnings of the New York Public Library, and Losada and

his editorial team likely would have been aware of the democratizing ambitions of the library movement in the city.

7 "Importante," *La Revista Ilustrada de Nueva York*, October 1890, 28.

8 Jenkins et al., *Participatory Culture*, 2. See also the discussion of participatory culture and its relevance to nineteenth-century print culture in this book's introduction.

9 Cutler, "Toward a Reading," 128.

10 "La Habana Elegante," *La Habana Elegante*, March 11, 1888, 4.

11 Ibid.

12 "Urbanidad pública," *La Habana Elegante*, December 25, 1887, 6.

13 Ibid.

14 Fleur de Chic [Héctor de Saavedra], "La Habana en 1893," *La Habana Elegante*, January 22, 1893, 10.

15 "Una nevada en la Habana," *La Habana Elegante*, May 29, 1887, 7.

16 Ibid.

17 Luis Baralt, "Carta de Nueva York," *La Habana Elegante*, July 7, 1889, 6.

18 Ibid.

19 Ibid.

20 Luis Baralt, "Carta de Nueva York," *La Habana Elegante*, July 21, 1889, 6.

21 "La Habana Elegante," *La Habana Elegante*, April 29, 1888, 9.

22 Baralt, "Carta de Nueva York," July 21, 1889, 6.

23 Ibid.

24 "Ramona," *La Habana Elegante*, September 23, 1888, 6.

25 "Nuestros huéspedes," *La Habana Elegante*, July 3, 1887, 8.

26 "A nuestros suscriptores," *La Habana Elegante*, July 15, 1894, 4.

27 Uricchio, "Storage," 130.

28 Ibid., 129.

29 Navitski locates a similar potentiality in discussions of film in the 1920s in the Mexican periodical *El Universal Ilustrado*, which "blurred the distinction between passive consumers and active participants in film culture." "'Ese pequeño arte,'" 315.

30 Casal, "La prensa," 291.

31 Ibid.

32 Ibid., 293.

33 Ibid.

34 Ohmann, *Selling Culture*, 8.

35 Nicanor Bolet Peraza, "Carta de Nueva York," *La Habana Elegante*, July 5, 1885, 4.

36 Ibid.

37 Ibid.

38 I., "Por teléfono," *La Habana Elegante*, February 12, 1893, 10.

39 Ibid. Luisa Campuzano has written about Cuban women travelers to the 1893 Chicago Exposition. See, for example, "'Valiant Symbol.'"

40 "Nuevo título," *La Revista Ilustrada de Nueva York*, December 1886, 1. Losada took over the publication in 1885 as part of his role leading the Latin American export

section of the Thurber Whyland company, which published, as a free advertising circular, what was originally called *Thurber-Whyland and Company's Spanish Review*. Although Losada did not rename the publication (which circulated under the name *La Revista Ilustrada Mercantil de Nueva York* when he took it over) to *La Revista Ilustrada de Nueva York* until December 1886, it is clear that he started laying the groundwork for his editorial strategy in the first issue that he edited in July 1885. Thus, I locate the beginning of *La Revista Ilustrada*'s run there. On the history of the magazine, see Chamberlin and Schulman, *La Revista Ilustrada*, 10–12. *La Revista Ilustrada* is available to scholars today thanks to their efforts to gather a near-complete run from private and institutional archives throughout Latin America.

41 "La Revista Ilustrada," *La Revista Ilustrada de Nueva York*, July 1887, 1.

42 Ibid. By reducing that community of print to "mere" entertainment, *La Revista Ilustrada* was articulating its own unique role within the period's print culture in a way that was similar to the approach used by Anglophone cultural magazines of the period to set themselves apart from mass-circulating newspapers. Among the period's leading English-language newspapers, another form of competition was taking place between an older guard of established newspapers, like the *New York Herald*, and new competitors, especially a revitalized *New York World* under the leadership of Joseph Pulitzer.

43 Ibid. Bolet Peraza was himself a political exile from Venezuela, and Martí was imprisoned and then exiled from Cuba as a young man for supporting independence from Spain.

44 "Importante."

45 On the relationship between such periodicals and *modernismo*, see Aching, *The Politics of Spanish American "Modernismo,"* 115–23; and Ramos, *Divergent Modernities*, 91–102.

46 "La Revista Ilustrada," *La Revista Ilustrada de Nueva York*, July 1887, 4.

47 On Mayorga Rivas and *La Revista Ilustrada de Nueva York*, see Valenzuela, *Reading Centroamericanismo*.

48 "El periodismo en América," *La Revista Ilustrada de Nueva York*, November 1887, 11.

49 "Importante."

50 "El número de enero," *La Revista Ilustrada de Nueva York*, January 1890, 6.

51 "Trabajos en nuestra imprenta," *La Revista Ilustrada de Nueva York*, March 1890, 6.

52 The word "elegant" in Spanish at the time was often employed almost synonymously with the word "French." On *La Habana Elegante*'s use of this word, see my "Networked Literature," 330.

53 On the mercantile origins of *La Revista Ilustrada*, see Chamberlin and Schulman, *La Revista Ilustrada*, 3–4.

54 Qtd. in Kanellos and Martell, *Hispanic Periodicals*, 67. This notice appeared in the March 1892 issue.

55 "La Revista Ilustrada," *La Revista Ilustrada de Nueva York*, July 1887, 4.

56 Elias de Losada et al., "Nuestras aspiraciones," *La Revista Ilustrada de Nueva York*, May 1892, 247.

57 "Lo que ofrecemos á los lectores," *La Revista Ilustrada de Nueva York*, January 1890, 13.

58 "Importante."

59 Ibid.

60 Ibid.

61 Ibid.

62 Román Mayorga Rivas, "La mujer hispano-americana," *La Revista Ilustrada de Nueva York*, February 1890, 15.

63 Amalia Puga, "La Revista Ilustrada de Nueva York," *La Revista Ilustrada de Nueva York*, February 1890, 8.

64 Ibid.

65 "Prensas de imprimir portatiles," *La Revista Ilustrada de Nueva York*, October 1886, 28. The home press was also widely advertised in the United States and Europe at the time.

66 "Sea Usted mismo su impresor!," *La Revista Ilustrada de Nueva York*, January 1890, 22.

67 Ibid.

68 "Sea Usted mismo su impresor," *La Revista Ilustrada de Nueva York*, December 1888, 34.

69 Chamberlin and Schulman, *La Revista Ilustrada*, 203.

70 See, for example, Belnap and Fernández, *José Martí's "Our America,"* 1–6.

71 See for example, Pease, "José Martí," 52.

72 "Nueva era."

73 José Martí, "Nuestra América," *La Revista Ilustrada de Nueva York*, January 1891, 3; Martí, "Our America," 288.

74 Martí, "Nuestra América," 3; Martí, "Our America," 288.

75 Martí, "Nuestra América," 5; Martí, "Our America," 293.

76 Martí, "Our America," 294.

77 Ibid., 292.

78 Ibid., 293.

79 Losada et al., "Nuestras aspiraciones." Chamberlin and Schulman also mention this investment endeavor in *La Revista Ilustrada*, 12.

80 Ibid.

81 Ibid.

82 Martí, "Discurso en el liceo cubano," 279.

83 "Nos interesa," *La Revista Ilustrada de Nueva York*, February 1890, 4.

84 Ibid.

85 Enrique Hernández Miyares, "New York—Primeras impresiones," *La Habana Elegante*, June 24, 1894, 7.

86 Ibid.

87 Mary Springer, "Semblanzas," *La Habana Elegante*, November 11, 1894, 9.

88 Ibid.

89 Ignotus, "La Habana elegante por teléfono," *La Habana Elegante*, February 3, 1895, 14.

90 Néstor Ponce de León, "En mi biblioteca," *La Revista Ilustrada de Nueva York*, February 1890, 31.

91 Ibid.

92 Kanellos and Martell, *Hispanic Periodicals*, 19. On the importance of Puerto Rican contributions to the Cuban movement, and their shared vision of independence in the Antilles, see Vega, *Memoirs*, chaps. 7–10.

93 For example, Aníbal González has observed that the need to establish the literary value of the *crónica* appears in mid-twentieth-century studies that describe the genre as "la nueva prosa" or "la prosa artística." *La crónica modernista*, 63. Such studies included Schulman, "Reflexiones" (1968); and Sirkó, "La crónica modernista" (1975). I have written about the *crónica* and its interpretation in the twentieth-century literary field in my "Networked Literature."

94 See Benjamin, "Paris."

95 Sotero Figueroa, "Reparos literarios I," *La Revista Ilustrada de Nueva York*, June 1890, 28.

96 Ibid.

97 Ibid.

98 Hoffnung-Garskof, *Racial Migrations*, 34.

99 Figueroa, "Reparos literarios I."

100 Ibid.

101 Ibid.

102 Sotero Figueroa, "Gutenberg," *La Revista Ilustrada de Nueva York*, January 1891, 48.

CHAPTER 4. REVOLUTIONARY WORKSHOPS

1 "'El cuarto poder . . . americano,'" *La Revista de Cuba Libre*, August 6, 1898, 1. While much debate surrounds the creation of the term "yellow press," one widely cited starting point was an 1897 editorial published in the *Tribune* by editor Ervin Wardman. According to Campbell, Wardman arrived at the phrase "yellow journalism" after experimenting with a number of options—including "nude journalism" and "yellow-kid journalism"—to provide "a pithy and insulting substitute for 'new journalism'" in his editorial attacks on the *World* and the *Journal*. Campbell, *Yellow Journalism*, 23, 26. The term, at least in part, refers to the star character in Alfred Outcault's *World* comic *Hogan's Alley*: a young boy who always wore an ankle-length gown. Milton argues that *World* pressroom secretary Charles W. Saalburgh chose to print the gown in yellow in order to test his new formula for a yellow ink that would not smear. See Milton, *The Yellow Kids*, 41.

2 Ibid.

3 On the impact of segregation on Tampa's Cuban community, see Greenbaum, *More Than Black*.

4 On Morúa Delgado, see Lamas's chapter on Morúa in *The Latino Continuum*; and Herrera McElroy, "Martín Morúa Delgado."

5 "Nuestra labor," *Doctrina de Martí*, July 25, 1896, 1.

6 On the change of leadership in *Patria* after Martí's death, see Hoffnung-Garskof, *Racial Migrations*. See also Muller, *Cuban Émigrés and Independence*, in which she argues that "there is more continuity between Martí and Estrada Palma's PRC than scholars have traditionally noted," as "both men viewed educated, middle-class professionals and elites as ideal representatives of the Cuban republic, although Martí had a broader vision of Cuban citizenship" (89, 91).

7 "Nuestra labor."

8 Qtd. in Campbell, "1897," 193.

9 Baldasty, "Nineteenth-Century Origins," 411.

10 "A nuestros amigos," *Doctrina de Martí*, September 30, 1897, 1.

11 Ibid.

12 Ibid.

13 "Nuestra prensa," *Patria*, March 14, 1892, 2. The article was unsigned. The Centro de Estudios Martianos's digital collection attributes this article to Martí.

14 José Martí, "Nuestras ideas," *Patria*, March 14, 1892, 1.

15 "Nuestro programa," *Cacara Jícara*, October 8, 1897, 1.

16 "A nuestros amigos."

17 Campbell, "1897," 190.

18 Ibid., 193.

19 Ibid.

20 Ibid., 191.

21 Ibid., 193.

22 Roggenkamp, "The Evangelina Cisneros Romance," 31. Moreover, as Leary has noted, "The *Journal*'s exploitation of Cosío played on . . . popular representational logics of the fallen woman and the chaste heroine." *A Cultural History of Underdevelopment*, n.p.

23 Hawthorne, "Julian Hawthorne's Introduction," 17.

24 Enrique Hernández Miyares, "España burlada," *Cacara Jícara*, October 30, 1897, 3.

25 Lowry, "The Flower of Cuba," 177, 178.

26 Ibid., 178.

27 Carey, "Breaking the News," 132.

28 Ibid.

29 In a sense, this constituted a mass media approach to painting modern life. While Baudelaire's model—and the versions reimagined in Spanish- and English-language illustrated newspapers in the 1880s—privileged individual observers, illustration here became part of a team effort that reflected the organization and division of labor of growing news organizations and differed from the collaborative models of Nueva York in that the team's primary purpose was to make the newspaper profitable.

30 Ferrer's *Insurgent Cuba* is a foundational study of this history.

31 In New York City, the year 1895 alone saw the introduction of *Cuba Libre, Guaimaro, Hijas de Cuba* (another publication of a women's club, directed by Emilia de Casanova Villaverde), and *Patria*. Based on available records, at least ten new publications dedicated to Cuban independence appeared in New York City between 1895 and 1898. In Tampa, six new publications dedicated to supporting the war effort appeared between those years.

32 "Saludo," *La Revista de Cuba Libre*, December 25, 1897, 1.

33 "Nuestro proposito," *La Revista de Cuba Libre*, December 25, 1897, 1.

34 "Por la patria," *La Revista de Cuba Libre*, January 8, 1898, 4.

35 "Directiva," *La Revista de Cuba Libre*, December 25, 1897, cover.

36 "Por la patria." The citation in the preceding sentence is also from this text and page.

37 Aurora, "De nuestra corresponsal," *La Revista de Cuba Libre*, December 25, 1897, 2.

38 Ibid.

39 As Alain Basail Rodríguez has argued in the context of *La Habana Elegante*, the widespread portrayal of the readership of such publications as primarily female is more likely "autopropaganda" (self-promotion) than historical reality: "Como rasgo general el público era masculino, distinguido y estable, formado por la clase media, la burocracia española y la élite social." (As a general trait, the audience was male, distinguished and stable, made up of the middle class, the Spanish bureaucracy and the social elite.) *El lápiz rojo*, 83.

40 Lola Rodríguez de Tió, "Nevando," *La Revista de Cuba Libre*, January 22, 1898, 4. All subsequent citations are from this one-page poem.

41 Hoffnung-Garskof. *Racial Migrations*, 12.

42 "Gacetillas," *La Revista de Cuba Libre*, January 22, 1898, 7.

43 "A nuestros suscriptores," *La Revista de Cuba Libre*, March 19, 1898, 7.

44 "40 pesos," *La Revista de Cuba Libre*, August 27, 1898, 6.

45 "Periódico fundado para arbitrar recursos a la causa de Cuba," *La Revista de Cuba Libre*, August 27, 1898, 10.

46 "Siempre en su puesto," *La Revista de Cuba Libre*, August 6, 1898.

47 Kreitz, "Revolutionizing Women's Roles," 229.

48 Qtd. in Robertson *Stephen Crane*, 147.

49 Kaplan makes this point in her reading of "Stephen Crane's Vivid Story of the Battle of San Juan," in which she argues that Crane "both played and parodied the heroic correspondent by theatrically exposing himself to bullets under fire and by 'capturing' a Puerto Rican town in a mock invasion." *The Anarchy of Empire*, 131. See also Robertson, *Stephen Crane*, chap. 5; and Gullason, "Stephen Crane's Private War."

50 Crane, *Reports of War*, 143.

51 Ibid.

52 Ibid., 145.

53 Ibid., 144.

54 Ibid.

55 Ibid., 145.
56 Ibid.
57 Ibid.
58 Rea, *Facts and Fakes About Cuba*, 22.
59 Ibid., 330.
60 Ibid., 329, 330.
61 Ibid. *Every Other Week*, in William Dean Howells's *A Hazard of New Fortunes*, had proposed a version of such an idea and explored its limitations nearly a decade earlier. But by now, it should no longer be news that Anglophone mass-circulation journalism followed fiction.
62 Mirabal, *Suspect Freedoms*, n.p.
63 Leary, *A Cultural History of Underdevelopment*, n.p.
64 Ibid.
65 "El cuarto poder . . . americano."
66 Ibid.
67 Ibid.
68 "Imprenta América," *Doctrina de Martí*, August 22, 1896, 4.
69 Beyond Serra and Figueroa, that team included Juan Bonilla and Francisco Gonzalo Marín, who had left the city to join the war effort and served as a correspondent from Cuba's battlefields.
70 Scholars have widely discussed the dearth of explicit discussion of race in *Patria* and in Martí's *oeuvre* more broadly. See, for example, Guerra, *The Myth of José Martí*.
71 Hoffnung-Garskof, *Racial Migrations*, 276.
72 "Nuestra labor."
73 Ibid.
74 Sotero Figueroa, "Por la revolución," *Doctrina de Martí*, July 25, 1896, 2.
75 Ibid.
76 Ibid.
77 Ibid.
78 Ibid.
79 "Sin justicia no hay union," *Doctrina de Martí*, June 15, 1897, 1.
80 Serra, *Ensayos Políticos*, 114.
81 Ibid., 113.
82 Ibid., 118.
83 "Nuestra labor."
84 Ibid.
85 Ramos, *Divergent Modernities*, 189, 188.
86 Ibid., 130.
87 I am thinking here of Bruno Latour's actor network theory, which investigates "situations where innovations proliferate, where group boundaries are uncertain." *Reassembling the Social*, 11.
88 See, for example, Pappademos, *Black Political Activism*.

89 For example, see Mirabal, *Suspect Freedoms*, chap. 4.

90 Hoffnung-Garskof, *Racial Migrations*, 195.

91 Qtd. in Marks, *The Black Press*, 67.

92 Ibid., 87.

CHAPTER 5. WORK IN PROGRESS

1 "La propaganda anarquista: La prensa," *El Despertar*, October 20, 1894, 1.

2 Ibid.

3 Ibid. Italics in original.

4 "Las ocho horas," *El Despertar*, November 11, 1891, 4.

5 See Lomas's chapter on *La América* in *Translating Empire*.

6 Casey and Salter, "Challenges and Opportunities," 102.

7 Ibid, 103.

8 Castañeda, "Anarchism," 81.

9 Ferguson, *Letterpress Revolution*, x.

10 Qtd. in Sánchez Collantes, "Spanish Republicanism," 42.

11 Castañeda, "Anarchism," 82.

12 Juan Bonilla, "Contestando una carta," *El Despertar*, April 15, 1893, 3.

13 Palmiro de Lidia [Adrián del Valle], "Industria periodística," *El Despertar*, October 10, 1894, 4.

14 José Cayetano Campos, "El literato por fuerza II," *El Despertar*, June 10, 1894, 3.

15 Ibid.

16 José Cayetano Campos, "El literato por fuerza IV," *El Despertar*, June 30, 1894, 1.

17 Lidia, "Industria periodística."

18 Ricardo Mella, "Como se afirma un metodo," *El Despertar*, August 30, 1901, 2.

19 Ibid.

20 Ibid.

21 Ibid.

22 A second edition of the magazine appeared in 1910, but as Mirabal has noted, "During the second phase *Minerva*'s commitment to feminism, racial enfranchisement, and maintaining diasporic connections changed dramatically. . . . Despite past commitments to empowering Afro-Cuban women, *Minerva*, like the [Cuban] republic itself, pushed Afro-Cuban women to the political, social, and economic margins." *Suspect Freedoms*, 161–62.

23 Barcia Zequeira, "Women of *Minerva*," 62.

24 On archival methods and challenges for recovering the political contributions of Afro-Cuban women, see Brunson, *Black Women*, 8. On *Minerva*, see also Barcia Zequeira, "Women of *Minerva*"; Mirabal, *Suspect Freedoms*; and Montejo Arrechea, "*Minerva*."

25 Brunson, *Black Women*, 13.

26 According to Mirabal, "Written for and by Afro-Cuban women on the island, *Minerva* was widely disseminated throughout New York and extremely popular with African-American women, who helped to finance it." "Archival Dilemmas," 347.

27 América Font, "Mis opiniones," *Minerva*, November 30, 1888, 3.

28 Natividad González, "La ignorancia," *Minerva*, December 15, 1888, 4.

29 O.R.P, "La familia," *Minerva*, December 30, 1888, 2. Mirabal discusses this aspect of *Minerva*'s position on women's education in *Suspect Freedoms*, 120.

30 Font, "Mis opiniones," 1–2.

31 Ibid., 2.

32 La Güinera, "Una carta," *Minerva*, April 15, 1889, 3.

33 Ibid., 4.

34 Ibid.

35 Ibid.

36 E. T. Elvina [Etelvina Zayas], "Notas quincenales," *Minerva*, February 7, 1889, 7.

37 Elvina [Etelvina Zayas], "Notas quincenales," *Minerva*, December 30, 1888, 6.

38 Ibid.

39 Mirabal, *Suspect Freedoms*, 120.

40 Elvina [Etelvina Zayas], "Notas quincenales," *Minerva*, November 30, 1888, 7.

41 "Nuestras colabadoras," *Minerva*, December 15, 1888, 1.

42 Elvina, "Notas quincenales," November 30, 1888, 7.

43 Elvina, "Notas quincenales," February 7, 1889, 6.

44 Elvina, "Notas quincenales," December 30, 1888, 7.

45 Ibid.

46 Maria Storini, "Una carta," *Minerva*, November 30, 1888, 3.

47 Ibid.

48 Ibid., 4.

49 Elvina [Etelvina Zayas], "Notas quincenales," *Minerva*, December 15, 1888, 5.

50 Ibid., 6.

51 Cecilia [Úrsula Coimbra de Valverde], "Gratitud," *Minerva*, February 15, 1889, 1–2.

52 Ibid., 2.

53 Ibid., 1.

54 Mirabal, *Suspect Freedoms*, 120.

55 Elvina [Etelvina Zayas], "Notas quincenales," *Minerva*, January 26, 1889, 7.

56 Mirabal, *Suspect Freedoms*, 135.

57 Duarte, "Carta abierta," x.

58 Ibid.

59 Domínguez, *Figuras y figuritas*, xv (hereafter cited parenthetically in the text as *FF*).

60 Hoffnung-Garskof, *Racial Migrations*, 276. A similar change happened within the party's military leadership. As Ferrer has shown in *Insurgent Cuba*, even before the US intervention, PRC leadership had begun to push Black officers out of leadership roles.

61 Mirabal, *Suspect Freedoms*, 135.

62 Hoffnung-Garskof includes this detail in *Racial Migrations*, 328.

63 On Schomburg's contributions to the Cuban and Puerto Rican independence movement and the connections between his early and later career, see Lisa Sán-

chez González, "Decolonizing Schomburg"; Helton and Zafar, "Arturo Alfonso Schomburg"; Hoffnung-Garskof, *Racial Migrations*; Winston James, *Holding Aloft the Banner*; Meehan, *People Get Ready*; Mirabal, *Suspect Freedoms*; Salgado, "The Archive"; and Valdés, *Diasporic Blackness*. Bernardo Vega also discusses Schomburg as a member of New York's early Puerto Rican community in his *Memoirs*.

64 Helton and Zafar, "Arturo Alfonso Schomburg," 3.

65 Meehan, *People Get Ready*, 54.

66 Ibid., 70.

67 Helton and Zafar, "Arturo Alfonso Schomburg," 8.

68 Salgado has noted that Schomburg's *New York Times* letters also indicate surprising acceptance from Schomburg in the years following 1898 of "US territorial expansion and neocolonial tutorship in Puerto Rico, the Philippines and Panama. . . . Rather than dispute post-1898 US sovereignty in Puerto Rico and other 'possessions,' he embraces it to argue in favor of lifting 'alien immigrations exams' for territorial natives wishing to move North, entitling them automatically with 'the privileges and immunities enjoyed by all citizens.'" "The Archive," 374.

69 Arthur A. Schomburg, "Questions by a Porto Rican," letter to editor, *New York Times*, August 9, 1902, 8.

70 Ibid.

71 Ibid.

72 Mirabal, *Suspect Freedoms*, 145. See also Mirabal's discussion of *New York Times* Cuba correspondent Dorothy Stanhope in chapter 4.

73 Arthur A. Schomburg, "Lynching a Savage Relic," letter to editor, *New York Times*, June 28, 1903, 8.

74 Ibid.

75 Ibid.

76 Ibid.

77 Arthur A. Schomburg, "Union League Club's Actions," letter to editor, *New York Times*, December 20, 1903.

78 Ibid.

79 Arthur A. Schomburg, "Tillman Trial and Verdict," letter to editor, *New York Times*, October 18, 1903, 25.

80 Ibid.

81 Ibid.

82 Valdés, *Diasporic Blackness*, 75.

83 Ibid., 72.

84 Arthur A. Schomburg, "General Evaristo Estenoz," *The Crisis* 4, no. 3 (July 1912): 143 (hereafter cited in the text as GEE).

85 Arthur A. Schomburg, "Takes Issue with Bishop Turner," letter to the editor, *New York Times*, September 3, 1901, 6.

86 Salgado, "The Archive," 372.

87 Meehan makes a similar observation, arguing that this was a point of intersection between Schomburg and his collaborators during the period of his involvement in

the Harlem Renaissance: "The idea that the archive might be a source of cultural raw material that could be fashioned into high art or fine art by talented creative genius is one that resonates with the core impulses of racial uplift ideologies espoused by Du Bois, Locke, and others" (67).

88 Arthur A. Schomburg, "The Negro Digs Up His Past," *Survey Graphic* 6, March 1925, 670 (hereafter cited in the text as NDHP).

89 Helton and Zafar, "Arturo Alfonso Schomburg," 15.

90 Valdés, *Diasporic Blackness*, 25.

91 Baeza Ventura et al., "A US Latinx Digital Humanities Manifesto," n.p. All subsequent citations are from this text, published online on Manifold, which does not have page numbers.

AFTERWORD

1 Richardson, *Democracy Awakening*, xi.

2 Ibid., xv.

3 Ibid., xvi.

4 Ibid., xiv.

5 "La Revista Ilustrada," *La Revista Ilustrada de Nueva York*, July 1887, 1.

6 Berry, *Understanding Digital Humanities*, 9.

7 "NPR Adds Radio Ambulante to Its Podcast Lineup," NPR, November 15, 2016, accessed June 2, 2024, www.npr.org.

8 Ibid.

9 Daniel Alarcón, "Junot Díaz and Francisco Goldman Live in New York," *Radio Ambulante* Soundcloud, accessed June 2, 2024, https://soundcloud.com.

10 Puerto Rican Literature Project, "About #PLPR," n.d., accessed December 31, 2024, https://plpr.uh.edu.

11 Picturing Mexican America, "About," n.d., accessed June 2, 2024, www.picturing-mexicanamerica.com.

12 Ibid.

13 Lincoln Center, "Legacies of San Juan Hill," n.d., accessed December 31, 2024, www.lincolncenter.org.

14 Discover the Latino Catksills, "About," n.d., accessed December 31, 2024, https://discover.latinocatskills.com.

REFERENCES

ARCHIVES, DATABASES, RARE BOOK LIBRARIES, AND
SPECIAL COLLECTIONS

Archives and Manuscripts on Microfilm. Washington University, St. Louis.

Arte Público Hispanic Historical Collection, Series 2. Digital archive. https://artepublicopress.com.

Instituto de Literatura y Lingüística. Havana, Cuba.

John Hay Library. Brown University, Providence, RI.

Manuscripts, Archives, and Rare Books Division. New York Public Library.

Milstein Microform Collection. New York Public Library.

Modernist Journals Project. Digital archive. https://modjourn.org.

Museo, Biblioteca y Archivo Histórico Municipal. San Isidro, Argentina.

Newberry Library, Chicago.

New York Times. Digital archive. www.nytimes.com.

Periodicals and Microforms Reading Room. Butler Library, Columbia University, New York.

Readex African American Newspapers, Series 1 and 2. Digital archive. www.readex.com.

Readex Hispanic American Newspapers, 1808–1980. Digital archive. www.readex.com.

Sala Cubana. Biblioteca Nacional, Havana, Cuba.

NEWSPAPERS AND OTHER SERIALS

La América Ilustrada, New York

Atlantic Monthly Magazine, Boston

Cacara Jícara, New York

The Century Illustrated Monthly Magazine, New York

The Cosmopolitan, New York

The Crisis, New York

El Despertar, New York

Doctrina de Martí, New York

El Fígaro, Havana, Cuba

La Habana Elegante, Havana, Cuba

Harper's Weekly, New York

The Journalist, New York

Minerva, Havana, Cuba

El Mundo Nuevo, New York

La Nación, Buenos Aires, Argentina

New York Age, New York

New York Journal, New York

New York Sun, New York

New York Times, New York

New York World, New York

Patria, New York

La Prensa, New York

La Revista de Cuba Libre, Tampa, FL

La Revista Ilustrada de Nueva York, New York

BOOKS AND JOURNAL ARTICLES

Aching, Gerard. *The Politics of Spanish American "Modernismo": By Exquisite Design.* Cambridge University Press, 1997.

Allen, Esther. "The Will to Translate: Four Episodes in a Local History of Global Exchange." In *In Translation: Translators on Their Work and What It Means*, edited by Esther Allen and Susan Bernofsky, 82–103. Columbia University Press, 2013.

Ambio, Marissa L. "Illustrating Identity in the Cuban Emigré Press: Latin American Transnationalism in El Ateneo." *Revista de Estudios Hispánicos* 48 (2014): 307–28.

Anderson, Benedict. *Imagined Communities: Reflections on the Origin and Spread of Nationalism.* Verso, 1983.

Arnold, Matthew. "Up to Easter." *Nineteenth Century* 21 (1887): 629–43.

Augst, Thomas. "Archives: An Introduction." *American Literary History* 29, no. 2 (2017): 1–9.

Bachiller y Morales, Antonio. *Guía de la ciudad de Nueva York y sus alrededores.* Néstor Ponce de León, 1876.

Baeza Ventura, Gabriela, María Eugenia Cotera, Linda García Merchant, Lorena Gauthereau, and Carolina Villarroel. "A US Latinx Digital Humanities Manifesto." In *Debates in the Digital Humanities*, edited by Matthew K. Gold and Lauren F. Klein. University of Minnesota Press, 2023. https://dhdebates.gc.cuny.edu.

Baldasty, Gerald J. "The Nineteenth-Century Origins of Modern American Journalism." *Proceedings of the American Antiquarian Society* 100 (1991): 407–21.

Barcia Zequeira, María del Carmen. "Women of *Minerva*." In *Afrocubanas: History, Thought, and Cultural Practices*, edited by Devyn Spence Benson, Daisy Rubiera

Castillo, and Inés María Martiau Terry, translated by Karina Alma, 59–73. Rowman & Littlefield, 2020.

Barrish, Phillip. *American Literary Realism, Critical Theory, and Intellectual Prestige, 1880–1995.* Cambridge University Press, 2001.

Basail Rodríguez, Alain. *El lápiz rojo: Prensa, censura e identidad cubana (1878–1895).* Centro Juan Marinello, 2004.

Baudelaire, Charles. "Le Peintre de la vie moderne." Available at Scribd, uploaded by Gérald Ledent n.d., 1–28. Accessed April 30, 2025. www.scribd.com.

Belnap, Jeffrey, and Raúl Fernández, eds. *Jose Marti's "Our America": From National to Hemispheric Cultural Studies.* Duke University Press, 1998.

Benjamin, Walter. "Paris: Capital of the Nineteenth Century." In *The Arcades Project*, translated by Howard Eiland and Kevin McLaughlin, 3–26. Belknap, 1999.

Bentley, Nancy. *Frantic Panoramas American Literature and Mass Culture, 1870–1920.* University of Pennsylvania Press, 2011.

Benton, Megan. "Unruly Servants: Machines, Modernity, and the Printed Page." In *Print in Motion: The Expansion of Publishing and Reading in the United States, 1880–1940*, edited by Carl F. Kaestle and Janice A. Radway, 151–69. University of North Carolina Press, 2009.

Berry, David M. *Understanding Digital Humanities.* Springer, 2012.

Blackwood, Sarah. *The Portrait's Subject: Inventing Inner Life in the Nineteenth-Century United States.* University of North Carolina Press, 2019.

Blanco, María del Pilar. *Modernist Laboratories: Science and the Poetics of Progress in Fin-de-Siècle Spanish.* Forthcoming.

Bly, Nellie. *Nellie Bly's Book: Around the World in Seventy-Two Days.* Pictorial Weeklies Co., 1890.

Bolter, J. David. *Remediation: Understanding New Media.* MIT Press, 1999.

Bonifacio, Ayendy. "'Se Habla Español': Hispanophone-Merchant Advertisements in José Ferrer de Couto's *El Cronista* (1878)." *American Periodicals* 30, no. 2 (2020): 118–21.

Brickhouse, Anna. "The Black Legend of Texas." *PMLA* 131, no. 3 (May 2016): 735–42.

Briggs, Asa, and Peter Burke. "Printing in Its Contexts." In *A Social History of the Media: From Gutenberg to the Internet*, 13–60. Polity Press, 2009.

Brinn, Ayelet. *A Revolution in Type: Gender and the Making of the American Yiddish Press.* New York University Press, 2023.

Brown, Joshua. *Beyond the Lines: Pictorial Reporting, Everyday Life, and the Crisis of Gilded Age America.* University of California Press, 2006.

Brunson, Takkara K. *Black Women, Citizenship, and the Making of Modern Cuba.* University of Florida Press, 2021.

Camacho, Jorge. *El poeta en el mercado de Nueva York: Nuevas crónicas de José Martí en El Economista Americano.* Editorial Caligrama, 2016.

Campbell, W. Joseph. "1897: American Journalism's Exceptional Year." *Journalism History*, no. 4 (2004): 190–200.

———. *Yellow Journalism: Puncturing the Myths, Defining the Legacies.* Praeger, 2001.

Campuzano, Luisa. "'Valiant Symbol of Industrial Progress'? Cuban Women Travelers and the United States." In *Women at Sea: Travel Writing at the Margins of Caribbean Discourse*, edited by Lizabeth Paravisini-Gebert and Ivette Romero-Cesareo, 161–82. Palgrave, 2001.

Carey, Craig. "Breaking the News: Telegraphy and Yellow Journalism in the Spanish-American War." *American Periodicals* 26, no. 2 (July 2016): 130–48.

Casal, Julián del. "La prensa." In *Poesía completa y prosa selecta*, edited by Álvaro Salvador, 290–93. Editorial Verbum, 2001.

Casey, Jim, and Sarah H. Salter. "Challenges and Opportunities in Editorship Studies." *American Periodicals* 30, no. 2 (2020): 101–4.

———. "With, Without, Even Still: Frederick Douglass, *L'Union*, and Editorship Studies." *American Literature* 94, no. 2 (2022): 245–72.

Castañeda, Christopher. "Anarchism and the End of Empire: José Cayetano Campos, Labor, and Cuba Libre." In *Writing Revolution: Hispanic Anarchism in the United States*, edited by Christopher J. Castañeda and Montse Feu, 81–99. University of Illinois Press, 2019.

Castañeda, Christopher J., and Montse Feu, eds. *Writing Revolution: Hispanic Anarchism in the United States*. University of Illinois Press, 2019.

Chamberlin, Vernon A., and Ivan A. Schulman. *La Revista Ilustrada de Nueva York: History, Anthology, and Index of Literary Selections*. University of Missouri Press, 1976.

Charvat, William. *Literary Publishing in America, 1790–1850*. University of Massachusetts Press, 1993.

Chenoweth, Katie. *The Prosthetic Tongue: Printing Technology and the Rise of the French Language*. University of Pennsylvania Press, 2019.

Connery, Thomas Bernard. *Journalism and Realism: Rendering American Life*. Northwestern University Press, 2011.

Conolly-Smith, Peter. *Translating America: An Immigrant Press Visualizes American Popular Culture, 1895–1918*. Smithsonian Press, 2004.

Conway, Christopher. "The Limits of Analogy: José Martí and the Haymarket Martyrs." *A Contracorriente: Una Revista de Estudios Latinoamericanos* 2, no. 1 (2004): 33–56.

Cordell, Ryan. "Reprinting, Circulation, and the Network Author in Antebellum Newspapers." *American Literary History* 27, no. 3 (2015): 417–45.

Coronado, Raúl. "Historicizing Nineteenth-Century Latina/o Textuality." In *The Latino Nineteenth Century*, edited by Rodrigo Lazo and Jesse Alemán, 49–70. New York University Press, 2016.

———. *A World Not to Come: A History of Latino Writing and Print Culture*. Harvard University Press, 2013.

Costanza-Chock, Sasha. *Design Justice: Community-Led Practices to Build the Worlds We Need*. MIT Press, 2020.

Crane, Stephen. *Reports of War*. University Press of Virginia, 1971.

Cutler, John Alba. "Latinx Modernism and the Spirit of Latinoamericanismo." *American Literary History* 33, no. 3 (2021): 571–87.

———. "Toward a Reading of Nineteenth-Century Latino/a Short Fiction." In *The Latino Nineteenth Century*, edited by Rodrigo Lazo and Jesse Alemán, 124–45. New York University Press, 2016.

Dana, Charles A. *The Art of Newspaper Making*. Arno, 1970.

Davis, Richard Harding. "A Derelict." In *Ranson's Folley*, 159–212. Charles Scribner's Sons, 1902.

Domínguez, Teófilo. *Figuras y figuritas: Ensayos biográficos*. Imprenta Lafayette Street 105, 1899.

Duarte, Pedro. "Carta abierta: Sr. Teófilo Domínguez." In *Figuras y figuritas: Ensayos biográficos*, by Teófilo Domínguez, vii–xi. Imprenta Lafayette Street 105, 1899.

Fagg, John, Matthew Pethers, and Robin Vandome. "Introduction: Networks and the Nineteenth-Century Periodical." *American Periodicals: A Journal of History & Criticism* 23, no. 2 (2013): 93–104.

Ferguson, Kathy E. *Letterpress Revolution: The Politics of Anarchist Print Culture*. Duke University Press, 2023.

Ferrer, Ada. *Insurgent Cuba: Race, Nation, and Revolution, 1868–1898*. University of North Carolina Press, 1999.

Feu, Montse. *Fighting Fascist Spain: Worker Protest from the Printing Press*. University of Illinois Press, 2020.

Fox, Claire F. "Commentary: The Transnational Turn and the Hemispheric Return." *American Literary History* 18, no. 3 (July 2006): 638–47. https://doi.org/10.1093/alh/ajl003.

Fraser, Nancy. "Rethinking the Public Sphere: A Contribution to the Critique of Actually Existing Democracy." *Social Text*, nos. 25–26 (1990): 56–80.

García Marruz, Fina. *Temas martianos*. 3rd series. Centro de Estudios Martianos, 1995.

Gilroy, Paul. *The Black Atlantic: Modernity and Double Consciousness*. Harvard University Press, 1993.

Gitelman, Lisa. *Always Already New: Media, History and the Data of Culture*. MIT Press, 2006.

Gitelman, Lisa, and Geoffrey B. Pingree. "Introduction: What's New About New Media." In *New Media, 1740–1915*, edited by Lisa Gitelman and Geoffrey B. Pingree, xi–xxii. MIT Press, 2004.

Glazener, Nancy. *Reading for Realism: The History of a US Literary Institution, 1850–1910*. Duke University Press, 1997.

Gluck, Mary. *Popular Bohemia: Modernism and Urban Culture in Nineteenth-Century Paris*. Harvard University Press, 2005.

Goble, Mark. *Beautiful Circuits: Modernism and the Mediated Life*. Columbia University Press, 2010.

González, Aníbal. *La crónica modernista hispanoamericana*. J. Porrúa Turanzas, 1983.

González, Juan, and Joseph Torres. *News for All the People: The Epic Story of Race and the American Media*. Verso, 2011.

González, Lisa Sánchez. "Decolonizing Schomburg." *African American Review* 54, nos. 1–2 (2021): 129–42.

Greenbaum, Susan D. *More Than Black: Afro-Cubans in Tampa*. University Press of Florida, 2002.

Guerra, Lillian. *The Myth of José Martí: Conflicting Nationalisms in Early Twentieth-Century Cuba*. University of North Carolina Press, 2005.

Gullason, Thomas Arthur. "Stephen Crane's Private War on Yellow Journalism." *Huntington Library Quarterly* 22, no. 3 (May 1959): 201–8.

Gunning, Tom. *D. W. Griffith and the Origins of American Narrative Film: The Early Years at Biograph*. University of Illinois Press, 1994.

Harris, Elizabeth M. *Personal Impressions: The Small Printing Press in Nineteenth-Century America*. Merrion Press, 2004.

Hartman, Saidiya. *Wayward Lives, Beautiful Experiments: Intimate Histories of Social Upheaval*. Norton, 2019.

Hartsock, John C. *A History of American Literary Journalism: The Emergence of a Modern Narrative Form*. University of Massachusetts Press, 2000.

Hawthorne, Julian. "Julian Hawthorne's Introduction." In *The Story of Evangelina Cisneros*, by Evangelina Betancourt Cosio y Cisneros and Karl Decker, 15–27. Continental Publishing Company, 1897.

Helton, Laura E., and Rafia Zafar. "Arturo Alfonso Schomburg in the Twenty-First Century: An Introduction." *African American Review* 54, no. 1 (2021): 1–18.

Herrera McElroy, Onyria. "Martín Morúa Delgado, precursor del afro-cubanismo." *Afro-Hispanic Review* 2, no. 1 (1983): 19–24.

Hiddleston, J. A. "Baudelaire and Constantin Guys." *Modern Language Review* 90, no. 3 (July 1995): 603–21.

Hochman, Barbara. *Getting at the Author: Reimagining Books and Reading in the Age of American Realism*. University of Massachusetts Press, 2001.

Hoffnung-Garskof, Jesse. *Racial Migrations: New York City and the Revolutionary Politics of the Spanish Caribbean*. Princeton University Press, 2019.

Holloway, Thomas. Introduction to *A Companion to Latin American History*, edited by Thomas Holloway, 1–9. Wiley-Blackwell, 2011.

Howells, William Dean. *Criticism and Fiction, and Other Essays*. Edited by Clara Marburg Kirk and Rudolf Kirk. New York University Press, 1959.

———. *A Hazard of New Fortunes*. New York: Harper, 1911.

Irwin, Robert McKee. "Almost-Latino Literature: Approaching Truncated Latinidades." In *The Latino Nineteenth Century*, edited by Rodrigo Lazo and Jesse Alemán, 110–23. New York University Press, 2016.

James, Henry. *The Art of Fiction*. Cupples and Hurd, 1885.

———. Henry James to Whitelaw Reid, August 30, 1876. In *Parisian Sketches: Letters to the New York Tribune, 1875–1876*, edited by Leon Edel and Ilse Dusoir Lind. New York University Press, 1957.

———. "Preface to Volume 5 of the New York Edition." The Ladder: A Henry James Website (archived), edited by Adrian Dover, n.d. Archive accessed April 30, 2025. https://web.archive.org/web/20050129212848fw_/http://www.henryjames.org.uk/prefaces/text05_inframe.

———. *The Princess Casamassima.* Harper, 1959.

James, Winston. *Holding Aloft the Banner of Ethiopia: Caribbean Radicalism in Early Twentieth Century America.* Reprint, Verso, 1999.

Jenkins, Henry. *Textual Poachers: Television Fans and Participatory Culture.* Routledge, 1992.

Jenkins, Henry, Mizuko Ito, and danah boyd. *Participatory Culture in a Networked Era: A Conversation on Youth, Learning, Commerce, and Politics.* Polity, 2015.

Johanningsmeier, Charles. "Henry James's Dalliance with the Newspaper World." *Henry James Review* 19, no. 1 (1998): 36–52.

"Joseph Pulitzer—National Monument (US National Park Service)." Accessed February 1, 2023. www.nps.gov.

Juergens, George. *Joseph Pulitzer and the New York World.* Princeton University Press, 1966.

Kaestle, Carl F., and Janice A. Radway. "A Framework for the History of Publishing and Reading in the United States, 1880–1940." In *Print in Motion: The Expansion of Publishing and Reading in the United States, 1880–1940*, edited by Carl F. Kaestle and Janice A. Radway, 7–21. University of North Carolina Press, 2009.

Kanellos, Nicolás, and Helvetia Martell. *Hispanic Periodicals in the United States, Origins to 1960: A Brief History and Comprehensive Bibliography.* Arte Público Press, 2000.

Kaplan, Amy. *The Anarchy of Empire in the Making of US Culture.* Harvard University Press, 2005.

———. *The Social Construction of American Realism.* University of Chicago Press, 1988.

Kern, Stephen. *The Culture of Time and Space, 1880–1918.* Harvard University Press, 1983.

Kreitz, Kelley. "Networked Literature: The Crónica Modernista and Nineteenth-Century Media Change." *Revista de Estudios Hispánicos* 50, no. 2 (2016): 321–46.

———. "The Metaphors We Use: Network." *American Periodicals* 30, no. 1 (2020): 5–8.

———. "Modernism's Workshops: Printing Latinx Literary Modernities in New York City." In *Latinx Literature in Transition, 1848–1992*, vol. 2, edited by John Alba Cutler and Marissa K. López, 242–59. Cambridge University Press, 2025.

———. "Revolutionizing Women's Roles in the Late Nineteenth-Century US-Based Spanish-Language Press." In *Immigration and Exile Foreign-Language Press in the UK and in the US: Connected Histories of the 19th and 20th Centuries*, edited by Bénédicte Deschamps and Stéphanie Prévost, 223–36. Bloomsbury Press, 2024.

Lamas, Carmen. *The Latino Continuum and the Nineteenth-Century Americas: Literature, Translation, and Historiography.* Oxford University Press, 2021.

Latour, Bruno. *Reassembling the Social: An Introduction to Actor-Network-Theory.* Oxford University Press, 2007.

Lazo, Rodrigo. "'La Famosa Filadefia': The Hemispheric American City and Constitutional Debates." In *Hemispheric American Studies*, edited by Caroline F. Levander and Robert S. Levine. Rutgers University Press, 2020.

———. "Introduction: Historical Latinidades and Archival Encounters." In *The Latino Nineteenth Century*, edited by Rodrigo Lazo and Jesse Alemán, 1–19. New York University Press, 2016.

———. *Letters from Filadelfia.* University of Virginia Press, 2020.

———. *Writing to Cuba: Filibustering and Cuban Exiles in the United States*. University of North Carolina Press, 2005.

Leary, John Patrick. *A Cultural History of Underdevelopment: Latin America in the US Imagination*. University of Virginia Press, 2016.

Library of Congress. "R. Hoe. & Co. Manufacturers of Single and Double Cylinder Printing Machines, Washington and Smith Hand Presses, Self-Inking Machines, Steam Engines, Cast Steel Saws, Machinery, &c. &c. &c . . . New York. Geo. W. Wood. Printer. [c. 1846]." Online text. Accessed March 24, 2022.

Lieberman, Jennifer L. *Power Lines: Electricity in American Life and Letters, 1882–1952*. MIT Press, 2017.

Lomas, Laura. "'El Negro Es Tan Capaz Como el Blanco': José Martí, 'Pachín' Marín, Lucy Parsons, and the Politics of Late Nineteenth-Century Latinidad." In *The Latino Nineteenth Century*, edited by Rodrigo Lazo and Jesse Alemán, 301–22. New York University Press, 2016.

———. *Translating Empire: José Martí, Migrant Latino Subjects, and American Modernities*. Duke University Press, 2008.

López, Marissa. *Chicano Nations: The Hemispheric Origins of Mexican American Literature*. New York University Press, 2011.

López Mesa, Enrique. *La comunidad cubana de New York: Siglo XIX*. Centro de Estudios Martianos, 2002.

Lowry, Elizabeth. "The Flower of Cuba: Rhetoric, Representation, and Circulation at the Outbreak of the Spanish-American War." *Rhetoric Review* 32, no. 2 (April 2013): 174–90.

Lutes, Jean Marie. *Front-Page Girls: Women Journalists in American Culture and Fiction, 1880–1930*. Cornell University Press, 2006.

Mainardi, Patricia. *Another World: Nineteenth-Century Illustrated Print Culture*. Yale University Press, 2017.

Margolis, Anne Throne. *Henry James and the Problem of Audience: An International Act*. UMI Research Press, 1985.

Margolis, Stacey. *Fictions of Mass Democracy in Nineteenth-Century America*. Cambridge University Press, 2015.

Marks, George P., III, ed. *The Black Press Views American Imperialism (1898–1900)*. Arno Press and New York Times, 1971.

Martí, José. "Class War in Chicago: A Terrible Drama." In *José Martí: Selected Writings*, edited and translated by Esther Allen, 195–218. Penguin, 2002.

———. "Discurso en el liceo cubano." In *Obras completas*, 2nd ed., 4:269–79. Editorial Ciencias Sociales, 1975.

———. "Un drama terrible." In *Obras completas*, 2nd ed., 11:333–58. Editorial Ciencias Sociales, 1975.

———. "Fiesta de la estatua de la libertad." In *Obras completas*, 2nd ed., 11:99–115. Editorial Ciencias Sociales, 1975.

———. "Fiesta de la liga de la propiedad literaria." In *Obras completas*, 2nd ed., 11:365–70. Editorial Ciencias Sociales, 1975.

———. "From *La América.*" In *José Martí: Selected Writings*, edited and translated by Esther Allen, 140. Penguin, 2002.

———. "A los lectores de 'La America.'" In *Obras completas*, 2nd ed., 8:266. Editorial Ciencias Sociales, 1975.

———. "New York Under Snow." In *José Martí: Selected Writings*, edited and translated by Esther Allen, 225–30. Penguin, 2002.

———. "Nueva York bajo la nieve." In *Obras completas*, 2nd ed., 11:417–22. Editorial Ciencias Sociales, 1975.

———. "Our America." In *José Martí: Selected Writings*, edited and translated by Esther Allen, 288–96. Penguin, 2002.

———. "Prólogo al 'Poema de Niágara' de Juan A. Pérez Bonalde." In *Ensayos y crónicas*, edited by José Olivio Jiménez, 59–78. Catedra, 2004.

———. "Prologue to Juan Antonio Pérez Bonalde's 'Poem of Niagara.'" In *José Martí: Selected Writings*, edited and translated by Esther Allen, 43–51. Penguin, 2002.

McLuhan, Marshall. *The Gutenberg Galaxy: The Making of Typographic Man*. University of Toronto Press, 1962.

Meehan, Kevin. *People Get Ready: African American and Caribbean Cultural Exchange*. University Press of Mississippi, 2009.

Mejías-López, Alejandro. *The Inverted Conquest: The Myth of Modernity and the Transatlantic Onset of Modernism*. Vanderbilt University Press, 2009.

Menke, Richard. *Telegraphic Realism: Victorian Fiction and Other Information Systems*. Stanford University Press, 2008.

Milton, Joyce. *The Yellow Kids: Foreign Correspondents in the Heyday of Yellow Journalism*. Harper & Row, 1989.

Mirabal, Nancy Raquel. "Archival Dilemmas and Possibilities." *Cultural Dynamics* 30, no. 4 (2018): 343–48.

———. *Suspect Freedoms: The Racial and Sexual Politics of Cubanidad in New York, 1823–1957*. New York University Press, 2017.

Mizruchi, Susan L. *The Rise of Multicultural America: Economy and Print Culture, 1865–1915*. University of North Carolina Press, 2009.

Monsiváis, Carlos. *A ustedes les consta: Antología de la crónica en México*. Ediciones Era, 1998.

Montejo Arrechea, Carmen. "*Minerva*: A Magazine for Women (and Men) of Color." In *Between Race and Empire: African-Americans and Cubans Before the Cuban Revolution*, edited by Lisa Brock and Digna Castañeda Fuertes, 33–48. Temple University Press, 1998.

Moran, James. *Printing Presses: History and Development from the Fifteenth Century to Modern Times*. University of California Press, 1978.

Muller, Dalia Antonia. *Cuban Émigrés and Independence in the Nineteenth-Century Gulf World*. University of North Carolina Press, 2017.

Muñoz Martinez, Monica. *The Injustice Never Leaves You: Anti-Mexican Violence in Texas*. Harvard University Press, 2018.

Murphy, Gretchen. *Hemispheric Imaginings: The Monroe Doctrine and Narratives of US Empire*. Duke University Press, 2005.

Murray, Janet. "Inventing the Medium." In *New Media Reader*, edited by Noah Wardrip-Fruin and Nick Montfort, 3–12. MIT Press, 2003.

Musser, Charles. *The Emergence of Cinema: The American Screen to 1907*. Scribner, 1990.

Navitski, Rielle. "'Ese pequeño arte que tanto amamos': Remediating Cinema in *El Universal Ilustrado*." *Revista de Estudios Hispánicos* 50, no. 2 (2016): 293–320.

Ohmann, Richard Malin. *Selling Culture: Magazines, Markets, and Class at the Turn of the Century*. Verso, 1996.

Panko, Julia. *Out of Print: Mediating Information in the Novel and the Book*. University of Massachusetts Press, 2020.

Pappademos, Melina. *Black Political Activism and the Cuban Republic*. University of North Carolina Press, 2011.

Pearson, Andrea C. "*Frank Leslie's Illustrated Newspaper* and *Harper's Weekly*: Innovation and Illustration in Nineteenth-Century American Pictorial Reporting." *Journal of Popular Culture* 23, no. 4 (1990): 81–111.

Pease, Donald E. "José Martí, Alexis de Tocqueville, and the Politics of Displacement." In *Jose Marti's "Our America": From National to Hemispheric Cultural Studies*, edited by Jeffrey Grant Belnap and Raúl A. Fernández, 27–57. Duke University Press, 1998.

Pérez, Lisandro. *Sugar, Cigars, and Revolution: The Making of Cuban New York*. New York University Press, 2018.

Petrik, Paula. "The Youngest Fourth Estate: The Novelty Toy Printing Press and Adolescence, 1870–1886." In *Small Worlds: Children and Adolescents in America, 1850–1950*, edited by Elliott West and Paula Petrik, 125–42. University Press of Kansas, 1992.

Poyo, Gerald Eugene. *"With All, and for the Good of All": The Emergence of Popular Nationalism in the Cuban Communities of the United States, 1848–1898*. Duke University Press, 1989.

Prettyman, Gib. "*Harper's Weekly* and the Spectacle of Industrialization." *American Periodicals* 11 (2001): 24–48.

———. "The Serial Illustrations of *A Hazard of New Fortunes*." *Resources for American Literary Study* 27, no. 2 (2001): 179–95.

Ramos, Julio. *Divergent Modernities: Culture and Politics in Nineteenth-Century Latin America*. Translated by John D. Blanco. Duke University Press, 2001.

Rea, George Bronson. *Facts and Fakes About Cuba*. G. Munro's Sons, 1897.

Reid, Whitelaw. Whitelaw Reid to Henry James, August 10, 1876. In *Parisian Sketches: Letters to the New York Tribune, 1875–1876*, edited by Leon Edel and Ilse Dusoir Lind. New York University Press, 1957.

Reynolds, Andrew R. "La Lente Indiscreta: Visuality and Mediality in Modernista Literary Expression." *Revista de Estudios Hispánicos* 50, no. 2 (2016): 347–70.

Richardson, Heather Cox. *Democracy Awakening: Notes on the State of America*. Viking, 2023.

Risam, Roopika. *New Digital Worlds: Postcolonial Digital Humanities*. Northwestern University Press, 2019.

Rivera, Jorge B. *El escritor y la industria cultural*. Atuel, 1998.

Robertson, Michael. *Stephen Crane, Journalism, and the Making of Modern American Literature*. Columbia University Press, 1997.

Roggenkamp, Karen. "Elizabeth Jordan, 'True Stories of the News,' and Newspaper Fiction in Late Nineteenth-Century American Journalism." In *Literature and Journalism: Inspirations, Intersections, and Inventions from Ben Franklin to Stephen Colbert*, edited by Mark Canada, 119–41. Palgrave Macmillan, 2013.

———. "The Evangelina Cisneros Romance, Medievalist Fiction, and the Journalism That Acts." *Journal of American and Comparative Cultures* 23, no. 2 (2000): 25–37.

———. *Narrating the News: New Journalism and Literary Genre in Late Nineteenth-Century American Newspapers and Fiction*. Kent State University Press, 2005.

Rotker, Susana. *The American Chronicles of José Martí: Journalism and Modernity in Spanish America*. University Press of New England, 2000.

Rowell, George Presbury. *Rowell's American Newspaper Directory*. Printers' Ink Pub. Co., 1871. https://babel.hathitrust.org.

———. *Rowell's American Newspaper Directory*. Printers' Ink Pub. Co., 1877. https://babel.hathitrust.org.

———. *Rowell's American Newspaper Directory*. Printers' Ink Pub. Co., 1879. https://babel.hathitrust.org.

Salgado, César A. "The Archive and Afro-Latina/o Field-Formation: Arturo Alfonso Schomburg at the Intersection of Puerto Rican and African American Studies and Literatures." In *The Cambridge History of Latina/o American Literature*, edited by John Morán González and Laura Lomas, 371–93. Cambridge University Press, 2018.

Sánchez Collantes, Sergio. "Spanish Republicanism and the Press: The Political Socialization of Anarchists in the United States (1880s–1910s)." In *Writing Revolution: Hispanic Anarchism in the United States*, edited by Christopher J. Castañeda and Montse Feu, 35–60. University of Illinois Press, 2019.

Schaffer, Kirwin. *Anarchists of the Caribbean: Countercultural Politics and Transnational Networks in the Age of US Expansion*. Cambridge University Press, 2020.

Schudson, Michael. *Discovering the News: A Social History of American Newspapers*. Basic Books, 1978.

Schulman, Ivan. "Reflexiones en torno a la definición del modernismo." In *El modernismo*, edited by Lily Litvak. Taurus, 1975.

Seltzer, Mark. *Henry James and the Art of Power*. Cornell University Press, 1984.

Serra, Rafael. *Ensayos políticos*. 2nd series. P. J. Díaz, 1896.

Shuman, Edwin Llewellyn. *Steps into Journalism: Helps and Hints for Young Writers*. Correspondence School of Journalism, 1894.

Silva Gruesz, Kirsten. *Ambassadors of Culture: The Transamerican Origins of Latino Writing*. Princeton University Press, 2002.

———. "Utopia Latina: The Ordinary Seaman in Extraordinary Times." *MFS Modern Fiction Studies* 49, no. 1 (2003): 54–83.

Sirkó, Oksana María. "La crónica modernista en sus inicios: José Martí y Manuel Gutiérrez Nájera." In *Estudios críticos sobre la prosa modernista*, edited by José Olivio Jiménez. Eliseo Torres and Sons, 1975.

Stern, Madeline Bettina. *Purple Passage: The Life of Mrs. Frank Leslie*. University of Oklahoma Press, 1953.

Streeby, Shelley. *Radical Sensations: World Movements, Violence, and Visual Culture*. Duke University Press, 2013.

Suárez León, Carmen. "La América: ¿Periódico de anuncios?" In *El periodismo como misión*, edited by Pedro Pablo Rodríguez, 159–70. Editorial Pablo de la Torriente, 2003.

Sundquist, Eric J., ed. *American Realism: New Essays*. Johns Hopkins University Press, 1982.

Supp-Montgomerie, Jenna. *When the Medium Was the Mission: The Atlantic Telegraph and the Religious Origins of Network Culture*. New York University Press, 2021.

Thorburn, David, and Henry Jenkins, eds. *Rethinking Media Change: The Aesthetics of Transition*. MIT Press, 2003.

Tilley, Wesley H. *The Background of The Princess Casamassima*. University of Florida Press, 1961.

Trilling, Lionel. *The Liberal Imagination*. New York Review of Books, 2008.

Uricchio, William. "Historicizing Media in Transition." In *Rethinking Media Change: The Aesthetics of Transition*, edited by David Thorburn and Henry Jenkins, 23–38. MIT Press, 2003.

———. "Storage, Simultaneity, and the Media Technologies of Modernity." In *Allegories of Communication: Intermedial Concerns from Cinema to the Digital*, edited by John Fullerton and Jan Olsson, 123–38. Indiana University Press, 2004.

Valdés, Vanessa Kimberly. *Diasporic Blackness: The Life and Times of Arturo Alfonso Schomburg*. State University of New York Press, 2017.

Valenzuela, Gabriela. *Reading Centroamericanismo: The Fugitive Genres of Nineteenth-Century US Central American Literature*. Forthcoming.

Vega, Bernardo. *Memoirs of Bernardo Vega: A Contribution to the History of the Puerto Rican Community in New York*. Translated by César Andreu Iglesias. Monthly Review Press, 1984.

Velleman, Barry L. "The Cuban Emigrado and the Cultural Unity of the Americas: The Work of Néstor Ponce de León (1837–1899)." *Revista Interamericana de Bibliografía/Inter-American Review of Bibliography* 4, no. 1 (1993): 103–16.

———. "*El Educador Popular*: Revista pedagógica de emigrados hispanos en Nueva York, 1873–1878." *Cuadernos Americanos*, no. 56, Nueva época (1996): 111–47.

Wells, Sarah Ann. *Media Laboratories: Late Modernist Authorship in South America*. Northwestern University Press, 2017.

Woo, Jewon. "The *Colored Citizen*: Collaborative Editorship in Progress." *American Periodicals* 30, no. 2 (2020): 110–13.

INDEX

access, to print, 126, 129, 133, 142, 139, 218

Aching, Gerard, 7, 15

actor network theory, 246n87

advertisements, 23, 80, 171, 181, 183; in *El Mundo Nuevo*, 42–43, 45; fundraising, 105–6, 109; portable printing press, 38, 131–32, *132*, 133; in *Revista Ilustrada de Nueva York*, 131–32, *132*, 133

advertising circulars, 183, 240n40

African Americans, Black Americans and, 4, 207–8, 227n8, 247n26; Black press and, 178–79, 207–8; racism faced by, 103, 210; rights of, 103, 152–53; Schomburg Center for Research in Black Culture and, 184, 203, 213, 219

Afro-Cubans, 59, 172, 184, 198–201, 204, 227n8; *Doctrina de Martí* established by, 152; independence movements and, 146; *New York Age* on, 152; night school for, 217; Schomburg on, 208–9; upper class Cubans on, 41; women, 4, 189–96, 247n22, 247n26

Afro-Puerto Ricans, 59, 146, 152, 173, 198, 204, 217

Alarcón, Daniel, 218–19

Allen, Esther, 10, 238n72, 238n84, 239n94

Ambas Américas (*Both Americas*) (New York, NY), *iv*, 37, 43

Ambio, Marissa L., 232n26

La América (*America*) (New York, NY), *iv*, 92, 103, 183

La América Illustrada (*Illustrated America*) (New York, NY), *iv*, 8, 10, 25–26, 38,
175, 234n70; illustrations in, 31, *32*, 49, 56–59, *58*; networking and, 45–51; *taller* model and, 33

American Newspaper Directory (Rowell), 38

americanos, 44–45

anarchism, 10–11, 66, 71–73, 78, 181–87; *El Despertar* and, 106–7, 110; Martí on, 97–103

anarchist presses, Spanish-language, 11, 26, 61, 66, 110, 181, 183–87

Anderson, Benedict, 15

Anglophone mass presses, 17, 65, 167, 217

Anglophone press, US, 230n50

anonymity, 50, 85, 106, 108, 181

antebellum, 66

anticolonialism, 10–12, 18, 27–28, 97, 211–12, 216

anti-imperialism, 27

Arango, Clemencia, 150–51, 160, 164–65

archives, 20–22, 25, 28, 183, 185; digital, 23–24, 36; Domínguez on, 196; Lazo on, 6; Mirabal on, 203

Argentina, 10, 49–50, 92–93

Armas y Céspedes, Juan Ignacio de, 31, 38

Arnold, Matthew, 235n6

Around the World in Eighty Days (Verne), 76

The Art of Fiction (James), 91

"El asesinato de los italianos" (The lynching of the Italians) (Martí), 103

The Aspern Papers (James), 71

El Ateneo (*The Athanaeum*) (New York, NY), 38

263

139, 146; telegraphy and, 100, 178. *See
also specific works*
Martí's Doctrine. See Doctrina de Martí
Massachusetts, 43, 46
mass-circulation presses, Anglophone, 25,
27, 32, 65, 67, 100–101, 181–82; exclusivity and accessibility in, 124–25; print
technology and, 114
mass media, 4–6, 9, 21, 145, 178–80, 217,
244n29
mass presses, 1, 3, 9, 40, 125, 128, 228n9;
Anglophone, 17, 65, 167, 217; Casal and,
121; Martí on, 103
McLuhan, Marshall, 1, 28
media change, nineteenth-century, 3, 5,
13–21, 24, 33, 35, 51, 134; Howell on,
87, 90–91; James on, 72, 74, 91; late
nineteenth-century, 148, 154–59; technology impacting, 28–29
media studies, 13–14, 19–24
media systems, 13, 227n6
Medina, Catalina (K. Latina), 183
Meehan, Kevin, 204, 249n87
Mella, Ricardo, 188–89
Menke, Richard, 13
Mexican-American War, 8–9, 18
Mexico, 46, 146, 227n7
middle class, 41, 89–90, 100–101
Milton, Joyce, 243n1
Minerva (Havana, Cuba), 4, 28, 183,
247n22, 247n26
Mirabal, Nancy, 168–69, 193, 196, 203,
247n22, 247n26
The Mirror (El Espejo) (New York, NY),
38–39
misinformation, 218
Mitre, Bartolomé, 49–50
mobile libraries, 26, 116, 135, 219
modernism, modernity and, 25–26, 52, 59,
85, 96, 102, 238n72
modernismo (literary movement), 15,
25–26, 34–35, 121, 127, 229n42; alternatives of, 142–49; *crónicas* and, 18–21,

53, 60, 176–77, 236n37; readership of,
116, 130; Spanish-language illustrated
presses and, 53, 62–63, 125; telephonic, 145–46
modern life, reporting, 51–60, 67–71
Mohammed, Khalil Gibran, 219
monarchies, 98
monopolies, 157
monthly publications, 125, 129, 154
Morse, Samuel, 2
Morúa Amendment, Cuba, 152, 160,
208–9
Morúa Delgado, Martín, 152, 190, 194,
208–9
Muller, Dalia Antonia, 227n7, 244n6
El Mundo Nuevo (The New World) (New
York, NY), iv, 25–26, 32–33, 36, 38–39,
55, 234n70; advertisements in, 42–43,
45; editors of, 40–42, 44, 47–48
murders, 55, 206–7
Murphy, Gretchen, 229n48
Murray, Janet, 14–15
Museo de las Familias (Museum for Fami-
lies) (New York, NY), 234n70
Museum of the City of New York, 220

La Nación (The Nation) (Buenos Aires,
Argentina), 10, 49, 92–103, 234n64
narration: impersonal, 79, 85; omniscient,
82, 83, 85–86
National Endowment for the Humanities
(NEH), US, 221
nationalism, 43, 186–87, 204
National Public Radio (NPR), US,
218–19
Navitski, Rielle, 229n42, 240n29
"The Negro Digs Up His Past" (Schom-
burg), 210–11
"El negro en los Estados Unidos" (The
Black man in the United States)
(Martí), 103
NEH. *See* National Endowment for the
Humanities

Néstor Ponce de León's Print Shop and Spanish-Language Bookstore, *iv*, 43, 92, 117
networked authors, 25–26, 66–67, 111
networks, 6, 13–19, 171; *La América Ilustrada*, 45–51, 58–60; social, 16, 33–34, 66
neutrality, gender, 7, 228n19
"Una nevada en la Habana" (A snowfall in Havana) (Anonymous), 61–62, 104–5, 116–17
"¡Nevando!" (It's snowing!) (Rodríguez de Tió), 162
new journalism, 66, 78–79, 83–84, 91–92, 108–11, 156, 235n6, 243n1
Newspaper Row, Lower Manhattan, 9, 31, 124, 182, 185
newspapers, daily, 14, 38–39, 49, 124, 154, 181, 232n22. See also *talleres* (workshops), newspapers as
newspapers, English-language, 3–4, 31, 67, 241n42
The New World. See El Mundo Nuevo
New York Age (New York, NY), 178
New York City/Nueva York. *See specific topics*
New York Herald (New York, NY), 1–3, 39, 44, 53, 241n42
New York Journal (New York, NY), 27, 150–51, 236n29, 244n22; Hearst purchasing of, 156–58, 165
New York Public Library, 211–12, 239n6; Schomburg Center for Research in Black Culture, 184, 203, 213, 219
New York Sun (New York, NY), 26, 69, 154, 236n42, 238n70
New York Times (New York, NY), 28, 32, 70, 231n1, 236n29, 249n68; foreign correspondents, 168–169; letters to the editor, 203–210
New York Times Building, Printing House Square, 31, 32, 46
New York Tribune (New York, NY), 39, 74–75, 231n1, 243n1

the *New York World* (New York, NY), 126, 231n1, 232n22, 236n29, 237n48, 241n42; Bly in, 64–65, 67–68, 83; circulation of, 75; *El Despertar* and, 106–9; *Hogan's Alley* comic in, 243n1; Pulitzer purchasing, 26, 181–82; Statue of Liberty in, 105–6; war correspondence for, 153, 166–67; yellow journalism in, 27, 150–51, 166–67
Nicaragua, 45–46
night schools, 217
nineteenth-century Spanish-language press, New York City, *iv. See also specific topics*
Las Novedades (weekly newspaper), 39
NPR. *See* National Public Radio
"Nuestra América" (Our America) (Martí), 3, 92, 134–36, 139, 146, 148, 176
la nueva prosa (genre), 243n93
Nueva York, Nineteenth-Century, *iv*, 10–11, 32. *See also specific topics*
"Nueva York bajo la nieve" (New York under the snow) (Martí), 93–96, 100, 104–5
Nuyorican Poets Café, 220

objectivity, journalistic, 168–69, 205
Ochs, Alfred, 236n29
omniscient narration, 82, 83, 85–86
one-sided reporting, 168
Outcault, Alfred, 243n1

"Pandora" (James), 236n42
Paris Herald (Paris, France), 1–2
Parsons, Albert, 101
Parsons, Lucy, 182, 185
participation, 16–17, 67; democratic, 26–27, 169–70, 214, 217–18, 221; mass, 138–39, 159; reader, 3–4, 109, 114, 131
participatory culture, 16–17, 25, 114, 139; participatory print cultures, 25, 114, 142–43, 177

ABOUT THE AUTHOR

KELLEY KREITZ is Professor of English and Affiliate Faculty in Latina/o Studies at Pace University in New York City.